Women, Media and Violence

Women, Media and Violence

Edited by

Vidya Jain

Rashmi Jain

RAWAT PUBLICATIONS

Jaipur • New Delhi • Bangalore • Guwahati • Kolkata

ISBN 978-81-316-0765-7

Published by
Prem Rawat for **Rawat Publications**
Satyam Apts, Sector 3, Jawahar Nagar, Jaipur 302 004 (India)
Phone: 0141 265 1748 / 7006 Fax: 0141 265 1748
E-mail: info@rawatbooks.com
Website: www.rawatbooks.com

New Delhi Office
4858/24, Ansari Road, Daryaganj, New Delhi 110 002
Phone: 011 2326 3290

Also at *Bangalore, Guwahati* and *Kolkata*

Typeset by Rawat Computers, Jaipur
Printed at Chaman Enterprises, New Delhi

Contents

Contributors vii

Introduction 1
Vidya Jain and Rashmi Jain

Section I
Theoretical Constructions

1 Gandhian Feminism: The Question of Women's Dignity and Honour 13
Vidya Jain

2 Engendering Security through Egalitarianism 28
Bernedette Muthien

3 Revisiting Feminist Thought in Contemporary Times 58
Rashmi Jain

Section II
Media and Literary Reflections

4 She Must Not Accept, She Must Challenge 75
Ranjit Kaur and Sapna Newar

5 Women's Indecent Portrayal in Media 89
Chanchal Sinha and Prateeksha Tyagi

6 Child Sexual Abuse: Unearthing the Quiet Corners of 'Home' 107
Ritu Sen

7 Indian Fiction: (W)Righting the Wrongs of Women's Word and World 116
Ruchi Sharma

8 Emotional Abuse: The Invisible Wounds of Women 133
Priyanka Sharma

Section III
Violence and Security Concerns

9 Traditions, Honour, and Women Security in a Global Context 151
Ramesh Kumar

10 Gender Inequality and Women's Empowerment: A Comparative Analysis of Kerala and Rajasthan 170
Rameshwar Jat and Rinku Bala

11 Social Protection of Women Workers in Informal Sector in India: Scenario and Significance 189
Subrata S. Satapathy

12 Work Without Fear: Combating Workplace Sexual Harassment 209
Shikha Sharma

13 Domestic Violence Against Women: A Study 225
Chandra Kumari

14 Nutritional Status of Middle Aged Urban Women in Jaipur 234
Kanika Varma and Aachu Agarwal

15 Twilight Years: Problems and Support System Focusing Women 246
Shubha Dube and Pooja Sharma

Index 257

Contributors

Vidya Jain is a Professor of Political Science in the University of Rajasthan, Jaipur. She is also Director, Centre for Gandhian Studies and Principal of University Maharani College, University of Rajasthan. Recently she has been elected as convenor of Nonviolence Commission of International Peace Research Association (IPRA). She was also Asia Pacific Peace Research Association (APPRA) Secretary General (2012–14). She is also a member of Board of Directors of IPRA Foundation. A well-known scholar of Gandhian, peace and gender studies, she has authored four books and innumerable articles in journals of national and international repute. She is on the editorial board of several journals. Professor Jain has organized several conferences, workshops, seminars and refresher courses on different themes of peace, gender and Gandhian studies. She is actively involved in spreading Gandhian ideas and practices throughout the globe.

Bernedette Muthien is head of Gender Mainstreaming in the Department of Women in the Presidency of South Africa. She serves on the Executive Council of the International Peace Research Association, is Co-Founder and Deputy Chair of the African Peace Research and Education

Association, and Convenor of the Global Political Economy Commission. She also serves on various international advisory boards, including the international journal *Human Security Studies*, as well as the International Institute on Peace Education. She chairs the Strategy and Policy Committee, as well as the Special Committee on Human Remains, of the Council of Iziko Museums of South Africa. She is part-time Commissioner for South Africa's Constitutional Commission for the Promotion and Protection of the Rights of Cultural, Religious and Linguistic Communities, and chairs its Research and Policy Development Committee.

Rashmi Jain is Director, Centre for the Study of Social Exclusion and Inclusive Policy, and Associate Professor, Department of Sociology, University of Rajasthan, Jaipur. Her core areas of interest are development communication, gender studies, sociology of law, leisure studies and European studies. At present she is Vice Principal, University Maharani's College, UOR, Jaipur and Dy. Coordinator in UGC SAP DRS II. She has been regularly taking part in conferences and seminars both in the country and abroad and has been active in organising national and international conferences. Her published work includes *Communicating Rural Development: Strategies and Alternatives* and more than twenty research papers in national and international journals. She is Convener of Research Committee on Sociology of Law of Indian Sociological Society. Besides being an academician, she has been working for raising voice for destitute women and citizen's issues by collaborating with civil society organizations of Rajasthan.

Ranjit Kaur, Assistant Professor, Department of English, St. Xavier's College, Jaipur has a rich experience of teaching a range of subjects of English in various colleges of repute. Having done SLET in English, postgraduation in English, History and Education, B.Ed. and PGDCA, she is currently doing PhD from University of Rajasthan. She has attended several national and international conferences, workshops and symposium and also presented papers.

Sapna Newar is Assistant Professor, Department of Economics, St. Xavier's College, Jaipur.

Chanchal Sinha, a graduate from Lady Irwin College, Delhi is a research scholar at Banasthali Vidyapeeth, Niwai, Rajasthan. She is actively involved in doing social work for the downtrodden sections of society.

Prateeksha Tyagi is a research scholar in the Department of Home Science at Banasthali Vidyapeeth, Niwai, Tonk.

Ritu Sen is Assistant Professor, Department of English, St. Xavier's College, Jaipur.

Ruchi Sharma is a Lecturer in the English Department at St. Xavier's College, Jaipur. She is also pursuing her PhD from IIS University, Jaipur, where she is working on Australian Indigenous writings. Her research and publication interests include women's writing, gender studies and ecocriticism. She has presented papers at national and international conferences, published papers in various journals and books.

Priyanka Sharma is an Assistant Professor at JECRC, Jaipur and has over seven years of teaching experience at leading academic institutions. She did her postgraduation in English Literature with specialization in linguistics and also did her B.Ed. and PhD from University of Rajasthan. Her research and writing interests cover a broad range of topics like diasporic literature, social theories, sociology of culture, feminist criticism and philosophy.

Ramesh Kumar is a Research Fellow at Department of Political Science, University of Hyderabad, Hyderabad. His areas of research are state, governance, and civil society in Rajasthan.

Rameshwar Jat is an Associate Professor in the Department of Economics, University of Rajasthan. He has published more than ten articles in international and national journals and is a regular participant and presenter in national and international conferences, seminars and symposiums.

Rinku Bala is a research scholar at Department of Economics, University of Rajasthan, Jaipur.

Subrata S. Satapathy, a postgraduate in Sociology from JNU, New Delhi and currently a PhD scholar at Utkal University has been working both in the academic as well as in the non-governmental sector. She has been teaching sociology, gender studies, social work and rural development for the last four years and has also worked as a research consultant in various projects.

Shikha Sharma is a social worker and writer. Currently she is a co-editor to an international multidisciplinary research journal and Post Doctoral Fellow from ICSSR, New Delhi. She has written several technical papers and participated in international and national conferences/symposiums to represent issues related to gender and development and feminist theories.

Chandra Kumari is Associate Professor, Human Development, Banasthali University, Niwai, Rajasthan. Her areas of interest are development issues, gender issues, action researches on current problems, community and rural issues.

Kanika Varma is Associate Professor, Department of Home Science, Maharani's College, University of Rajasthan. Her research areas are women health, clinical nutrition, cancer, liver diseases, geriatric nutrition and role of nutrition in non-communicable diseases. She has also been trained in IMNCI and Facility-based Care of SAM children. She has 17 international and two national publications to her credit. She is also actively involved in giving lectures for general public, police personnel, elderly and school children regarding nutrition and healthy lifestyle. She is the President of Indian Dietetic Association, Jaipur Chapter.

Aachu Agarwal is PhD in Food Science and Nutrition from University of Rajasthan, Jaipur. She has been involved in various epidemiological studies, community-based studies and clinical trials in association with eminent organisations like Fortis Escorts Hospital, Jaipur, Monilek Hospital & Research Centre, Jaipur, UGC, DST and UNICEF. She has more than 15 national and international research publications to her credit. Presently she is working with Department of Medical Health and Family Welfare, Rajasthan under National Health Mission.

Shubha Dube is an Associate Professor in the Department of Home Science, University of Rajasthan. She has 22 research papers published and has attended and chaired sessions in several seminars and conferences. Her research areas are human behavioural genetics, gerontology, psychobiology of inter-group attitudes and behaviour.

Pooja Sharma is an Assistant Professor in the Department of Home Science, Churu Girls College, Churu, Rajasthan since 2009. She is also pursuing her PhD from University of Rajasthan, Jaipur.

Introduction

VIDYA JAIN AND RASHMI JAIN

In patriarchal societies, all over the world, women experience subordination on a daily basis regardless of the class to which they belong. Women have been treated as the 'other' who required subordination, control and differential treatment. The subordination and victimisation takes several forms – discrimination, disregard, insult, control, exploitation, oppression, violence – within the family, at the place of work and in society. Sylvia Walby in her book *Theorizing Patriarchy*, calls it "a system of social structures and practices in which men dominate, oppress and exploit women." The experience of patriarchy in India is further deepened by the notion of caste purity, the idea of chastity and honour that is considered intrinsic to women's body and behaviour and, to some extent, the economic dependence of women.

Feminism as a social movement is associated with changes in society. Many aspects of what were once considered to be 'private life', associated with male/female relations in household, family, and other social relationships have been transformed and have acquired a public aspect and there has been an increased involvement of women in public life. Feminists argue that there is still a long road ahead before the goal of equality of males and females is achieved, but there can be no doubt that major advances have occurred toward such equality. A large part of feminist theory and research has been devoted to explaining how the status, role, and position of women in the social world was socially constructed, and was not natural or unchangeable. Femininity has now become a standardised visual image. We learn the rules of what a 'woman' is through bodily discourse – images tell us what face, body shape and clothes we need to have. Feminists have articulated concerns about women being seen as an object. Such gender biases and stereotypes are amply reinforced in the mass media. Print and electronic media in most countries do not provide a balanced picture of women's diverse lives and contributions to society in a changing world.

Violence against women has been one of the mechanisms that are often employed to control women and to demonstrate male power. A 1994 United Nations Development Programme (UNDP) report noted: "In no society are women secure or treated equally to men. Personal insecurity shadows them from the cradle to the grave, and from childhood through adulthood they are abused because of their gender." The indicators of status of women have shown considerable improvement since independence but a lot needs to be done. Despite constitutional provisions and affirmative action by the government to bring in gender equality we find that women still face a lot of challenges. Her struggle for survival begins as soon as she is conceived in the womb which continues till her death. It is indeed an irony that despite significant achievements by women in all realms, safety of women within the home and outside has emerged as the most serious concern for policy makers, law enforcers and women activists. The recent spate of brutal gang rapes provoking widespread public outrage and unprecedented protests has led to a serious debate over the strategies and approaches that need to be evolved to counteract threats towards the safety of women. The complex issues of bodily integrity that women have identified as critical to their intimate security: reproductive rights, body image, violence against women in the family in particular need closer inquiry.

Gender justice is another key aspect of improving women's security concerns. Gender justice refers to legal processes that are equitable, not privileged by and for men, and which distinguish gender-specific injustices that women experience. Girls and women are usually rendered invisible or are marginalized within judicial processes. Also, girls' and women's empowerment through the promotion of gender equality and reduction of gender discrimination is crucial to their security and the protection of their political, civil, economic, social, and cultural rights. Because women's peace-building initiatives are key in addressing and reducing gender inequities and discrimination and related direct and structural violence, their peace-building work must be encouraged and supported by policies and programmes that underscore its importance in improving human security.

There is a plethora of laws regarding women which seek not only to provide justice to women but also to empower them. However, these laws have not been able to bring in a lot of change in the lives of women due to various reasons. The legal/judicial system has to become more responsive and gender sensitive to women's needs, especially in cases of domestic violence and personal assault. Existing laws should be reviewed to ensure that justice is quick and the punishment meted out to the culprits is commensurate with the severity of the offence. The police play a crucial role in promoting peace and security. They are at the frontline of the criminal justice system. Their attitude and response to all involved can have a dramatic impact on ensuing developments, including the prevention of future violent acts and the protection of victims.

Without clear targeted efforts to alter institutional culture and practice to introduce gender mainstreaming, most legal and political reforms are of little worth. Legislative measures are ineffectual unless they are accompanied by alterations in law enforcement standards, values and conduct. A combination of laws prescribing tough retribution, training in ethical and moral education, attitudinal change through socialisation is the need of the hour.

In Indian society, patriarchy, far from becoming liberal and gender equitous is unfolding into a more oppressive, exploitative and violent system. Women in India today are becoming the most vulnerable section as far as their safety and security is concerned. Cases of female foeticide, dowry harassment, sexual assault, molestation, rapes, trafficking, ill treatment of women in houses, violence against women in remote areas, etc. imply that there has been an increasing trend of violence, patriarchal oppression and sexual overdrives in contemporary times.

Low status of women, gender discrimination, violence against women and women's security are serious subjects of research in social sciences in contemporary times. While contemporary social changes have exposed women to unprotected socio-economic, cultural and political environment, there are no corresponding protective social systems and institutions of social justice to safeguard their interests. There are many who are sceptical about women's ability to exercise equal rights with men and about their capacity to play equal role with men. But such apprehensions are ill-founded in the context of the broader opportunities available for women following mechanization of industry and agriculture, enabling women to compete with men successfully.

In spite of the UN Charter of Human Rights and the provisions of the Indian Constitution, women continue to be victims of exploitation. The view that the future generation of a family is carried on and preserved by boys-only has degraded the position of women in society. Whether it is economic security, health security, personal or political security, women and young girls are affected in a very specific way due to their physical, emotional and material differences. Similarly, it is noticed that majority of the women are lacking in the spirit of rebellion. If careful attention is not paid and major steps are not taken, the situation will become extremely critical. Therefore, any attempt to assess the status and problem of women in a society should start from the social framework. Social structure, cultural norms, and value systems are crucial determinants of women's role and their position in society. In respect of the status there is a gap between the theoretical possibilities and their actual realization. The present book is an attempt to understand the myriad aspects of issues related to security of women.

Vidya Jain puts forward her argument that in India, whenever we want to search for an indigenous model of feminism, Gandhian principles can be of great use. Gandhi mingled women's issues with national freedom movement. In his constructive programme, women issues held a dominant place. As Gandhi stood for an egalitarian, non-exploitative and humane society, working for the dignity of women was of extreme importance. While the western feminism is moving towards promoting a more feminist consciousness of the human existence, the Gandhian feminism has potential to go beyond gender and help in building a society in which gender difference becomes redundant for meaningful existence of humans. In a society which is steeped in inequality and underdevelopment, a society where the majority are fighting for their basic necessities of survival, women constitute the most exploited and oppressive section. Women must concern themselves about creating equality not only with respect to gender but also with respect to caste, class, religion and technological colonialism or globalisation. The socio-economic and political scenario all over the world has undergone tremendous changes during last decades. Traditional values are replaced by new set of attitudes and lifestyles which are steeped in materialism and consumerism. Where Vidya Jain's paper deals with these pertinent questions and the solutions offered by Gandhian philosophy, Bernedette Muthien presents an international perspective on women security issues and also takes forward the ideal of satyagraha as a tool for achieving egalitarian partnership.

Muthien in her paper critically interrogates constructions of security generically, and human security specifically, in relation to women and notions of women's security. She documents the space provided to women's representation in security, and argues that among other transformative changes, engendered security will of necessity involve change in the way we think of the world and such issues as national and human security.

Rashmi Jain in her article revisits feminist thought and examines it in current scenario. Tracing the emergence of feminist thought from 1880s by extending support to equal legal and political rights for women; women's right to bodily integrity and autonomy, abortion rights, and reproductive rights (including access to contraception and quality prenatal care); protection of women and girls from domestic violence, sexual harassment and rape; workplace rights, including maternity leave and equal pay, to name a few, we have come a long way. The author also looks at development of feminism in India and discusses the three phases in Indian feminist movement. The first three papers deal with theoretical aspects of issues of feminity and feminism debate.

The second section devotes itself to media and literary reflections on gender issues. Feminists have articulated concerns about women being seen as an object. Such gender biases and stereotypes are amply reinforced in the mass media. Print and electronic media in most countries do not provide a balanced picture of women's diverse lives and contributions to society in a changing world. Ranjit Kaur and Sapna Newar present their views on representation of women in mass media. Although the images of women and types of messages transmitted through various mass media, such as print media, electronic media and films, are not very different, it would be worthwhile to examine the specificity of media in reinforcing existing gender ideology. This paper also discusses the provisions of the Indecent Representation of Women (Prohibition) Act, 1986 and also the purpose for which the Act was introduced.

Chanchal Sinha and Prateeksha Tyagi in their paper too present the observation that mass media has failed to portray the true image of women as they are often portrayed as schemers, manipulators, home breakers or as vamps. Advertisements often commodify them by exploiting their sexuality and the music videos usually show them skimpily dressed with tantalizing choreography. The Indecent Representation of Women (Prohibition) Act, 1986 provides for the regulation of representation of women in media. The need of the hour is to take certain steps that can maintain the dignity of women, such as: creating conditions that enable projection of women in a decent way; form appropriate policies and guidelines for ensuring no negative portrayal of women; and introduce a system of rewards for those who portray women in a positive manner.

Ritu Sen's article seeks to examine the representation of the women in mainstream media (newspapers/magazines/films) and unearths reasons for the gross under-addressal of the issue. She uses two significant depictions, Pinki Virani's *Bitter Chocolate* (2000) and Mira Nair's film *Monsoon Wedding* (2001) to present her case. The research explored *Bitter Chocolate* which exposes the nexus between patriarchal systems and sexual offenders which allow extensive proliferation of child sexual abuse (CSA) in India. It also offers an insight into the socio-psychological repercussions on the life of an abused child.

Ruchi Sharma expresses her ideas on feminine struggle against oppression through interpretation of Raj Kamal Jha's *The Blue Bedspread*. It explores and identifies the malaise in women's life around a common terrain of restrictions posed by the society. The prevailing attitudes and social arrangements presented in the novel further pin down their sense of need and potential in life with limited social opportunities to be grabbed at the mercy of patriarchal set up of society.

The marginalisation of women and the cultural pressure to accept this secondary status has a global perseverance in human history. Women across the world have struggled for ages to live a life of dignity. Priyanka Sharma addresses the concealed yet extremely damaging facet of women's victimisation and analyses the complex hegemony of masculinity maintained by socio-structural control. Like any other form of abuse, emotional abuse is aimed at manipulation of the 'self' of the female individual through an on-going process of belittling her essential feelings, perceptions and ideas. Emotional abuse inflicts greater psychological injury upon the victimised woman than physical violation. She also traces the structural processes and patterns of emotional abuse in women and discusses how social directives shape a woman into a passive, unassuming being.

Ramesh Kumar argues that practices of traditions, honour, and women security are intrinsically interrelated. According to him, any attempt towards maximising women security needs to begin with by *re-visioning* the ideas of honour and traditions. The article does not aim to prescribe any immediate remedial measures towards maximising women security; it is rather a modest attempt towards highlighting the need for evolving a conceptual framework that could be used as a tool to minimise the problems generated due to the intricacies of traditions, honour, and women security in a global context.

Moving away from the victimisation and exploitation of women, Rameshwar Jat and Rinku Bala in their paper "Gender Inequality and Women's Empowerment: A Comparative Analysis of Kerala and Rajasthan" attempt to understand the demographic changes, gender inequality, women's empowerment and relationship between gender inequality and women's empowerment in the states of Rajasthan and Kerala for the decades 1991–2001 and 2001–2011 through analysing secondary data collected from Census of India reports and other published documents. Over the past decade, gender equality and women's empowerment have been explicitly recognised as key not only to the health of nations, but also to social and economic development. Low gender disparity in Kerala reveals higher women empowerment compared to Rajasthan.

One of the factors found to have a positive relationship with women empowerment is employment. In India it is observed that nearly 93 percent of women are engaged in informal sector. According to Subrata S. Satapathy, the informal sector is characterised by vulnerability and the women workers engaged in it are not protected by health and safety legislation. They hardly get paid for their overtime work; have no access to minimum wages, worker benefits like paid vacation and sick leave, health insurance, unemployment insurance, maternity benefits and parental leave. The provision of social protection, including health insurance, pensions, and maternity benefits, improving occupational safety and reducing work hazards, improving access to child care, and building informal workers' organizations, alliances and networks are some of the ways that can be undertaken to improve the conditions of women informal workers.

Gender is an element of social relations based on perceived differences between the sexes. This sheds light on the role gender plays in shaping social interactions. As women have crossed the boundary from the domestic sphere to the professional arena, expectations and representations of women have changed as well. Shikha Sharma's paper contextualises working women's dealings with issues, more importantly, sexual harassment at workplace and its iteration and effects. Sexual harassment limits identity and aspirations of working women and reinforces power relations. Even after legal empowerment (redressal of grievances, laws, policies) it has been felt that women at work have not been protected and present paper attempts to create a discourse on affects of workplace harassment and the legal mechanisms created for safe working environment.

Chandra Kumari in her article expresses the view that violence against women is an act of gender-based violence that results in or is likely to result in physical, sexual or psychological harm or suffering to women in public or private life. She presents findings of a study conducted on women in the NGO's (Mahila Samakhya and Disha) from Saharanpur (U.P.). The findings demonstrate that most of the respondents suffer from physical violence, particularly by alcoholic husbands. A great number of respondents preferred to remain silent while facing violence.

In India, it is observed that the health of women and families is compromised by inadequate, inaccessible and unaffordable medical care, lack of sanitation, unsafe drinking water, poor nutrition, insufficient research and education about women's health practices. Kanika Varma and Aachu Agarwal argue that gender discrimination from birth to adulthood; poverty, unemployment, stress, restricted access to resources and illiteracy, etc. in countries like India make women vulnerable to poor health and nutritional status. Nutrient intake of adult women after the age of child-bearing has not been studied extensively. Health and nutrition programmes in India focus on pregnant and lactating women and women after the period of child-bearing and rearing are neglected. This is particularly important in present scenario as the non-communicable disease burden is increasing in India at younger age.

Shubha Dube and Pooja Sharma argue that despite constitutional guarantee of equality, exploitation of women continues. Elder women are facing domestic violence of different kind and have to adjust with them as they find no other solution to it due to their unawareness to certain laws and illiteracy among them. State government has framed few programmes but they are just eyewash and not sufficient enough to bring satisfactory changes. Emotional abuse – the hidden side of women victimisation is another crime against women which most of the women neither understand nor can it be proved.

Promoting gender equality and advancing the status of all women and girls around the world remains one of the greatest unmet challenges of our times, and one that is vital to achieving nation's overall developmental policy objectives. This requires that a nation ensures women and girls, including those most marginalized, are able to participate fully in public life, are free from violence, and have equal access to education, economic opportunity, health care, broader economic prosperity as well as political stability and security.

Section I

Theoretical Constructions

CHAPTER 1

Gandhian Feminism

The Question of Women's Dignity and Honour

VIDYA JAIN

Gandhi stood for an egalitarian, non-exploitative and humane society and hence working for the dignity of marginalised sections like dalits, peasants and women was of extreme importance. Gandhi's concept of womanhood as well as his initiatives and ideas in the economic, political and the social realms produced a distinctive indigenous theory of feminism. While the western feminism is moving towards promoting a mere feminist consciousness of the human existence, the Gandhian feminism has potential to go beyond gender and help in building a society in which gender differences become redundant for meaningful existence of humans. Feminist discourse has been dominated by western hegemonistic feminist theories which ignore the local, particular and indigenous identities. In India when there is a search for an indigenous model of feminism, Gandhi's principles are of great use. Gandhi mingled women's issues with the national liberation movement. In his constructive programme women's issues had a very dominant place. The present article seeks to analyse and interrogate Gandhian model of feminism and concept of egalitarian social ethos as a solution to the specific problems and challenges of Indian women.

I

Women have been treated as the 'Other' who required subordination, control and differential treatment. The cumulative effect of such mindsets resulted in the marginalisation of women from the public sphere and their confinement to the private sphere. It appears that, from the moment of human interaction and language, women have always been associated with the private, and men with the public. The traditional divide between public and private has caused women to be largely excluded from the public domains of economy and politics, and confined to their 'private' roles as homemakers and mothers, resulting in male domination of the system. There is no clear origin of this public/private division; it could have been, as Germaine Greer humorously suggested, 'while the male-hunter-gatherer strolled along burdened with no more than his spear and a throwing stick, his female mate trudged along after him carrying their infant, their shelter, their food supplies and her digging stick.' The separation of social space into public and private has also been referred to as *ghar/bahar*, inner/outer and internal/external dichotomies. The relegation of women to the so-called sacred or private sphere of the home has also been defined as the domestic ideology or the cult of domesticity which characterises family and home as the proper/appropriate domain of women and it was based on the premise that women were innately weaker – both physically and intellectually – and less capable of taking care of themselves in the rough and tumble of the public life. Women's confinement to the private sphere was reinforced by the so-called enlightened and progressive upheavals in history. Martin Luther who had raised the standard of rebellion against Papacy and the Catholic Church in the sixteenth century never got tired of repeating that Lord intended women to confine her activities to cooking, child-bearing and sewing. He remarked, 'Take women out of the kitchen and they are good for nothing'. The leaders of the French Revolution felt that the delicate constitution of women was suitable for perpetuation of species and household chores. The sphere of politics, property and public life were regarded as inappropriate for women.

In most societies there has been a clear demarcation of the public domain – war, production and politics- and the private domain of the family, domestic labour, reproduction and sexuality. The unequal and arbitrary division of labour on the basis of sex precluded women from access to power and resources leading to subordination, vulnerability and powerlessness. Mary Wollstonecraft asserted that exclusion from women from production led to their disempowerment and oppression. Fredrick Engels too considered the creation of private property and sexual division of labour as the primary conditions that led to subordination and subjection of women and also adversely affected their freedom of movement. Moreover confinement of women to the domain of family and home led to the invisibility of women's work. Most productive work done by women is neither recognised nor remunerated. Moreover, women's work as child-rearers and producers is not considered economic contribution at all. Since the beginning of first wave feminism and fight for women's suffrage in the West, women's movement has challenged the gendered division between the private sphere attributed to women and the public sphere of men. One of the earliest manifestations of liberal first-wave feminism in Europe, Mary Wollstonecraft's *A Vindication of the Rights of Woman* (1792), was written in the wake of the French Revolution and is still read as a seminal text. Virginia Woolf's *A Room of One's Own* (1929) and Simone de Beauvoir's *The Second Sex* (1949) are central to the canon.

II

Women's situation, in addition to these universal deprivations, is also defined by culture specificities. Plurality in Indian women's situation has rendered it inappropriate to construct any facile stereotype of the typical Indian woman. Nevertheless, certain ideals that define and inspire the normative model of Indian womanhood have shown remarkable continuity over centuries. These ideals not only enjoy widespread recognition at the societal level but have impinged deeply on the psyche of women themselves. Most dominant and pervasive of these ideal are the *Pativrata* or the ideal of a devoted wife and self-sacrificing mother. Women, as mothers, have commanded unusual honour and veneration (also a role in decision-making). Certain characters from Indian mythology like docile and acquiescent Sita and a devoted Savitri are the salient models for Indian women. In spite of modernisation the all-pervading impact of these models has not changed drastically.

The historical reconstruction of the status and condition of women in Indian society has underscored a trajectory of gradual deterioration since the post-Vedic period. The golden age of Indian womanhood in the Rig Vedic period was followed by epochs that witnessed the subordination of women within the family and exclusion from the spheres of power, resources and education. The low status of women was signified by the emergence of specific social practices like *sati*, prohibition of widow marriage, preference for child marriage etc. Significantly, these practices continued unabated till the 19th century. These practices that largely revolved around the institution of marriage and women's exclusion from formal system of education remained the focus of the reformers in the social reform movement of the 19th century.

In the pre-independence period, three historical processes have sought to redefine femininity in Indian society. Firstly, the vibrant movement for social reform in the nineteenth century, while conceding extensive space to women's issues, sought to construct a new femininity without deconstructing the traditional virtues, images and roles of women as competent house makers, devoted wives and benevolent mothers. The objective of the reformers was not deconstruction of traditional virtues, images and roles of women as devoted wives and nurturing mothers and homemakers. The regressive nature of women's discourse in the 19th century is exemplified in the debates on women's education and the alternatives that were put forth for widows. The miserable condition of widows aroused some of the most graphic responses in the social reform movement. However, the option of remarriage remained a sensitive issue and characterised by considerable reluctance and confusion even among the reformers. Similarly, education was espoused not because of its liberatory content but to confer dignity on women within the family and also to improve efficiency in their traditional roles as mothers, wives and home-makers. Only a few reformers like Agarkar, Ramabai, Phule and Dwarkanath Ganguly conceived of new social roles for women and therefore advocated a curriculum that would equip them for these extra-familial roles.

The emergence of the women's organisations in the 1920s, 'inspired, formed and dominated by women, unlike the previous women's organisations which owed much to male leadership, was another historical milestone that led to the transformation of the women's movement.' The establishment of Women's India Association, (1917), National Conference for Women and All India Women's Conference, within a short span of a decade, catapulted women as agents of change rather than as passive recipients of reform. Women's issues not only acquired urgency but the pioneers of the movement had a holistic approach to the various women's issues which were viewed as interlinked. In addition to other issues, especially female education, its concern for women's health was also very obvious. Limited space in the homes resulting in inferior living and work areas for women remained a major preoccupation of the All Indian Women's Conference. The need for a safer environment and better working conditions for women industrial workers were also articulated. In addition to reproductive health the women's movement tried to address the issue of women's occupational health, both outside and at home.

Last but not the least, agitation against British imperialism, particularly during the Gandhian phase, was a catalytic process that brought forth women from the invulnerable confines of the *Zenana* to the vanguard of nationalist politics. Gandhi's emergence on the Indian political scene revolutionised and intensified women's commitment to the freedom struggle. He brought forth a unique political process based on concepts of *Ahimsa* and *Satyagraha* that were more conducive to women's participation. He felt that women had great ability to suffer and could therefore, play a vital role in the movement. Women participated in large numbers in the mass movements of the 1920s and the 1930s. Jawaharlal Nehru, while recounting women's phenomenal contribution to the Civil Disobedience Movement of the 1930 wrote: 'Most of us men folk were in prison. And then a remarkable thing happened. Our women came to the front and took charge of the struggle. Women had always been there, of course, but now there was an avalanche of them, which took not only the British Government but their own men folk by surprise. Here were these women, women of the upper and middle classes, leading sheltered lives in their homes – peasant women, working class women, rich women, pouring out in their tens of thousands in defiance of the government order. It was not only that display of courage and daring but what was even more surprising was the organisational power they showed." As has been rightly observed, 'Viewed from the perspective of women's participation, the freedom struggle crystallised into a tremendous confidence building process which radicalised women's own perception of their self image. Participation in the large liberation struggle not only generated amongst them the confidence to lead their own struggle against patriarchal domination but it also symbolised a significant breakthrough in the entire public/private debate by producing social sanction for new extra familial roles.'

In the post-independence period, the commitment of the Indian freedom struggle to the equality of the sexes was enshrined in the Constitution of India, enacted in 1950. The Preamble to the Constitution of India resolved to secure to all its citizens justice – social, economic and political and equality of status and opportunity. Article 14 of the Indian Constitution ensures equality before law for all its citizens and Article 15 prohibits any discrimination, Besides, the Directive Principles of State Policy embody the principles and policy goals of the welfare state. With the attainment of independence and constitutional provision of a formal structure of equality, it was felt the goals of social equality and egalitarian structure of society would be automatically accomplished. The visibility of educated middle class women's entry into professions further strengthened the myth of improvement in women's status. The consequent complacency on women's issues among the policy makers and among the women leaders themselves led to the weakening of the women's movement and the women's question gradually faded from the arena of public debate.

The next major development in the post-independence period which reopened women's issues and laid out the concerns of the resurgent women's movement of the 70s was the publication of the report of a Committee on the Status of Women in India (CSWI) in 1974. The investigations of the committee collated a large body of data on different aspects of women's lives and identified disturbing demographic indicators like the accelerated decline in sex ratio and increasing gender gaps in life expectancy, child mortality, literacy and economic participation. The findings of the CSWI expressed serious doubts over the 'development ' and 'modernisation' models ushered in after independence and confirmed their failure to arrest the process of economic marginalisation of women.

The celebration of the International Year of Women in 1975 drew global attention to the predicament of women and further sharpened the awareness of women's unequal status in India society. The shocking revelations of the CSWI report and the internationalisation of the women's question as a result of the decadal thrust provided by the preparations for the U.N. Conference in Mexico (1985) infused new life and vigour into the Indian women's movement. The second wave of women's movement questioned the patriarchal value structure, inegalitarian structure of society and unequal social and economic relations based on oppression of women. From its earliest phase, the growing violence against women through the institutions of family, society and state and the increasing marginalisation of women in the economic sphere formed major concerns of the women's movement.

Since the 1990s, the processes of liberalisation and globalisation have unleashed forces of materialism and consumerism that have sought to impact women's status in Indian society. In this all pervading materialistic, agnostic and consumerist culture women's images are deconstructed and reconstructed by media everyday. The whole politics of beauty is propagated. In search of impossible figures – features – fairness women's dignity is at stake. Media and market are the new structures of patriarchy adding to the already existing old structures of patriarchies. Globalisation is a masculine concept. Globalisation is new slavery, new holocaust and new apartheid. It is a war against nature, workers, farmers, *dalits*, poor and women. To break this trinity of poverty, powerlessness and patriarchy we have to reclaim Gandhian ideas.

III

The historical role of Gandhi in revolutionising women's roles in India, in addition to his vision of an inclusive society, decentralised polity and economy has the potential to empower women. To gain insights into Gandhian model of feminism, it would be instructive to classify it under three heads: Gandhi's concept of ideal women, his views on inhibitive and debilitating social evils and his efforts to involve women in the freedom struggle.

Gandhi believed in equality between genders. He believed that women possessed the same intellectual faculties as men have. Addressing the annual gathering of the Bombay Bhagini Samaj held on February 20, 1918 he had remarked, 'Woman is the companion of man gifted with equal mental capacities. She has the right to participate in the minutest detail of the activities of men and she has the same right of freedom and liberty.' Similarly his belief in gender equality was evident in his distaste for son preference. He remarked, 'I make no distinction between son and daughter. Such distinction in my opinion is invidious and wrong. The birth of a son or a daughter should be welcomed alike.' In fact, Gandhi even asserted the superiority of women over men. In a radical reconstruction he gave women a confidence in herself, empowering her in family and involved her in political life. He says 'My contribution to the great problem (of women's role in society) lies in my presenting for acceptance of truth and ahimsa in every walk of life. Women will be unquestioned leader'. On another occasion he wrote, 'To call woman the weaker sex is a libel; it is man's injustice to woman. If by strength is meant brute strength, then, indeed, is woman less brute than man. If by strength is meant moral power, then woman is immeasurably man's superior. Has she not greater intuition, is she not more self-sacrificing, has she not greater courage? Without her man could not be. If non-violence is the law of our being, the future is with woman... Who can make a more effective appeal to heart than woman?' (YI, 10–4–1930: 121) Nevertheless, he asserted that 'while men and women are equal they are not identical. Equality of sexes does not mean equality of occupations. There may be no legal bar against a woman hunting or wielding a lance. But she instinctively recoils from a function that belongs to man, nature has created sexes as complements of each other. Their functions are defined as are their forms.' (H, 2–12–1939: 359) Gandhi saw home and household activities as the main sphere of women's activities. His notion of gender equality does not extend to equality in employment. In this context Madhu Kishwar has observed, 'He wanted first and foremost, to change the moral condition of women's lives, and to do away with the vile abuses of power by men, but not so much to alter the basic relationship from which that power was derived. He attempted to extend the power of women as wives, mothers and sisters within the household rather than to have women acquire political power in their own right. Gandhi did not envisage a radical change in their social role even though he was in favour of removing all legal and juridical disabilities against them'. In advocating and upholding women's traditional roles as wives, mothers and homemakers, Gandhi reinforced the views of the nineteenth century reformers.

Gandhi often presented ideals before women, drawn from Indian traditions, mythology and history. He invoked the instances of ancient role models who were epitomes of Indian womanhood. He often talked about Sita, Draupadi, Damayanti and Mirabai as great women. According to Usha Thakkar, 'There is nothing new for a social reformer drawing inspiration from the tradition. What is new here is the fact that this innovate interpretation of these characters gives a glimpse of the dynamic element in his thinking. He did not accept the negative elements of the Hindu tradition. He visualised the Indian women as new Sitas, Draupadis and Damayantis, pure, firm and self-controlled'. For Gandhi, Sita was not a weak and dependent creature, but a strong woman who thus kept her heart and body pure. Moreover, she should defy the might of Ravana by sheer moral courage and she would not waste 'a single moment on pleasing Rama by physical charms'. Implying thereby that a woman could assert herself in doing what she considered right even if the husband thought otherwise. Another ideal model presented by Gandhi was Draupadi who was not dependent on men and saved herself by an appeal to Krishna when the Pandavas failed to protect her. Here the appeal to Krishna is to be understood as following one's own conscience. However, Gandhi also invokes Meerabai very often as an ideal character for Indian women. Meera deviated from the ideal of a devoted wife to rebel against the tyranny of her husband and family yet she is one of Gandhi's favourite symbolic figures. He held her as up as a symbol of non-violent resistance to injustice and hence a *satyagrahi*. He also saw her as an example of wife's assertion of her individuality and as a symbol of power of love and sacrifice. Gandhi desired the fearless and sacrificing Mira to be seen as a role model by Indian women. The manner in which Gandhi applauded Meera's rebellious and assertive spirit and by upholding her as a role-model for women is significant. Meera has been often hailed as the original feminist and women's struggle for independence and identity have been often traced to her. Thus while Gandhi, like the nineteenth century reformers, sought to project indigenous symbols rooted in Indian tradition, he digressed from them in two ways. Firstly, it is evident that while Gandhi invoked those female characters from mythology and tradition who have been revered for their *pativratya* or devotion to their husband, he reinvented these characters to construct a new kind of wife – assertive, firm, pure and strong. Secondly, he digressed from the prevalent discourse on women when he selected Meera as one of the role models for Indian women. Gandhian feminism thus emerges as a Gandhi also came down heavily on social customs that sought to denigrate and inhibit women. Most of these social evils derived sanction and legitimacy from *shastras*. In this context his approach to *shastras* needs to be spelt out. He warned against blind adherence to the tenets of the *shastras* and instead advocated that 'we must test on the anvil of reason everything that is capable of being tested by it and reject that which does not satisfy it even though it may appear in an ancient garb'. He cautioned that all that is printed in the name of scriptures need not be taken as the word of God or the inspired word. He had immense historical insight to understand that shastric injunctions were promulgated to suit the challenges and problems of their times. Commenting on Manu's injunction on curtailment of freedom for women, he remarked, 'It only shows that probably at the time when it was promulgated women were kept in a state of subjection.' In the twentieth century most of the social reformers had realised the futility of justifying reforms on the basis of *shastras* and instead upheld caste as the real roadblock in the way of reform. Moreover, the *shastras* had multiple and contradictory voices and could be effectively employed by opposing parties.

Like nineteenth century reformers, Gandhi came down heavily on the evil practices associated with the institution of marriage. He denounced child marriages and upheld that marriage was a sacrament that could be performed only when the girl was fully developed. He considered child marriages as the root cause of the deplorable condition of child widows. Gandhi was not in favour of remarriage of all the widows but he considered remarriage of virgin widows as not only desirable but the bounden duty of all parents who happen to have such widowed daughters. It is true that Gandhi was not in favour of remarriage of consummate widows but at the same time he was against second marriage of widowers. He was in favour of strict monogamy both for men and women. His attitude towards remarriage reflects the widespread and deep-seated prejudice in contemporary upper-class society. Those reformers who took progressive stand on the issue of widow remarriage made strange exceptions. Peary Chand Mitra, a member of Young Bengal, who even published a woman's journal, *Masik Patrika,* supported women's education and opposed early marriages but would not advocate widow remarriage. Even Bankim Chandra in his essay *Samya,* generally considered his most radical piece of writing, does not admit of widow remarriage as readily as women's education. The essay in fact contends that a widow who was chaste and loved her deceased husband could hardly marry a second time. Similarly, Vivekanand saw in the love and fidelity of the widow, the Absolute or an immutable God. He actually supported Sasipada Banerjee's Widow Home, which was trying to give helpless widows some dignity and social resettlement. Even Tagore, in his lecture 'Hindu Vibaha' delivered in 1887 felt that while second marriages were acceptable in the case of men, remarriages of women were socially more disruptive as they involved transference of name, lineage, loyalty and property to the other family. Like Vivekanand, Gandhi too appreciated the restraint and sufferings of the Indian widows and considered them as one of 'gifts of Hinduism to humanity'.

Gandhi, however, came down heavily on child marriages as immoral and inhuman which made innocent girls objects of men's lust. He advocated eradication of this malpractice through mobilisation of public opinion and through agitations. Gandhi stood for the rights of women over her own body. He even exhorted women that they should resist the husbands in marriage and should not succumb to their carnal desires. He considered child marriage as a veritable obstacle in the path of swaraj. Gandhi also decried evils like extravagant and opulent marriage as also the custom of dowry which defiled the pure character of the institution of marriage. He also came down heavily on the custom of *purdah* as a means to protect women's purity. Gandhi upheld that women should strive to bring about change in their own situation and work for the welfare of their own sex.

The above discourse testifies to Gandhi's strong denunciation of social evils that sought to inhibit and denigrate women. Gandhi conformed to the reformist mindset of the Indian renaissance as far as his views on child marriage, widow remarriage and purdah were concerned. Moreover, he sought to reinforce and idealise the traditional images of women and upheld home as the centre of women's activities. He never desired that women forsake their conventional feminine virtues, images and roles. Despite his apparently regressive stand on women's position, Gandhi digressed from their approach in some ways. Firstly, he upheld women's rights over their bodies and he saw women not as recipients of reform but as active agents in reforming their own condition. Moreover, he emerged as one of the key figures who successfully challenged the public private divide which led to social sanction for women's public roles.

The most important contribution of Gandhi was his success in involving women in the freedom movement. Gandhi espoused a distinctive method of protest, dissent and change called Satyagraha which he upheld as a moral ethical struggle. Its basic meaning is holding on to truth, hence truth force. Gandhi says, 'I have also called it love force or soul force. In the application of Satyagraha, I discovered in the earlier stages that pursuit of truth did not admit of violence being inflicted on one's opponent but that he must be weaned from error by patience and sympathy'. In the method of Satyagraha fraud, lying, deceit, and all the ugly brood of violence and untruth have absolutely no room. He upheld that women's innate qualities of suffering and sacrifice were more suited than men to take part in a non-violent struggle. As Pratibha Jain has observed, 'Suffering as a method of protest in Gandhi's non-violent struggle was intended to leave a deep impact on the adversaries, whether they were the British imperialists, the high caste Hindus, the liquour traders or the foreign cloth merchants. He evolved a collective style of suffering for attainment of larger goal – both social and political'. The womanly qualities which so far were considered as their weakness were redefined and remoulded by Gandhi as their superior virtues which made them stronger than men. Gandhi in fact desired universalisation of these so-called womanly traits.

Gandhi's advocacy of non violence created favourable conditions for participation of women in all movements he launched. They came out from homes instead of hiding in fear. Women played a pivotal role in Gandhian movements as 'dictators, organisers, captains, messengers and a whole lot of things'. In all the agitations against British imperialism they took part in multiple processes like laying *dharnas*, going to jails, facing police brutalities and walking in the processions. Gandhi was able to inculcate so much confidence in women that during the Civil Disobedience Movement, they were no longer satisfied by limited roles and instead demanded more challenging, courageous and leadership roles. Women started taking initiative not only in direct action struggle but also in organisational matters. In fact, women demonstrated immense organisational aptitude through their organisations like Rashtriya Sevika Sangh and Desh Sevika Sangh which had played a seminal role in planning and executing programmes of boycott and *dharna*.

Gandhi's encouragement to women in political movement too has been critiqued on many grounds. Madhu Kishwar has upheld that despite great concern for women's rights Gandhi never encouraged women to organise as a political force in their own right for their rightful place in society. As a result women remained almost invisible in positions of power and decision-making even within the Congress organisations. On one occasion Kamla Devi Chattopadhyaya registered her protest and deep anguish when Nehru while constituting his working committee in 1936 did not include a single woman. Similarly Sarla Devi Chaudhrani's famous remark that 'Congress wants women to be law breakers but not law makers' also conveys deep frustration felt by women on being marginalised by the Congress leadership at decision-making levels. Even within the movement, women were expected to be more active in the constructive programme. Probably, as Kishwar has concluded, 'Gandhi found the world of politics too ruthless and corrupt. They were to be the moral force in the movement by staying away from the struggle for power and by transforming people's hearts through their quiet, non-violent strength.'

In summation one can say that at the level of ideas and images, Gandhi articulated a concept of womanhood that reinforced traditional stereotypes of women. He saw home as the main sphere of women's activities. While western feminism has laid stress on equality of roles since they felt that sexual division of labour was asymmetric, hierarchical and unequal. The binary of public and private to denote men's and women's roles, once established by violence was perpetuated through the institutions of family, state, religion and other powerful ideological systems. Gandhi however at the level of precept reinforces the traditional divide between *ghar* (home) and *bahar* (outside). He sought to uphold a model of gender equality which emphasised complementarity rather than similarity of roles. In fact during the freedom struggle Indian feminists too believed in complimentarity rather than competition between the sexes. It can also be explained as a pragmatic political necessity to nullify the disintegrating forces based on gender, caste and religion and avoid all divisive tendencies threatening the unity of the national movement which was passing through a decisive phase. During the struggle for suffrage, the women leaders too projected the demand in terms of 'social feminism' rather than radical equality. The demand was presented not in a spirit of aggression, competition or encroachment upon male privileges. Even confident and competent women leaders committed to the struggle for gender equality canvassed in favour of the demand as an extension of women's traditional roles as nurturers of children and custodians of morality and justice in society. Sarojini Naidu, while canvassing in favour of the demand remarked, 'We ask for franchise, we ask for vote, not that we might interfere with you in your official functions, your civic duties, your public place and power, but rather that we might lay the foundation of national character in the souls of the children that we hold upon our laps and instill them with the ideas of nationality ... that we might be able by our own implacable ideas of moral purity to cleanse our public life ...' . Similarly the employment of traditional paradigm metaphor and language by Gandhi was, perhaps, designed to diffuse male hostility.

At the level of practice however Gandhi played a transformative role as far as women's role was concerned. He successfully drew a wedge in the divide between the public and the private spheres and gave moral legitimacy to women's public roles. The fact that women came out in large numbers to participate in the numerous processes of the freedom movement led to social acceptance of their new roles in public life. This was the reason that women's entry into politics, administration and other spheres in the post-independence period was smooth and almost unopposed.

Gandhi's model of feminism was thus defined by considerable restraint and caution wherein he refrained from advocating radical or revolutionary changes. He had adopted similar caution towards other issues also – caste reform, land reform and labour problems. He believed in gradual reform rather than revolutionary changes.

References

Forbes, Geraldine. 'Votes for Women'. In Vina Mazumdar (ed.), *Symbols of Power*. New Delhi: Allied Publishers, 1979.

Jain, Pratibha (ed.). *Selections from Nehru's Writings and Speeches*. Jaipur: Kumar and Company, 1989.

——. 'Gandhi on Women: Imaging a New Identity'. In Pratibha Jain and Rajan Mahan (eds), *Women Images*, Jaipur: Rawat, 1996.

Kasturi, Leela and Vina Mazumdar. *Women and Indian Nationalism*. Indian Association for Women's Studies. Delhi: Vikas, 1994.

Kishwar, Madhu. 'Gandhi on Women'. *Economic and Political Weekly*, 12 October 1985.

Kumar, Radha. *History of Doing*. New Delhi: Kali for Women, 1993.

CHAPTER 2

Engendering Security through Egalitarianism

BERNEDETTE MUTHIEN

Introduction

This paper will critically interrogate constructions of security generically, and human security specifically, in relation to women and notions of women's security. The constructs national security and human security will be critiqued, whose interests these serve, and how these constructs are specifically gendered (and class-based) and neglect issues relevant to women specifically, and other marginalised members of the international community.

Johan Galtung's (1996) triangular model of violence, with its antitheses peace, will be examined, in order to explicate violence generically, which will lead to an examination of gender-based violence more specifically, premised on a deconstruction of patriarchal ideology, and drawing on the peace and feminist anthropologies of egalitarian studies.

What will be evinced is that violence and oppression brutalises everyone, from victims/survivors to perpetrators to witnesses, and that all will benefit from transforming societies into equitable peaceful spaces, as even 'freeriders' (e.g. the millions of black South Africans who were not part of the anti-Apartheid struggles) have benefited from the end of Apartheid.

The final section seeks to rethink activisms, employing the work of Mahatma Gandhi, Martin Luther King, Nelson Mandela and Ang San Suu Kyi.

State-centred security concerns itself with armies, guns and war, and excludes people's basic needs. This paper argues that the imperatives for peace are egalitarianism, which by its very nature engenders human security and justice.

Is Security Gendered?

At workshops in Cape Town, South Africa, grass roots women identified their needs for spouses or partners to be faithful, monogamous, and non-violent. Given the high rate of generic-societal violence, as well as the health implications of HIV and AIDS, these community women also requested more mortuary vans and ambulances. There were also specific calls for an end to violence, an end to the gangsterism that plagues their communities, and critically, given the pandemic of gender-based violence in South Africa, an end to violence against women and children.

A study on violence against women in metropolitan South Africa found that almost 60 per cent of women felt 'very unsafe' while walking in their own neighbourhoods at night, with only five per cent of women feeling 'very safe' in their neighbourhoods at night (Bollen et al., 1999: 75, 78). The alarming statistics on violence against women illustrates that a lack of women's security affects the entire Southern African region. Goldblatt and Meintjes (1998: 8) discuss the present effects on women, of Apartheid violence against communities, the condition of women in the aftermath:

> The entrenchment of violence creates new daily insecurities for women – constant and overwhelming fear, exposure to abuse and obscenities, and threats of rape, kidnapping or death for themselves, their children or other relatives.

Security and Peace Studies have been dominated by men, and men's interests; particularly their emphasis on guns and war. As with most fields of study, women's interests and needs have been largely neglected and ignored.

Contesting Security

Barry Buzan (1983) recognises security as an underdeveloped and contested concept. Buzan draws critical conceptual distinctions between defence and security, individual and national security, national and international security, violent means and peaceful ends. He applies his concept across a range of military, political, economic and social sectors. According to Buzan (1983: 20) the national security problem is a systemic security problem in which individuals, states and the system, all play a part. Thus Buzan (1983: 187) proposes the holistic notion of systemic security so that the:

> national security problem defines itself as much in economic, political and social terms as in military ones.

National Security

Security has tended to be defined in terms of the nation state. Thus the notion of national security, emanating predominantly from the field of Strategic Studies, is dominated by a neo-realist mode of thought,[1] with its focus on power and institutions of power, especially the military. Neo-realist thought and notions of the state derive from Thomas Hobbes (1651). His infamous postulate that life in a state of nature is 'nasty, brutish and short', epitomises the neo-realist hypothesis of an international state system of anarchy. Classical American neo-realist theorists, especially Carr (1939), Morgenthau (1948) and Waltz (1954, 1979) built on the Hobbesian notion of an anarchic state system. Reacting to this position, Maxi Schoeman (1998: 7, 22–23), who has extensively researched women's security in Southern Africa, criticises Waltz in particular for 'de-historicising' the international state system and assuming its:

> inevitability, rather than admitting that it is a human construct and a product of a specific era and context.

The British academic, Hedley Bull (1977), tried to theorise a form of anarchy characterised by at least some interdependence and co-operation in his writings on an 'international society' of states. Bull's key contention centres on his notion of 'society' versus that of the traditional, more anarchic system, thus arguably placing his thinking between neo-liberal[2] and neo-realist thought. Issues about what constitutes cooperation, and whose interests it serves, can be derived from rudimentary studies of the world system's theory of

Wallerstein (1979). More recent critical theory is fundamentally concerned with historicising the *status quo*, and seeking structural transformation.

This traditional notion of national security, in terms of armies, guns and war, emphasises the state as both the primary actor and level of analysis. Narrow state-centrism excludes other important actors and levels of analyses, including individuals and groups (ethnicities and religious groupings, political and ideological groups, and non-state actors like corporate mercenaries), as well as other institutions (e.g. transnational corporations (TNCs) and multi-national corporations (MNCs), international financial institutions (IFIs) such as the World Bank, as well as the global arms trade – from manufacturers to marketers to purchasers). The modern move away from inter-state war to intra-state conflict, in particular, stresses the importance of group and institutional analyses, e.g. the conflict in the Democratic Republic of Congo (DRC) involves regional, linguistic, economic, gender, group, state and international dimensions. It involves various political and military groups, as well as especially diamond and oil TNCs, as well as other African states, notably Namibia, Zimbabwe, Angola, Uganda, Rwanda, South Africa, as well as non-African states such as the United States, Belgium and France. It includes non-state actors such as mercenaries, arms and other suppliers, locally and internationally. More recently entrenched in the DRC are also scores of humanitarian and faith workers from around the world, engaged in everything from health care (treating, e.g. fistula due to sexual violence and/or early pregnancy), to economic development and other social programmes. These volunteers and professionals also critically need to be accounted for in any substantive analyses of the country, region and continent.

The skewed focus on the state usually excludes the worst affected – women and children – especially in rural areas where women and children are the ones who have to seek fresh water and wood for fuel, which exposes them to landmines (and sexual assault). Hence the irony of men who plant landmines to deter other men, but which largely kill and maim women and children trying to survive during and after conflicts.

The traditional definition of security also emphasises protection from harm for citizens of a country within national boundaries. National boundaries in Africa are colonial legacies, often arbitrary, and variously disputed, e.g. the Kasikili/Sedudu Island conflict between Namibia and Botswana. Sovereignty of borders is often bestowed, with little or no consultation, and with little regard by the international community to the impacts on the inhabitants within the borders. Eritrea, for example, is deemed a sovereign state after its secession from Ethiopia, while Somaliland, where women contributed significantly to brokering peace, is not officially recognised. The ongoing conflicts between Sudan and the newly independent South Sudan further epitomise the complexities of arbitrary borders, contested state sovereignty and international recognition, in theory and law, but more so in practice.

The idea of protection from harm for citizens is narrowly defined, and effectively means protection from foreign attack, but does not preclude offensive measures deemed in the interests of citizens and state. For example, South Africa and Botswana's military intervention in Lesotho during 1998, as well as Namibia's incursions into Angola against UNITA, in addition to South Africa's intervention in the attempted military coup in Lesotho during September 2014. So too, the traditional definition of harm does not include other aspects of safety, security or well-being, including the environment, basic needs (for example food and housing), identity and dignity. A more holistic definition of protection from harm would mean more than the traditional protection from war and invasion by foreign armies. It would mean, to name a few examples, protection from hunger, protection from poverty, protection from sexual assault for women, children and men.

The traditional national security definition of protection from harm refers to a state-level notion of harm, and does not protect citizens from homelessness, illiteracy and unemployment. Nor does it protect citizens' fundamental human rights, as enshrined in the South African Constitution, to be free of discrimination on the grounds of race, class, gender, spirituality or sexuality. Negative peace, or the absence of war, conforms to traditional definitions of security in general and traditional protection from harm in particular. Positive peace, on the other hand, means both negative peace, as well as the realisation of even the most basic of social justice needs.

Traditional notions of security are based on conventional (though flawed) distinctions between public and private spheres.

The state has traditionally been concerned with the male-dominated public realm. Thus issues outside of the public realm, including domestic violence, job discrimination, the status of women, have not been viewed as concerns of national security.

According to veteran peace educator and activist, Betty Reardon,[3] the three major problems with the international security system are:

> (Firstly) it is dominantly masculine rather than human in conception; (secondly) it is designed to achieve the security of the state rather than that of persons or human groups; and (thirdly), what is most readily evident, it addresses only one of four fundamental sources of human wellbeing. The condition of world-wide insecurity exists because the present state-centred security paradigm places a priority on protection against harm from others over all other sources of human wellbeing. The militarised international security system is maintained at the expense of the abuse of the natural environment. It sets limits on meeting the economic and social needs of the world's poor. It disregards and violates fundamental, universal human rights, and provides inadequate protection against the harms of ill health, poor infrastructures, and accident and disaster provision, as inordinate resources, research, human talent and human effort are squandered on the armed defence of 'national security'. The system is inadequate, indeed, dangerous because it is imbalanced. It is derived by exclusively masculine, outwardly directed standards applied by the predominantly male 'national security' establishments who have not been socialised to focus on human needs.

Human Security

A second approach that contests the national security model is proposed by Johan Galtung, who matured from radical analyses of (under) development since the 1960s to groundbreaking peace studies during the 1990s. Based on the work of other researchers [especially the work of Robert Johansen of the Peace Studies Programme at Notre Dame (1975–1996)] over two decades, Galtung (1996) took the debate into new realms of understanding the requirements for peace when he proposed what has come to be called the human security model. This model, Reardon asserts, focuses on environmental security, basic needs, issues of dignity and identity, and finally, protection from harm.

The human security paradigm is designed to provide a more holistic, comprehensive definition of security and protection from all forms of harm. These include indirect or structural, cultural, and direct or personal, and their respective antitheses, as postulated in Galtung's (1996) model. Structural violence (with its antithesis structural peace) refers to, for example, discrimination based on class, ethnicity or gender, violence embedded in the very structure of society. Personal or direct violence implies a direct verbal or physical attack of one person on another. Cultural violence 'serves to legitimise direct and structural violence' (Galtung, 1996: 31).

Illustration 1

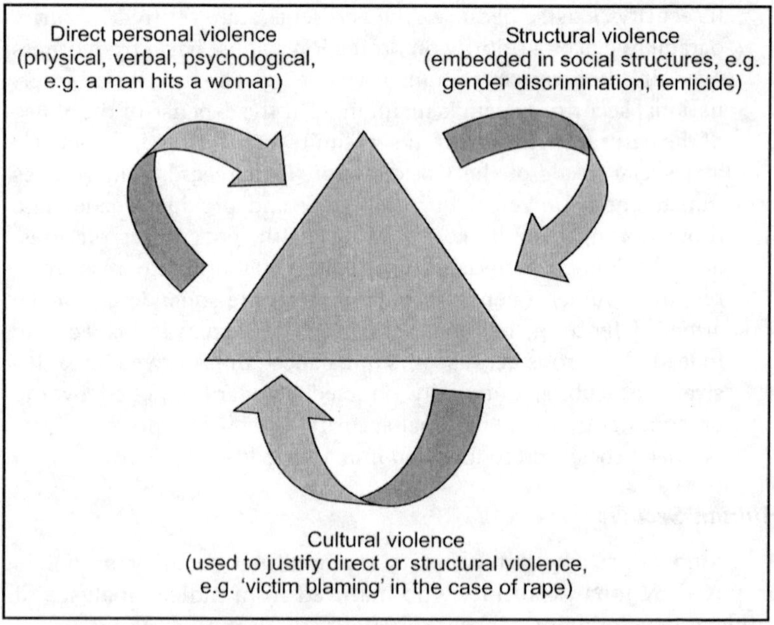

While violence against women is direct and personal (e.g. a man assaults a woman), it also embodies structural sexism and gynocide,* as well as cultural legitimisation which seeks its

* With gynocide is meant the mass killing/s of females, including female infants, derived from its Greek roots: gyn = female or feminine; cide = kill or murder. This particular form of the terms alludes to genocide, the mass killing/s of humans. Also called gynecide or femicide.

continuous replication. A subtle example of structural violence in this instance would be victim blaming which is institutionalised in law and legal practice. More pronounced forms include common practices which are sometimes codified in law, such as female genital mutilation, forced child brides, and femicide/infanticide, which includes the elective abortion of female foetuses in favour of male progeny. In relation to cultural violence, this is evident for example when survivors internalise their personal and systemic brutalisation. This relates to the sexist attitudes that keep women's opportunities limited, with many women professionals around the world getting a fraction of what their male peers earn.

The antithesis of violence, of course, is peace,[4] and the three forms of violence outlined above would also have corresponding forms of peace. If one eliminates physical assault (including physical forms of gender-based violence) one will experience personal/direct peace. If one eliminates structural violence (including sexism, racism and homophobia) and transforms institutions appropriately, one will experience structural peace. And if one eradicates cultural violence (including ways of thinking and being) one will experience cultural peace.

No form of violence, or its respective antithesis, is entirely isolated from the other. For example, one cannot eliminate gender-based violence without transforming institutions, as well as ways of thinking and being. And if one changes cultures of violence into cultures of balance and harmony in line with egalitarian societies, one will necessarily eliminate gender-based violence, since there will no longer be polar opposites, distrust and devaluation of others.

What is also evident is that violence traumatises not only the victim, but, where relevant, the perpetrator too. Even onlookers or bystanders may experience vicarious trauma from witnessing violence. So that violence impacts on everyone: victims/survivors, perpetrators, and even witnesses. Hence the benefits of peace and non-violence for everyone in society, because no human is secure, unless everyone is secure.

The human security paradigm attempts to address critical questions about who is secure, and who not, and whose interests are served. Reactively, human security would include the absence of physical violence, or negative peace. But proactively, human security involves establishing mechanisms (policies, structures and indeed ways of thinking and being) that will ensure that individuals and communities enjoy personal, structural and cultural security, in other words, positive peace.

A question that could be asked is: how is security constructed, and how does it exclude women and other marginalised groups (such as indigenous peoples or migrants)?

Reardon** speaks of four sources of human security: the environment, basic needs (for example food and housing), identity and dignity, and finally, protection from harm. She asserts that human security of groups and individuals is essentially the expectation of well-being:

> Everything that is done in the name of security is ostensibly to fulfil that expectation. Human security derives primarily from the expectation that four fundamental conditions of security will be met: one, that the environment in which we live can sustain human life; two, that our basic physical survival needs for food, clothing and shelter will be met; three, that our fundamental human dignity and personal and cultural identities will be respected; and four, that we will be protected from avoidable harm. If a society can meet these conditions for most of its population it is generally a secure society; and, as it intentionally seeks to meet them for all the population, it moves toward being a just society. By these standards there are no truly secure societies in the world and probably none that are fully committed to achieving authentic human security.

In a departure from traditional practice, the post-Apartheid South African National Defence Force (SANDF), with assistance from civil society, drafted its security legislation in a radically new way. They redefined security in terms of development, and acknowledged the absence of an external aggressor, and the very real threat of poverty to internal stability. As founding chairperson of the National Conventional Arms Control Committee (NCACC),[5] Minister Kader Asmal (1996: 33), puts it:

> ... non-military sources of instability in the economic, social, humanitarian and ecological fields have become threats to peace and security.

** Interview, January 1999.

Galtung's model is still by far the most comprehensive in terms of inclusivity, and he painstakingly demonstrates his respect for and desire to include women in his analysis. However, it is precisely the 'phallogocentrism' of generic knowledge and thought which precludes complete transcendence of his own masculine and other subjectivities. The term 'phallogocentrism' stems from the Greek words *phallos* (phallus) and *logos* (word) or *logy* (discourse), and thus implies that traditional (male-stream) knowledge and logic, constructed by men for men, is fundamentally imbued with male bias, and will necessarily ignore the inclusion of women, or women's perspectives. It follows that universal objectivity, constructed by male theoreticians throughout history, is neither universal nor objective, but gendered, and specifically male, and hence serves particular (male) interests. One can think, for example, of the founding fathers of modern democracy and social science: Greek philosophers (male) from Plato to Aristotle, and European scholars (male) from Locke to Rousseau. An example closer to home is that of African griots (male), with Senegalese griots' strategic extrusion of Senegal's part in African slavery from their oral history. Confucious, Gautama, Jesus and Muhammed were all male too.

Engendering Security

Grass root women in Southern Africa define security as:

1. more than individual, and including families and communities;
2. more than physical, and including economics and health;
3. dependant on gender justice;
4. including the quotidian or everyday (from access to food and prevention of sexual assault).

In South Africa a woman is raped every 26 seconds, and a woman is murdered by her male partner every six hours (Medical Research Council), while police deal with a 3 per cent increase of sexual offences cases that average eight per day.[6] This can be compared with developed countries like Sweden, Belgium, Germany and the USA, where at least 30 per cent of women are battered by their male partners. The United Nations estimates, based on multi-country studies, that 'up to 70 per cent of all women experience violence in their lifetime'[#], and that 'women aged 15–44 are more at risk from rape and domestic violence than from cancer, car accidents, war and malaria, according to World Bank data'.

The Uncivil War Against Women: Gender as Society's Battle Line

When countries are not officially at war with one another, can it justifiably be called peace when women and children are beaten and raped every few seconds in every village and city in the world?

To answer this question, it is necessary to examine the origins of violence. As a starting point, the following working definition of 'violence' is offered: *the harmful action or actions of one person or group against another person or group*. Looking at this definition one can see that it speaks of one person or group, versus or against another person or group.

The construction of binary oppositions may stem from a particular identity formation, the ways in which people are taught to view themselves and the world. The conventional modern formation of identity is premised on an understanding of 'I am because I am not'. So one can find statements such as, 'I am female because I am not male'; 'I am black because I am not white'; 'I am African because I am not European'. This construction of Self fundamentally needs an Other against which to measure itself and its value. In a socially constructed competitive environment, if the Self is to succeed and be valued, it needs to transcend or overpower the Other, and if the Self is to be valued and triumph, the Other of necessity needs to be devalued. This process can be termed 'Othering'.

Such identity construction premised on polarity[7] or 'Othering' fosters conflict over access to and control of resources. In this way power also becomes a resource, as in 'power to' and 'power over'. This belief system, based on 'I am because I have and you don't', can be juxtaposed with one in which there is a more equitable

---

[#] 'Violence Against Women: The Situation', a United Nations Secretary General's Campaign Unite fact sheet, http://www.un.org/en/women/endviolence/factsheets.shtml, endviolence.un.org, Published by the UN Department of Public Information, DPI/2546A, November 2011.

distribution of resources, i.e. a more 'diffuse' form of power. Power as a relation between people became a contest over resources because it is premised on a flawed belief system centred on 'Othering' and the devaluation of the Other.

Othering and Oppressions

The origins of Othering and Oppressions centres on the explication of two fundamental belief systems. Riane Eisler (1995), based on the work of anthropologist Marija Gimbutas, posits two models, the *partnership* model and the *dominator* model. When Eisler refers to the dominator model, she means 'either patriarchy or matriarchy – the ranking of one half of humanity over the other'. She describes the partnership model, on the other hand, as one in which social relations are primarily based on the principle of linking rather than ranking.

> In this model – beginning with the most fundamental difference in our species, between male and female – diversity is not equated with either inferiority or superiority. (1995: xvii)

Eisler continues to argue that the dominator model is based on domination and force and the power to take life (death, killing), rather than the power to give life (birth) as in the partnership model, where actualisation and maximisation of individuals' potentials are primordial.

Western and modern thinking and beliefs are premised on the dominator model. Societies based on this paradigm are intrinsically unequal, hierarchical and oppressive. A historical precedent is found in the shift in ancient Aztec society from partnership to dominator models. More recently, modern European imperialism, which constructed the present state system in Africa, provides further examples.

Significantly, the discourse of colonisation similarly operates on a system of binary oppositions, such as female-male, black-white, infidel-believer or barbarity-civilisation. This particular way of constructing personal and group identity fosters conflict rather than cooperation, and by its very nature leads to violence. Think, for example, of the Hutu and Tutsi in the Great Lakes.[8]

However, while one bears in mind that colonisation of Africa engendered much violence, one must also not forget that some

African forebears traded in other Africans, as the histories of slavery evince. Some Africans, who operated on the construct of 'I am because I am not', also oppressed and waged wars against their kinsfolk whom they felt threatened by and whose property they wished to confiscate, practices which were exploited and exacerbated by colonisation, and which continue to this day.

Indigenous Egalitarianism

The dominator model can be juxtaposed with the partnership model, or egalitarianism, ancient and indigenous ways of thinking that precede colonisation, still found in diverse societies such as that of the KhoeSan of Southern Africa, the Iroquois of North America, the Minangkabau of Indonesia, and the Pnar, Khasi, Garo and Nayars of India.

Anne Baring and Jules Cashford (1991: 157), in their narration of the migrations and invasions into Europe by Aryans and Semites during the Bronze and Iron Ages, are effectively describing the shift from the egalitarian to the dominator model:

> Both invading peoples introduced the idea of an opposition between the powers of light and darkness, imposing this polarity on the older view in which the whole contained both light and darkness in an ever-changing relationship.

Egalitarian societies are premised on harmony and balance, on mutual respect for, and interdependence of, each other and the environment, on cooperation rather than conflict. It is personified in the yin/yang symbol, which epitomises a harmonious integration of all elements into one being, all dancing fluidly together to create a dynamic organism. While Descartes said 'I think therefore I am', egalitarian societies embody a different tenet: 'I am because I care; I am because I belong'. This sense of caring community in ancient societies[9] is something Carol Lee Flinders has also touched on in her book, *The Values of Belonging: Rediscovering Balance, Mutuality, Intuition, and Wholeness in a Competitive World*. In egalitarian societies, peace and respect are fundamental organising principles, where power is cooperatively shared.

Two renowned peace researchers, Graham Kemp and Douglas Fry, in their joint and respective multi-country studies, show the direct relationships between social egalitarianism and less violence or peace. They each and together draw significantly on Scandinavian as well as indigenous societies, as models of egalitarianism and peacefulness. However, in line with most other predominantly male scholars that lead the peace research field, Kemp and Fry individually and collectively fail to take cognisance of gender in their analyses, a substantial oversight. A pro-poor post-colonial African leader, Thomas Sankara, devoted to egalitarianism and women's rights, famously pronounced in a speech during the 1980s:

> The revolution and women's liberation go together. We do not talk of women's emancipation as an act of charity or because of a surge of human compassion. It is a basic necessity for the triumph of the revolution. Women hold up the other half of the sky.

Sankara was from Burkina Faso, one of many countries across the world where matrilineal and egalitarian peoples like their native Dagara live to this day. A society cannot be generically egalitarian if at least one half of its population, notably women, are treated as less than equal or routinely violated. Hence the importance of including gender, that is women, in any analysis, and of noting the direct relationships between social and gender egalitarianism, with less violence and peace.

Many egalitarian societies explicitly call themselves matriarchal, including the Iroquois of North America, as well as the Pnar, Garo and Khasi of Northeast India. In this model, matriarchy is not necessarily the opposite of patriarchy. Ancient and modern matriarchal societies were and are not hierarchical, oppressive and violent (towards men). Instead, they have been shown to be cooperative and peaceful, societies in which men and women are equal and equitably share resources,[10] even as females are key leaders, spiritually and otherwise, of their societies.[11] However, the term 'matriarchy' to describe ancient and existing egalitarian and cooperative societies as the antithesis of patriarchy is variously contested, and several scholars have posited alternative terms, agreeing in essence that non-patriarchal societies were and are both matrilineal and matrilocal (with patriarchal societies being patrilineal and patrilocal).[12]

The Origins of Gender Oppression

Ancient societies were not always patriarchal or necessarily gendered. African history records the matriarchal rule of, for example, Amanitare and other ancient Nubian queens, as well as the rule of Ashanti in North Ghana. Katarina Tomasevski refers to the civilian rule of Neber in Egypt during the Old Kingdom (c. 3100–2345 BC). She argues that indigenous Egyptian society was strongly matriarchal:

> Some historians argue that women may, in fact, have 'discovered' agriculture in prehistoric times. There are even instances of matrilineal and matriarchal societies in Malaysia, Java, the Philippines, and India. (1993: 1,2).

In the context of gender, the patriarchal dominator model presupposes a rigid distinction between the two genders. There are countless examples of modern colonisers imposing and maintaining this separation to the expense of the egalitarian partnership model of thought.

In the context of gender, the patriarchal dominator model presupposes a rigid distinction between the two genders. There are countless examples of modern colonisers imposing and maintaining this separation to the expense of the egalitarian partnership model of thought.

In Burma, for example, British colonisers noted how 'barbaric' the native Burmese were because their genders were not rigidly separated and hierarchised, so too were the KhoeSan of Southern Africa. In both cases the colonisers, aided by the requirements of capitalism, worked immensely hard at inculcating gender distinctions in these societies and communities, with horrific results. Heike Becker has shown in her studies of gender-based violence and the San that colonisation and capitalism (as well as Apartheid in Southern Africa) caused and exacerbated gender-based violence in the KhoeSan communities in Southern Africa, through the introduction and fostering of rigid and controlled gender distinctions.

Especially in Africa, the impact of colonialism, grounded in monotheistic and patriarchal religious systems,[13] extended beyond the imposition of rigid gender polarities to also subvert traditional constructions of family and partnerships. The Judeo-Christian and colonial model of heterosexual, male-dominated families can be contrasted with indigenous African family practices such as woman-to-woman 'marriage'.

While studies about marriages between women have always been limited, Anthonia Uzuegbunam (2001) documents this phenomenon amongst the Igbo in Nigeria, and traces documents relating cases from the 1930s. She asserts that marriages between women are common in East, Southern and West Africa, as well as Sudan (2001: 3). She argues that these marriages are initiated by women who are not able to bear children, who join in a (traditional) union with a younger woman who bears the family children after insemination by a carefully selected man. According to Uzuegbunam:

> ... woman–woman marriage in Igboland is portrayed as a flexible option available to women to pursue any number of interests, political, social, economic and personal. The guiding principles therefore are flexibility, heterogeneity and ambiguity. (2001: 11)

She asserts that these relationships are more egalitarian than conventional heterosexual ones, and that the childbearing partner enters entirely freely into the union, and continues to explain that:

> ... woman–woman marriage in Igboland is not like lesbianism where love and sexual relations are exchanged by same male sex (sic). Rather, woman–woman marriage has stories of love, children, companionship, commitment, sexual freedom, vulnerability and empowerment. The woman initiator invites a male with the arrangement for procreation and for pleasure. (2001: 11)

> Things are not as clear-cut as they seem. They are neither circumscribed nor separated from each other by lines. Lines are drawn in the mind. *There are no lines in nature* ... (Everything emerges) from a matrix of conditions and in turn becomes part of another matrix of conditions from which something else emerges.
>
> **Stephen Batchelor (1997: 76)**

This centuries-old practice of woman-woman marriage, with its intrinsic mutuality and egalitarianism, has been steadily eroded by the colonisation of indigenous African societies.

Man's fear of penetration and/or violation by the 'impure' (bisexual) Other, does seem to cast some light on the reason(s) for his rejection of her. A useful analogy can be drawn between black and white, or colonised and coloniser. The need to increase and maintain the distance between these opposites stems from the fear of the (strangeness/difference of the) Other. China Galland (1998: 117) recalls an ancient Indian story:

> Ramakrishna explained (Kali's) darkness as the result of distance. When we are far away from an object, it appears dark to us. 'Go near and you will find her devoid of all color,' he said. 'The water of a lake appears black from a distance. Go near and take the water in your hand, and you will see it has no color at all. Similarly, the sky looks blue from a distance. But look at the atmosphere near you; it has no color.

Galland's story serves to illustrate that something only looks alien when it is not examined closely enough. Galland (1998: 80) cites a wise Tibetan: 'Our confusion lies in believing something to be separate from ourselves,' he begins, explaining the Buddhist view that sees mind and matter as one continuum, continually arising and falling back into itself, like waves into water.' Dynamic and fluid, inseparable and one.

What is the origin of this fear of the Other? The answer could be found in dominant ideology itself. Ideology is advanced by (a group of) individuals (whether they are autonomous or form classes and/or genders) and those individuals would wish to perpetuate their own (positions of) power and privileged access to resources. If they create a new market (or dumping ground) for commodities through colonisation, they would need to subjugate the colonised Other, and the ideology of fear (and hierarchical oppositions) lends itself well to this form of exploitation. So is the case with oppression of women.

Galland (1998: 50) recounts the words of Wisdom Moon, the Mother of all Buddhas – known as Drolma or Mother in Tibet, Kwan Yin in Chinese, Tara (Liberator or Saviour) in Sanskrit, Wisdom or Sophia in the Old Testament, and the Goddess of Compassion everywhere:

> Nowhere can I find what is male; nowhere can I find what is female. These are simply forms, no more separate from one another than a wave is from water. But since most Buddha's have chosen to come (to earth) as a man, perhaps it would be more helpful if I became enlightened in a woman's body.

Gender-Based Violence

This understanding of violence and peace now allows a more in-depth examination of the concept of 'gender-based violence'. According to the Committee on the Elimination of Discrimination Against Women (CEDAW)(General Recommendation No. 12), gender-based violence is defined as:

> violence that is directed against a woman because she is a woman, or that affects women disproportionately. It includes acts that inflict physical, mental or sexual harm or suffering, and threats of such acts, coercion or arbitrary deprivation of liberty.

The Declaration on the Elimination of Violence Against Women notes three key spheres in which gender-based violence may occur or which may perpetrate and/or condone such violence: the family, the community and the state.[14] December Green adds one further site of gender-based violence, i.e. the economy. The concept of gender-based violence should accordingly be broadened to also include the notion of economic abuse, which has been defined in the South African Domestic Violence Act (1998) to include 'the unreasonable deprivation of economic or financial resources or the unreasonable disposal of household effects in which the victim/survivor has an interest'.[15]

Gender-based violence therefore occurs through the act of being gendered. Through the kinds of identity construction where the Self cannot exist without the Other, and where the Self cannot be valued without devaluing the Other, women are valued as less than men. (It may be useful to note that men too get raped, especially during times of conflict. This is because these more vulnerable men are made into the Other, and so feminised or turned into surrogate women. This happens in prisons throughout the world, in gangs and in other areas of conflict.)

The CEDAW definition above focuses on women as the subjects of gender-based violence; however, it should be recognised that such violence also affects men, not only as potential victims, but also when they act as perpetrators.

It is ironic that the dominator model, and the ways in which it articulates itself in the construction of contemporary societies, brutalises everyone, even the dominant or oppressor. If one is taught violence, control and domination as a way of life, one becomes brutalised by it, on all sides of the equation. In this way even oppressors are victimised by the system and their own violent behaviours (whether physical, institutional and/or cultural), since they cannot perceive of a more harmonious and compassionate existence. This is most readily evident in cases of family violence, especially in intensely patriarchal contexts where the role of father and provider turns on itself when the patriarch murders the entire family he is meant to protect.[16] The same is the case when fathers rape daughters as an expression of their right of ownership over female offspring. It is also commonly known that a large proportion of perpetrators of incest are themselves survivors of such violence. The same can be said about war, where no party involved in the conflict is left unscathed by the violence, murder and carnage.[17]

Violence, murder and rape exact a toll on the psyche of both perpetrator and survivor/victim, and everyone is (re-) brutalised in the process, even spectators through vicarious trauma, as those working to combat gender-based violence will attest. As Jane Bennett puts it:

> Both women and men are vulnerable to the way dominant norms of gender relation, within their contexts, are working. Within South Africa, men are as likely to become blunt assailants of women (and often, of men), as women are to become victims of sexual abuse, domestic battery, economic abuse, and incest. Clearly, those who actively assault retain responsibility for their violence – that is a matter of principle and law. But the challenge for South Africans committed to the transformation of oppressive social norms is to untangle both 'victim' and 'perpetrator' from their terrible interlock of violence, no matter how shocking the 'perpetration' or how resonant the 'victimhood/survivorship'. (2000: 4)

Gender-based violence, as is commonly known, is not about sex or about conflict. It is about control and about power, in keeping with the dominator model. Vicky Randall asserts that 'if woman is associated with nature as opposed to culture, and culture is compelled to maintain itself, it follows that culture will devalue the nature it seeks to transcend, and hence man will subordinate woman' (1982: 23).

Gender-based violence is fundamentally premised on the ideology of male control over women's productive and reproductive powers, of male control over women's skills and resources, and especially of control over our power to produce future generations of producers. It is also about male control over women's sexuality, which is the key aspect of reproductive powers.

Women's productive powers include agricultural labour, wage labour in domestic service and other industries, as well as the informal sector (e.g. selling goods for small profits). Women's reproductive powers centre on our abilities to give birth and raise children, children who constitute the next generation of producers. And hence this particular function is of critical importance to patriarchy, and control of not only the present productive capacity, but that of future generations too, is very important.

As consumers, women buy and use commodities in the home. Hence women are also caught up in the endlessly repetitive task of using (if not producing) and reproducing (by baking, cooking, etc.) the commodity, and are at least equally alienated from the product. Women also support the production process, apart from their 'invaluable' roles as consumers, through their domestic work, thus freeing men for labour in the production process and the public sphere. So too women reproduce the labour force by bearing the next generation of workers (and consumers or surplus accumulators).

A critical psychological dimension of the control of women's sexuality is male insecurity about the origins of their children. Women become impregnated, and without complex and expensive medical tests, a man will never know certainly whether he is the actual father of his female partner's children. This is prominent in male anxiety over and control of female sexuality. But far more fundamental in this dominator model is the need to limit women's mobility and choice to ensure their consistent producing and reproducing (of future generations of producers, reproducers and surplus accumulators).

So too, with the kind of identity formation discussed earlier of Self-Other, with women devalued as lesser beings than men, women's sexuality is also devalued and of less consequence than that of men.

According to some writers, there are four clear indicators of gender-based violence. In societies where these circumstances prevail, gender-based violence is more likely to occur and/or to occur in more severe forms. The indicators are:

1. Economic inequality.
2. Existing patterns of using physical violence to resolve conflicts.
3. Male authority and control over decision-making (and excluding women from this process).
4. Restrictions on women's ability to leave the family setting.

All four indicators fit in with the patriarchal dominator model, from inequality (economic and other forms); employing violence (physical, structural and cultural) as conflict resolution methods; male control over women and others; as well as restrictions on women's (and others') mobility and freedom. In this sense, since violence generically, and gender-based violence specifically, function on the three axes of Galtung's triangle of violence/peace (personal/direct/physical, structural/institutional, and cultural), it is imperative that attention be paid to factors that exacerbate and contribute to violence, from issues of development and poverty, to HIV/AIDS. And hence even the International Monetary Fund's Structural Adjustment Programmes or SAPs (with decreased state spending on social security) contribute to gender-based violence, as Heidi Hudson (1998: 70) has shown in Zimbabwe, where the first two years of the introduction of SAPs led to health spending being cut by a third and the maternal mortality rate (a form of gender-based violence) doubled.

Rethinking Activisms: Agency and Compassion

Existing ways of thinking are too often premised on polarity, the kind of thinking and activism that engenders conflict rather than cooperation, and which prohibits or inhibits efforts to seek true transformative solutions for social change.

Activism can be viewed as inherently adversarial, where two sets of 'enemies' square off in battle, with neither side able to claim victory without defeat of the other, in other words a perpetuation of the dominator model, which by its very nature perpetuates violence in a continuous cycle, as evinced by the current conflict between Israel and Palestine. Mohandas (Mahatma) Gandhi's concept of satyagraha (truth-force),[18] in which a non-violent mass campaign of non-compliance is waged, was originally conceptualised as an alternative to the idea of 'passive resistance', which implies passivity and victimhood over agency and action. Instead, satyagraha is designed as not merely an alternative to violence or force, but as superior to it.[19] In the words of Geoffrey Ashe:

> The Satyagrahi – in theory – not only consents to suffer at the wrongdoer's hands, but conquers through suffering ... Yet his (sic) victory is not the opponent's defeat. It is the opponent's conversion ... Victory does not mean that one side triumphs at the other's expense, but that both sides are reconciled in a new harmony, with the Wrong cancelled ... Gandhi, British-conditioned, believed in the reign of law as a moral concept. But – he insisted – some laws can and should be broken, in the name of a higher law with which they conflict. (1968: 101)

This expression of Gandhi's satyagraha is certainly in keeping with a partnership model. Martin Luther King Jr. drew on Gandhi's satyagraha in his own non-violent defiance of racism in the United States. His words still ring powerfully true today:

> We must develop and maintain the capacity to forgive. He who is devoid of the power to forgive is devoid of the power to love. There is some good in the worst of us and some evil in the best of us. When we discover this, we are less prone to hate our enemies.

Nelson Mandela, first President of a democratic South Africa since 1994, transitioned from an adversarial position during the 1960s, with the formation of the African National Congress' (ANC) military wing, Umkhonto we Sizwe (MK), to a philosophical and political perspective perfectly typical of the partnership model more latterly during his 27 years of imprisonment by the apartheid regime. Since the 1980s Mandela consistently sought reconciliation through dialogue and negotiation with his erstwhile oppressors, eventually leading to a government of national unity, based on proportional representation, including the former apartheid leader as one of two Deputy Presidents, and senior cabinet positions for leaders of opposition parties, in the first democratic government of 1994.

Mandela's selfless desire to seek alternatives to apartheid without wreaking vengeance on perpetrators of brutality led him to a search for common ground, reconciliation and nation building across ethnicities. Thus both Gandhi and Mandela embody the principles of partnership, and both have proven to be formidable activists in the struggles for equity, justice and peace. Both viewed human rights through the prism of the partnership model, which allows for more creative ways of including human rights in activisms.

A key activist who embodies the principles of the partnership model in her struggle for justice and peace is Aung San Suu Kyi, who quoted her father during a speech to a mass rally during 1988: 'Democracy is the only ideology which is consistent with freedom. It is also an ideology that promotes and strengthens peace. It is therefore the only ideology we should aim for' (1991: 200).

Aung San Suu Kyi's methods of resistance included several hunger strikes while unlawfully imprisoned for several years by the military dictatorship in Burma. Her struggle for human rights is firmly located in the principles of democracy, non-violence and collective discipline, as Philip Kreager summarises in Aung San Suu Kyi's book:

> These principles reflect the inspiration which Aung San Suu Kyi derived from her study and reflection on Gandhi's philosophy and practice of non-violent civil disobedience ... Under such severe pressures (imprisoned, killed or driven into hiding), and against tremendous odds, Aung San Suu Kyi's reasoned insistence on the sole legitimacy of non-violent means and the priority of human rights has proven the only enduring answer: by her example, and her prevention of bloodshed, she was able to establish a real alternative for the people, who otherwise face only submission. (1991: 287, 288)

Aung San Suu Kyi also modelled her activism on the ideas espoused by Martin Luther King. Firmly rooted in the intrinsic egalitarianism of Buddhism, she noted the absence of hierarchical structures in precolonial Burmese society. She is a Nobel Peace Laureate (1991) along with other notable activists such as South Africa's Albert Luthuli, Desmond Tutu and Nelson Mandela.

Ironically, many supposedly radical thinkers have written and spoken of the necessity of 'love' or 'compassion' as a prerequisite for societal transformation through the ages, including Karl Marx, Frantz Fanon, Che Guevara, and former Black Panther, Angela Y. Davis.

Davis discusses Christopher Cauldwell's notion of 'tenderness as the essence of the (pre-capitalist indigenous) relation', and asserts that 'love alone is impotent, yet without it, no revolutionary process could ever be truly authentic' (2000: 167). Here Davis suggests that as capitalism has engendered various forms of alienation, so too it centrally cleaved 'love' or 'tenderness' from economic (and other) relations. So even activists and thinkers not necessarily associated with non-violence, argue that 'love' or compassion needs to be reclaimed, especially in struggles for societal justice.

The examples of non-violent strategies, as well as radical efforts to reclaim compassion, illustrate that activism does not need to be violent in order to be effective. To achieve reconciliation between conflicting parties, one needs a redistribution of power, i.e. one party has to voluntarily relinquish some of its power and resources. The dominant party often needs to be forced to agree to redistributive justice. However, that force does not need to be violent, as argued above.

Conclusion

The construction of identities based on polar opposites, and creation of Self versus Other, engenders oppression, inequality and violence. To get away from this, to get to the root of the violence in all societies, one needs to begin thinking of more harmonious ways of thought and living and being. And move away from patriarchal domination towards egalitarianism and partnership.[20]

While patriarchy, and the dominator model, has been around for thousands of years, evidence of egalitarian societies modelled on partnership clearly shows that patriarchal rule is not inevitable, and that other more cooperative possibilities do exist. Historical reflections of non-patriarchal societies and periods of rule help support a belief in, and conception of, forms of existence and societies that transcend patriarchal rule.

One should remind oneself that change is possible. Think, for example, of Chinese foot binding, which is now extinct. The practice of facial scarring of indigenous women in Sudan and some parts of South Africa, traditionally used as a form of adornment like modern day cosmetics or makeup, is now almost extinct. As are other practices from some ethnic groups in South Africa, like the severing of a finger or part of a finger to signify marriage.

The key to success is to move away from the adversarial nature of the prevailing dominator system, with its inherent violence and oppression, and to move towards partnership by embracing the timeless values of satyagraha. In the words of Ang Suu Kyi:

> If a people or a nation can reach their objectives by disciplined and peaceful means, it would be a most honourable and admirable achievement ... Those who have the greater strength should show restraint and tolerance towards those who have less strength ... Democracy is an ideology that allows everyone to stand up according to his beliefs. They should not be threatened or endangered ... Do not because of your greater strength be vengeful towards those who are of weaker strength. (1991: 201, 204)

God has chosen what the world regards as foolish to shame the wise, and what the world regards as weak, God has chosen to shame the strong, and what the world regards as low, contemptible, mere nothing, God has chosen ...

(First Lesson, I Corinthians I: 27–28)

Ethical integrity originates in empathy, for then we take the well-being of others to heart and are moved to be generous and caring. Our thoughts, words, and deeds are based on a sense of what we have in common rather than what divides us ... Ethical integrity requires both the intelligence to understand the present situation as the fruition of former choices, and the courage to engage with it as the arena for the creation of what is to come. It empowers us to embrace the ambiguity of a present that is simultaneously tied to an irrevocable past and free for an undetermined future. Ethical integrity is not moral certainty. *A priori* certainty about right and wrong is at odds with a changing and unreliable world, where the future lies open, waiting to be born from choices and acts. Such certainty may be consoling and strengthening, but it can blunt awareness of the uniqueness of each ethical moment. When we are faced with the unprecedented and unrepeatable complexities of this moment, the question is not 'What is the right thing to do?', but 'What is the compassionate thing to do?'

Stephen Batchelor (1997)

Notes

1. Schoeman acknowledges that 'the literature (attempting to expand the existing narrow scope of Security Studies) is still rather thin to non-existing when it comes to broadening or exploring the agents of security' (1998: 5).
2. Schoeman, citing Robert Keohane, suggests that one objective of neo-liberalism 'is to ensure that the state-system and the capitalist world economy function smoothly in their co-existence by diffusing any conflicts, tensions, or crises that may arise between them' (1998: 7).

   Hence, the need to maintain the international states system, with Bull's (1977) idea of a loose society of states, cooperating to perpetuate the status quo.
3. Interview, January 1999, through e-mail communication.
4. Conflict, which is not the same as violence, is not necessarily and intrinsically bad, and may contribute to creativity if resolved peacefully. All relations, and all societies, will invariably experience conflict at least some of the time, in part due to difference(s). It is in acknowledging conflict (and differences), and dealing with it constructively and peacefully that creativity and growth can be fostered.
5. A cabinet committee charged with ratification of all sales and purchases of arms, the NCACC has, in direct contravention of its own guidelines, ratified sales of weapons to countries with contested human rights records.
6. http://www.news24.com/multimedia/south-africa/infographic-crime-stats-2013-20140918.
7. According to the *Oxford English Reference Dictionary* polarity implies two poles with contrary qualities, two opposite tendencies/ opinions, while dualism implies being twofold, duality; theory regarding two independent underlying principles, e.g. mind and matter, form and content, theological forces of good and evil equally balanced in the universe, Christ as both divine and human. So what we have is polarity and what we are striving (back) towards is duality.
8. Whether the identities of 'Hutu' and 'Tutsi' in Rwanda are based on caste or class, ethnicity, or on resources, and whether their identities preceded colonisation, is contested by Rwandans themselves, most of who argue that their ethnic identities are colonial constructs.
9. It is useful to note that Gimbutas, Eisler, Goettner-Abendroth and others who have studied ancient Europe and the Middle East assume

time frames going back to 6000 BCE at their earliest. However, more recent excavations in Africa (arguably the birthplace of humankind), including the very recent discoveries at the Sterkfontein Caves in South Africa, show evidence of an intelligent, creative and cooperative indigenous society dating back to more than 70,000 BCE.

10. As to the relations between women and men in Old Europe, the archaeological evidence suggests that there was no apparent social superiority of males over females, and, generally, the distribution of goods in the cemeteries of Old Europe points to an egalitarian and clearly non-patriarchal society (Baring and Cashford, 1991: 56).
11. The National Centre for Women Development in Abuja, Nigeria, has a display of prominent women throughout recorded history, including Moremi of Ife, Mai Bintu the 'King' of Hunters, Fatima Mohammed Nur (first woman to memorise the entire Koran), Chief Mercy Eneli (the premier Ibo female in the cabinet of Igwe the Kingmaker), Maira Aisa Kili Ngirmaramma (1501–1558, who ruled Kanem-Borno for 7 years, 7 months and 7 days), Queen Amina of Zaria, and Emotan of Benin (who ruled the old Benin Empire), as well as various female chiefs from the 19th century forward.
12. To more accurately describe patriarchy, Eisler (1995: 105) proposes the term *androcracy* (Greek *andros* = man; *cratos* = rule), and she depicts the prepatriarchal non-hierarchical social constructions as *gylany* (Greek *gyne* = woman; *an* from *andros* and *l* as a linking of the two genders).
13. Tomasevski (1993) emphasises that the subjugation of women did not begin 'until the advent of the religions, and became more intense as the centuries rolled on'.
14. Article 2(a) – (c) of the Declaration on the Elimination of Violence Against Women UN General Assembly Resolution 48/104, 20 December 1993.
15. Section 1(ix)(b) of the Domestic Violence Act 116 of 1998.
16. South Africa is an example of a particularly patriarchal society where family murder by a patriarch is routine, especially amongst sectors of society that are highly militarised and/or hierarchised, e.g. the police force.
17. The excessively high levels of generic societal violence in South Africa, as well as the pandemic of gender-based violence in the country, is said to be one legacy of Apartheid, where white boy-soldiers were systematically brutalised in a similar way to the liberation movements' (largely black) youthful combatants. The Vietnam War is said to have had similar effects in both the USA and Vietnam.

18. The Hindi word *satya* means love or deity.
19. Cf., e.g. *Gandhi* by Geoffrey Ashe. And one of many of Gandhi's own writings, including 'Civil Disobedience and Non-Violence'.
20. It may be appropriate to acknowledge that both models, when used in this contrasting way, are in themselves polar or binary oppositions.

Further Reading

Amadiume, Ifi. *Reinventing Africa: Matriarchy, Religion and Culture*. London and New York: Zed Books, 1997.

Amnesty International. *Making Violence Against Women Count*. 2004. www.amnesty.org

Ashe, Geoffrey. *Gandhi*. New York: Stein and Day, 1968.

Ashrawi, Hanan. *This Side of Peace*. New York: Simon & Schuster, 1995.

Aung San Suu Kyi. *Freedom from Fear and Other Writings*. New York: Penguin, 1991.

Baring, Anne and Jules Cashford. *The Myth of the Goddess: Evolution of an Image*. London: Arkana, 1991.

Batchelor, Stephen. *Buddhism without Beliefs: A Contemporary Guide to Awakening*. London: Bloomsbury, 1997.

Bennett, Jane. 'Gender-based Violence in South Africa'. *The African Gender Institute Newsletter*, 6 May 2000.

Bollen, S., L. Artz, L. Vetten and A. Louw. *Violence Against Women in Metropolitan South Africa: A Study on Impact and Service Delivery*. Monograph 41, Pretoria: Institute for Security Studies, September 1999.

Bull, Hedley. *The Anarchical Society: A Study of Order in World Politics*. New York: Columbia University Press, 1977.

Buzan, Barry. *People, States and Fear: The National Security Problem in International Relations*. Sussex: Wheatsheaf, 1983.

Carr, E.H. *The Twenty Years' Crisis 1919–1939: An Introduction to the Study of International Relations*. London: Macmillan, 1939.

Davis, Angela Y. 'Women and Capitalism: Dialectics of Oppression and Liberation'. In Joy James and T. Denean Sharpley-Whiting (eds), *The Black Feminist Reader*. Malden, MA: Blackwell, 2000.

Diop, Cheidkh Anta. 'Origin of the Ancient Egyptians'. In G. Mokhtar (ed.), *General History of Africa: II Ancient Civilizations in Africa, Abridged Edition*. Glosderry, South Africa: New Africa Books. A UNESCO publication, 1981 and 1990, republished 2003.

Eisler, Riane. *The Chalice and the Blade: Our History, Our Future*. San Francisco: HarperCollins, 1995.

Flinders, Carol Lee. *The Values of Belonging: Rediscovering Balance, Mutuality, Intuition, and Wholeness in a Competitive World*. San Francisco: Harper, 2002.

Fry, Douglas P. *Beyond War: The Human Potential for Peace*. New York: Oxford University Press, 2009.

Galland, China. *The Bond Between Women: A Journey to Fierce Compassion*. New York: Riverhead, 1998.

Galtung, Johan. *Peace by Peaceful Means*. London: Sage, 1996.

Gandhi, Mohandas. 'Civil Disobedience and Non-Violence'. In *The International University Society Reading Course: The Commonwealth Story*. Vol. 9, Edinburgh: International University Society, nd.

Göttner-Abendroth, Heide (ed.). *Societies of Peace: Matriarchies Past, Present and Future*. Toronto: Inanna, 2009.

Göttner-Abendroth, Heide. *Matriarchal Societies: Studies on Indigenous Cultures Across the Globe*. New York: Peter Lang, 2012.

Green, December. *Gender Violence in Africa: African Women's Responses*. London: Macmillan, 1999.

Hobbes, Thomas. *Leviathan*. Oxford: Oxford University Press, 1952 (1651).

Hudson, Heidi. 'A Feminist Reading of Security in Africa'. *Caring Security in Africa*. Monograph 20, Pretoria: Institute for Security Studies, February 1998.

James, Joy and T. Denean Sharpley-Whiting (eds). *The Black Feminist Reader*. Malden, MA: Blackwell, 2000.

Kemp, Graham and Douglas Fry (eds). *Keeping the Peace: Conflict Resolution and Peaceful Societies Around the World*. New York and London: Routledge, 2003.

Matthews, Shanaaz, Naeemah Abrahams, Lorna Martin, Lisa Vetten, Lize van der Merwe and Rachel Jewkes. 'Every 6 Hours a Woman is Killed by Her Intimate Partner: A National Study of Female Homicide in South Africa'. MRC Policy Brief No. 5, Medical Research Council, June 2004.

Morgenthau, Hans J. *Politics Among Nations: The Struggle for Power and Peace*. New York: Alfred A. Knopf, 1948.

Muthien, B. 'The Privatisation of War in Southern Africa'. Paper presented on Demilitarisation and Peacebuilding at the Conference in Southern Africa, Pretoria: Bonn International Centre for Conversion (BICC) and Centre for Conflict Resolution (CCR), 2000.

Muthien, B. and H. Combrinck. 'When Rights are Wronged: Gender-based Violence and Human Rights in Africa'. In M.B.

Kuumba and M.M. White (eds), *Transnational Transgressions: African Women, Struggle and Transformation in Global Perspective*. Trenton, NJ: Africa World Press, 2003.

Muthien, B. and I. Taylor. 'Executive Outcomes: The Return of Mercenaries and Private Armies'. In T. Biersteker, R. Hall and C. Murphy (eds), *Private Authority and Global Governance*. New York: Alfred A. Knopf, 2002.

Muthien, Bernedette. 'The KhoeSan and Partnership: Beyond Patriarchy and Violence'. Masters Thesis, Political Science Department, Stellenbosch University, 2007.

Pech, K., W. Boot and A. Eveleth. 'South African Dogs of War in Congo'. *Mail and Guardian* (28 August 1998): 6–7.

Randall, Vicky. *Women and Politics*. New York: St. Martin's, 1982.

Schoeman, M. 'An Exploration of the Link between Security and Development'. In H. Solomon and M. Schoeman (eds), *Security, Development and Gender in Africa*. Pretoria: Institute for Security Studies, 1998.

Smith, Linda Tuhiwai. *Decolonizing Methodologies: Research and Indigenous Peoples*. London and New York: Zed Books, 1999.

Tomasevski, Katarina. *Women and Human Rights*. London and New Jersey: Zed Books, 1993.

Turshen, M. and C. Twagiramariya (eds). *What Women Do in Wartime: Gender and Conflict in Africa*. London: Zed Books, 1998.

Tutu, Desmond Mpilo. *No Future without Forgiveness*. New York and London: Image Doubleday, 1999.

Uzuegbunam, Anthonia. 'Conflict Management Implications of Woman: Woman Marriage Among the Igbos of Nigeria'. WAAD 3rd International Conference, Antananarivo, Madagascar, 8–17 October 2001.

Vaughan, Genevieve. *Women and the Gift Economy: A Radically Different Worldview is Possible*. Toronto: Inanna, 2007. www.gift-economy.com

Vickers, J. *Women and War*. London and New Jersey: Zed Books, 1993.

Wallerstein, I. *The Capitalist World Economy*. Cambridge: Cambridge University Press, 1979.

Waltz, K. *Man, the State and War*. New York: Columbia University Press, 1954.

——. *Theory of International Politics*. New York: Random House, 1979.

World Health Organization. *World Report on Violence and Health*. Geneva, 2002.

CHAPTER 3

Revisiting Feminist Thought in Contemporary Times

RASHMI JAIN

The term feminism can be used to describe a political, cultural or economic movement aimed at establishing equal rights and legal protection for women (Bardon, 1978: 23). Feminism involves political and sociological theories and philosophies concerned with issues of gender difference, as well as a movement that advocates gender equality for women and campaigns for women's rights and interests (Stambler, 1970: 102–105). During much of its history, most feminist movements and theories had leaders who were predominantly middle-class white women from Western Europe and North America. However, at least since Sojourner Truth's 1851 speech to American feminists, women of other races have proposed alternative feminisms (Sinclair, 1975: 235–238). This trend accelerated in the 1960s with the Civil Rights movement in the United States and the collapse of European colonialism in Africa, the Caribbean, parts of Latin America and Southeast Asia (Salper, 1972: 43–48).

The term 'Feminist' came into use in the English language during the 1880s indicating support for women's equal legal and political rights with men (Bryson, 1992). Throughout history, women have largely been excluded from making war, amassing wealth, from governments, art and science (Kelly-Godal, 1976). The emergence of women's studies in the 1960s had a dual goal, namely, to restore women to history and restore our history to women (Kelly-Godal, 1976). Seeking to add women to the existing repository of historical knowledge has theoretical significance. Although the terms 'feminism' and 'feminist' did not gain widespread use until the 1970s, they were already being used in the public parlance much earlier (Baumgardner and Richards, 2000: 28); for instance, Katherine Hepburn speaks of the 'feminist movement' in the 1942 film 'Woman of the Year'. Feminism has altered predominant perspectives in a wide range of areas within western society, ranging from culture to law. Feminist activists have campaigned for women's legal rights (rights of contract, property rights, voting rights); women's right to bodily integrity and autonomy, abortion rights, and reproductive rights (including access to contraception and quality prenatal care); protection of women and girls from domestic violence, sexual harassment and rape; workplace rights, including maternity leave and equal pay, to name a few.

One of the key texts in the history of feminist thought was Mary Wollstonecraft's *Vindication of the Rights of Women* (1792) that challenged the biological explanation of women's suitability in the public sphere. She wrote her book at the time of industrialisation, which although opening some opportunities for working women, also subjected them to poor conditions and low wages. Women in the emerging middle classes began to see the separation of home and work. The basis of (capitalist) class differences between women started to emerge. But political goals were never far from the surface. Women's pressure groups began to be formed and preceded the emergence of the Edwardian suffrage societies. Women in cities like Bristol played an active part in political movements in the late Eighteenth Century (Malos, 1983). From the 1860s in Bristol, groups of women began to work together to reflect upon the factors that limited their involvement in society and politics. Their predominant concerns were with issues such as a lack of higher education for women and their exclusion from the professions, such as law and medicine. At that time the franchise for all men was also a contentious issue. Numerous women were convinced that the winning of the vote should be their priority.

After the gaining of the vote and the intervening two World Wars, feminist activity seemed to have entered a harmonious period. In the immediate post-World War II epoch, there was no mass feminist movement as had been the case in the early part of the century. The vote had been gained, and although opportunities were still unequal it could be argued that key pressures of earlier feminists had been met. New sources of employment for middle-class women through the 'typewriter revolution' had taken place. Women had gained a significant degree of legal independence and importantly changes in social behaviour and expectations of women had transformed women's lives. It seemed to many that a new age had begun and that the drudgery of domesticity had been removed and women could make choices about the career they wished to follow. There was pressure for equal pay, primarily, although not exclusively, from professional women. The developing welfare state ensured that there was some recognition of, and financial support for women, based primarily on their maternal role. In addition, there was a rise in living standards and the availability of consumer goods. It seems that any consciousness-raising and protests were isolated and confined to a small minority. For most women there was no ready access to feminist debates and few knew anything of feminist history and the importance of Simone de Beauvoir's book *The Second Sex*. This book, published in 1949, was the only available feminist text for the generation of women.

In the 'new history' emerging in the 1960s and the late 1970s the accounts of women's history rested upon whether gender could be developed as a category of analysis. A developing interest in the intersection of race, class and gender was the first commitment to history that included stories of the oppressed. This included an attempt to understand how the inequalities of power were organised. Concepts of class most often rested upon Marxist economic principles, working with or against a set of definitions that involved causal explanation beginning from the economic base to the social and gendered superstructure (Scott, 1986). Marxist feminists asked the question 'how do ghettoes of women's work arise?' In the early years they attributed this, often in a functionalist manner, to the needs of capitalism itself. Employers benefited from the existence of a pool of unskilled labour and their subsequent actions caused gendered inequalities in pay and conditions (Phillips and Taylor, 1979). Later, this Marxists feminist perspective was revisited by feminists such as Heidi Hartmann (Hartmann, 1981) who highlights the need to re-think economic categories relating to women's work. She argues that we must use Marxist analysis to understand the economic laws of motion and the feminist analysis for its strength in understanding the particular predicament of women (Hartmann, 1979). But this does not explain why women end up at the bottom of the hierarchy (Phillips and Taylor, 1979).

The 1960s was a period of the development of consciousness-raising women's groups. They began with the notion of sisterhood and a common struggle against men's power and began to redefine women's liberation without using categories like class. The proliferation of women's groups and centres campaigned on major issues as they affected women. This led to the recognition of a common sisterhood and the idea that, in general, women had different interests as compared to men (Hartmann, 1981). 'Feminism was intended to develop as a universal theory to show women the nature of their oppression and as an international political practice to achieve their liberation (Ramazanoglu, 1989). This second wave of feminism produced overwhelming evidence of widespread social discrimination against women but also raised new questions – although various groups often differed in the ways they accounted for women's oppression (Ramazanoglu, 1989).

Early work by Firestone (1979), Morgan (1970) and Millett (1976) broke a new ground in feminist theory. Although the analysis they provided was an incomplete analysis, they outlined the basis for a critical analysis of male power. Their work also provided the beginning of self-awareness of socialist feminism. The 1960s saw the emergence of the New Left that became associated with a number of movements (Bryson, 2003). Heidi Hartmann (1981), for example, outlined her theme of the unhappy marriage between Marxism and feminism. Her discussion was formed around the experiences of women's movements in the 1960s, where some women working in revolutionary politics began to question the theory and their role in day-to-day socialist work. They began to raise questions such as: Who writes the manifestos and who cleans the office? For them, revolutionary zeal was replaced by a requirement by middle class males for women members to take on a nurturing role. The women of the Left soon realised that whilst women might occasionally participate on the front lines as 'revolutionary cheerleaders', in general they would keep the home fires burning and be revolutionary nurturers as secretaries and typists; filing, phoning, feeding, loving, and providing support. Betty Friedan identified a strange stirring in the American suburbs where housewives nurtured their husbands and families and struggled alone. They were even afraid to ask the silent question 'Is that all' and this she identifies as 'the problem with no name' in her book, *The Feminine Mystique* (Friedan, 1963).

The revival of an organised feminist movement after the 1960s bought the term 'patriarchy' back into popular and academic work and was beginning to be used as an analytical tool. Feminists were looking to distinguish between women's subordination as a sex and their oppression as a class. The argument over patriarchy was not new and there have been three forms of patriarchal argument (Pateman, 1988). The first form emerged in the seventeenth century involving traditional thoughts of family and the authority of the father, followed by the second classic debate starting in 1860s and was a theory of political right and political obedience. The third form, modern patriarchy, is the current form that underpins much feminist debate. The third form sees patriarchy as fraternal, contractual and structures capitalist civil society. Pateman argues that older forms of patriarchy are a relic of old world status or part of the natural order of subjection and this older family form gave way to a more public form. Patriarchy seems to pre-date capitalism, suggesting that it is universal and that there is a necessary connection between patriarchy and capitalism (Pateman, 1988). However, despite problems, the term 'patriarchy' has enabled women to 'see' the (alleged) common oppression of all women in relation to all men and this has been discussed and acted upon in a variety of ways (Ramazanoglu, 1989).

The concept of patriarchy, whilst essential and problematic in the development of feminist thought, has not been without its critics. Theorising patriarchy was the first step to understanding the subordination of all women rather than the subordination of working class women. As the term continued to be used, serious difficulties with the concept became evident (Beechey, 1979). Radical feminist versions were seen as pursuing a kind of universal claim, where men oppressed women everywhere in more or less the same ways (Acker, 1989). The term has also been criticised as a reflection of white, middle class women's reality (Acker, 1989). The Marxist tradition linking of patriarchy to modes of production was also difficult because production and patriarchy operate as separate systems. At the end of the 1980s feminists from a number of disciplines began to develop new theories about the large-scale societal process. For instance, Walby introduced a model of patriarchy as six partially independent structures that have causal effects upon each other. The first is in the household where housewives are the producing class, whilst husbands are the expropriating class. The second relates to the economic dimension of patriarchical relations within paid work. The third refers to the role of the state in maintaining systematic bias towards patriarchal interests and policies. The fourth relates to the role of male violence and the relations of sexuality that follow this. The final structure is the set of cultural institutions which create the representation of women in a variety of arenas, such as religion, education and the media (Walby, 1990). The model showed that patriarchy could be systematically elaborated to deal with historical and cross-cultural variations and, therefore, overcome some objections to the concept of patriarchy (Walby, 1990).

The development, between 1960s and 1970s, of the links between feminism and socialism increased into an understanding of the relationships between a system of power that was derived from capitalist patriarchy and how the capitalist class structure reinforced the sexual structure (Eisenstein, 1979). From this a synthesis of Marxist class analysis and radical feminist patriarchal analysis evolved into Socialist feminism (Eisenstein, 1979). Three predominant theories developed, Radical, Liberal and Marxist, and there were variations within each of these. It is possible to sub-divide and distinguish between different strands of radical feminism, and to differentiate between Marxist feminism and Socialist feminism (Ramazanoglu, 1989). Marxist feminists believed in the importance in the struggle against capital as 'workers' and not as 'women'. Socialist feminists agreed with radical feminists that there was a system of oppression called patriarchy but they also agreed with Marxists feminists that there was class oppression. They attempted to combine the two approaches in their analysis of society (Hartmann, 1981).

The three approaches of Liberal, Radical and Marxist offer different political strategies. Liberal feminists work towards reform without changing the fundamentals of capitalism; Radical feminists strive for the overthrow of patriarchy, which they believe will involve changing only the patriarchal parts of capitalism; and Marxist feminists fight for the overthrow of capitalism as a means of removing its patriarchal parts (Eisenstein, 1979). The dichotomy between women's issues and the different versions of Marxism makes the relationship difficult to determine. Marxists analysis seeks to explain power relationships in terms of class relations and Radical feminism in the 1970s dealt with the biological reality of power. An assumption of the classic Marxist interpretation was that whilst capitalism strove for profit it became 'sex blind'. Capitalists will employ anyone in their drive for profit and increasingly brought women and children into the paid labour market who were therefore subjected to exploitation (Bryson, 1992). The debate over women's domestic labour in general led to the common idea that housework done by women is not a personal service to men, but serves the interests of the capitalist class. What is, arguably, more important is that the domestic labour debate drew attention to a neglected and previously rejected activity, meaning that domestic labour could not be sidelined (Bryson, 1992). This meant that the objectives of the three different approaches were different. Ramazanoglu (1989) argues that both Radical and Marxist interpretations are feminist because they question every aspect of male power, whereas, Liberal feminist accept the status quo and believe that the use of legal pressures as a political strategy can be ineffective. She argues that Liberal feminism is attractive to the middle classes within national movements, but has little appeal for the mass of women.

Table 1 shows the ideological lines on which feminist thought is divided.

Feminist Movement in India

Indian feminist scholars and activists had to struggle to carve a separate identity for feminism in India. They define feminism in

Table 1

Different Feminisms

Different Feminisms and their Central Concerns	*Views on Identity*	*Structures to Overcome this Difference*	*Commonalities to all Feminisms*
Liberal (advocate equal rights and equal opportunities)	Men and women not different 'by nature' – equal capabilities; do not focus on discriminations based on race, class, etc.	Institutions and women get equal status in institutions	Understanding that women historically occupy a secondary position in the society; gender-based discrimination unjustified.
Marxist (critique class structure and the sexual division of labour)	Identity mediated by class structure; women bear double burden of class and sexual oppression	Class and gender struggles and women be part of process of class liberation and equity process	Resistance to patriarchal structures
Radical ('patriarchy' as the root of all systems of oppression)	Identity shaped by 'sex-gender systems' and 'patriarchy'	Power and getting rid of patriarchy and replacing it with feminist ideology	Linking feminist theory to feminist practice
Essentialist Standpoint (emphasise difference rather than equality in women's experiences; interlink biology, and sociology and psychology	Identity formed through a process of 'Other'-ing; 'self' is either connected (female/relational) or separate (male/disjointed)		Intersectionality with all other progressive movements

Cont'd...

...Cont'd

Postmodern (critique universalism and celebrate differences, no 'authentic woman's voice', often run the risk of overstating differences to render impossible any common threads)	Resist universal categorisations; identity mediated through class-caste gender-race-community-culture-religion and various other factors.	Get women's experience; history and voices in all identity mediated organisations; women have to make a choice in keeping their traditions or changing to modernity	Women's liberation form all forms of injustice and discrimination
Critical (aims to strike a balance between a universal gender analysis and differences among women's experiences across the world)	-do-; primacy of gender as an analytical category is not lost	-do-	Women's equal participation in all spheres public and private

Source: Anuradha M. Chenoy, 'Identity Politics and Feminist Praxis Peace Prints', *South Asian Journal of Peacebuilding*. No. 3, Vol. 2, Winter 2010; Available at http://www.wiscomp.org/peaceprints.htm

time and space in order to avoid the uncritically following of Western ideas. Indian women negotiate survival through an array of oppressive patriarchal family structures: age, ordinal status, relationship to men through family of origin, marriage and procreation as well as patriarchal attributes – dowry, siring sons etc. – kinship, caste, community, village, market and the state. It should however be noted that several communities in India, such as the Nairs of Kerala, certain Maratha clans, Bengali families and some tribal societies exhibit matriarchal tendencies, with the head of the family being the oldest women rather than the oldest man. Sikh culture is also regarded as relatively gender-neutral.

The heterogeneity of Indian experience reveals that there are multiple patriarchies and so also are there multiple feminisms. Hence feminism in India is not a singular theoretical orientation; it has changed over time in relation to historical and cultural realities, levels of consciousness, perceptions and actions of individual women and women as a group. Suma Chitnis (1951) writes, 'The most distinctive feature of this movement was that it was initiated by man. It was only towards the end of the century that the women joined the fray. Men like Raja Ram Mohun Roy, Ishwar Chandra Vidya Sagar, Keshav Chandra Sen, Matahari, Phule, Agarkar, Ranade, Karve to mention a few championed the cause of women and initiated reforms. They made efforts to abolish the practice of Sati, the custom of child marriage, custom of distinguishing widows, the ban on remarriage of the upper caste Hindu widows and many other civil practices that affected women.

First Phase of Indian Feminism: 1850–1915

The colonial venture into modernity brought concepts of democracy, equality and individual rights to the fore. The rise of the concept of nationalism and introspection of discriminatory practices brought about social reform movements related to caste and gender relations. This first phase of feminism in India was initiated by men to uproot the social evils of Sati (widow immolation), to allow widow remarriage, to forbid child marriage, and to reduce illiteracy, as well as to regulate the age of consent and to ensure property rights through legal intervention. Women in this phase were categorised along with lower castes as subjects of social reforms and welfare instead of being recognised as autonomous agents of change. The emphasis was on recreating new space in pre-existing feminine roles of caring. The women involved were those related to male activists, elite, western educated, upper caste Hindus.

Second Phase of Indian Feminism: 1915–1947

During this period the struggle against colonial rule intensified. Nationalism became the pre-eminent cause. Claiming Indian superiority became the tool of cultural revivalism resulting in an essentialising model of Indian womanhood similar to that of Victorian womanhood, special yet separated from public space. Gandhi legitimised and expanded Indian women's public activities by initiating them into the non-violent civil disobedience movement against the British Raj. He exalted their feminine roles of caring, self-abnegation, sacrifice and tolerance; and carved a niche for those in public space. Women-only organisations like All India Women's Conference (AIWC) and the National Federation of Indian Women (NFIW) emerged. Women were grappling with the issues relating to the scope of women's political participation, women's franchise, communal awards, and leadership roles in political parties.

Women's participation in the freedom struggle developed their critical consciousness about their role and rights in independent India. This resulted in the introduction of the franchise and civic rights of women in the Indian Constitution. There was provision for women's upliftment through affirmative action, maternal health and child care provision (crèches), equal pay for equal work etc. The state adopted a patronising role towards women. Women in India did not have to struggle for basic rights as the women in the West. The utopia ended soon when the social and cultural ideologies and structures failed to honour the newly acquired concepts of fundamental rights and democracy.

In India, the concept of 'equality' was completely alien until liberally exposed Western-educated Indians introduced it in the early nineteenth century. However, the term did not gain meaning or become an operational principle in Indian life until the country gained independence in 1947 and adopted a democratic government. The Indian Constitution then granted equality and freedom from discrimination based on gender or religion, and guaranteed religious freedom. Also, Five Year Plans made provisions to provide health, education, employment opportunities to women and also look after their welfare. Women were even declared as 'partners in development' in the Sixth Five Year Plan.

It is crucial to note that Indian women themselves do not agree with the Western concept of feminism. The concept of 'feminism' is unique within the context of Indian culture; it cannot be directly compared to feminism in Western culture.

India has had a vibrant women's movement that goes back to the pre-independence movement with protests for social reform in the nineteenth century. The movement has been marked by tragedies that have led to campaigns resulting in new laws: the Mathura rape case of 1972, the protests against the dowry-related death of Tarvinder Kaur, who was burned to death in her marital home in 1979, the protests sparked by the act of Sati (where a widow is cremated on her husband's funeral pyre) by Roop Kanwar in 1987 and the protests against the Bhanwari Devi gang rape in 1992 and the latest case of Nirbhaya in 2012.

The challenges that the feminist movement now faces stem from the vast diversities within India. Feminism within India is divided along class, caste, sexuality and disability. As parts of India develop at a faster rate, increased social and economic inequality is giving rise to new problems like sexual harassment at the workplace and in public spaces, which need to be analysed further.

References

Acker, J. 'The Problem with Patriarchy'. *Sociology*, 23: 235–240, 1989.

——. *Class Questions Feminist Answers.* Oxford: Rowman and Littlefield, 2006.

Amanda, Vickery. *Women, Privilege and Power: British Politics, 1750 to the Present.* California: Stanford University Press, 2001.

Bardon, E.J. *The Sexual Arena and Women's Liberation.* Chicago: Nelson Hall, 1978.

Beechey, V. 'On Patriarchy'. *Feminist Review*, 1: 66–82, 1979.

Baumgardner, J. and Richards Amy. *Manifesta: Young Women, Feminism and the Future.* New York: Farrar, Straus and Giroux, 2000.

Bradley, H. *Gender.* Cambridge: Polity Press, 2007.

Bradley, K.A. *History of the Women's Suffrage Movement in Cornwall 1870–1914*. Cornwall: The Patten Press for Hypatia Trust, 2000.

Bryson, V. *Feminist Political Theory: An Introduction*. Hampshire: Palgrave McMillan, 1992.

Bryson, V. *Feminist Political Theory: An Introduction* (2nd edition). Hampshire: Palgrave McMillan, 2003.

Cancain, F.M. 'Methodologies that Challenge Inequality'. *Gender and Society,* 6(4), 1992.

Chitnis, Suma. 'Alphabet of Lust'. *Kenyan Review,* Vol. VIII, 1951.

Crawford, E. *The Women's Suffrage Movement in Britain and Ireland: A Regional Survey*. Oxford: Routledge, 2006.

Crompton, R. *Class and Stratification*. Cambridge: Polity Press, 1998.

Denis, A. Review Essay: Intersectional Analysis: A Contribution of Feminism to Sociology. *International Sociology*, 23: 667, 2008.

Eisenstein, Z.R. *Capitalist Patriarchy and the Case for Socialist Feminism*. New York, London: Monthly Review Press, 1979.

Firestone, S. *The Dialectic of Sex: The Case for Feminist Revolution*. New York: Bantom, 1979.

Hartmann, H. and Lydia Sargent. 'The Unhappy Marriage of Marxism and Feminism: Towards a More Progressive Union'. In *Women and Revolution: A Debate on Class and Patriarchy*. London: Pluto Press, 1981.

Healy, G., Bradley, H. and Forson, C. 'Intersectional Sensibilities in Analysing Inequality Regimes in Public Sector Organisations'. *Gender, Work and Organisations*, 18(5), 2011.

Holton, S.S. 'Silk Dresses and Lavender Kid Gloves: The Wayward Career of Jessie Criagen'. Working Suffragist, *Women's History Review*, 5(1): 129–150, 1996.

Kelly-Godal, J. 'The Social Relations of the Sexes: Methodological Implications of Women's History'. *Signs,* 1(4): 809–823, 1976.

Lawrence, J. 'Contesting the Male Polity: The Suffragettes and the Politics of Disruption in Edwardian Britain'. In A. Vickery (ed.) *Women, Privilege and Power: British Politics, 1750 to the Present.* Stanford: Stanford University Press, 2001.

Lewis, G. 'Celebrating Intersectionality? Debates on a Multi-faceted Concept in Gender Studies: Themes from a Conference'. *European Journal of Women's Studies,* 16: 203, 2009.

Liddington, J. 'Rediscovering Suffrage History'. *History Workshop Journal*, 4: 192–202, 1977.

Malos, E. Bristol Women in Action (1839–1919). Bristol Broadsides (Co-op) Ltd: Bristol, 1983.

Maynard, M. 'Beyond the Big Three: The Development of Feminist Theory into the 1990s'. *Women's History Review* 4(3): 259–281, 1995.

McCall, J. 'The Complexity of Intersectionality'. *Signs: Journal of Women in Culture and Society,* 30(3), 2005.

Millett, K. *Sita.* London: Virago, 1976.

Morgan, R. *Sisterhood is Powerful: An Anthology of Writings from the Women's Liberation Movement*. New York: Random House, 1970

Morgan, S. 'Theorising Feminist History: A Thirty-year Retrospective'. *Women's History Review,* 18(3): 381–407, 2009.

Nash, J.C. 'Re-thinking Intersectionality'. *Feminist Review,* 89, 2008.

Park, J. 'The British Suffrage Activists of 1913: An Analysis'. *Past & Present,* 120: 147–162, 1988.

Pateman, C. *The Sexual Contract*. Cambridge: Polity Press, 1988.

Phillips, A. and Taylor, B. 'Sex and Skill: Notes towards a Feminist Economics'. *Feminist Review,* 79–88, 1979.

Ramazanoglu, C. *Feminism and the Contradictions of Oppression,* London: Routledge, 1989.

Rowbotham, Sheila, 'The Trouble with Patriarchy'. In R. Samuel (ed.) *Peoples History and Social Theory.* London: RKP, 1981.

Salper, Roberta L. *Female Liberation: History and Current Politics.* New York: Knopf, 1972.

Scott, J.W. 'Gender: A Useful Category of Historical Analysis'. *The American Historical Review,* 91(5), 1986.

Sinclair, Barbara. *The Women's Movement: Political, Socio-economic and Psychological Issues.* London: Harper & Row, 1975.

Stambler, Sukie. *Women's Liberation: A Blueprint for the Future.* New York: Ace Publishers, 1970.

Taylor, V. 'Feminist Methodology in Social Movements Research'. *Qualitative Sociology,* 2, 1998.

Walby, S. *Theorising Patriarchy.* Oxford: Blackwell, 1990.

Walby, S. *Gender Transformations.* London: Routledge, 1997.

Walby, S. *The Future of Feminism.* Cambridge: Polity Press, 2011.

Wollstonecraft, Mary. *Vindication of the Rights of Women.* Boston: Peter Edes, 1792.

Section II

Media and Literary Reflections

CHAPTER 4

She Must Not Accept, She Must Challenge

RANJIT KAUR AND SAPNA NEWAR

> Woman must not be awed by that which has been built up around her; she must reverence that woman in her which struggles for expression.
>
> —Margaret Sanger

With the advent of new communication technologies, the mass media have acquired global dimension. Although the form and substance of mass media have changed severely over the years, they have played a crucial role in reinforcing gender stereotype and in strengthening patriarchal culture by constructing new meanings and images and by setting the agenda for public opinion through selective themes and viewpoints.

This article tries to provide a wide picture of representation of women in the mass media. It argues that women and their concerns are no longer invisible in the mass media. With the growing commercialisation of the mass media, there has been increasing commodification of women in the mass media. With the propagation of 'women's genres', she has emerged as important patron of mass entertainment, but feminist activists and academicians are concerned with the negative portrayal of women in media.

Development of women cannot happen in seclusion. Community and society has to work hand-in-hand with the government to inculcate sustained awareness and then women themselves will be able to usher a change for their betterment.

Although the images of women and types of messages transmitted through various mass media, such as print media, electronic media and films, are not very different, it would be worthwhile to examine the specificity of each media in reinforcing existing gender ideology. It attempts to delineate the representation of women in the mass media. Accordingly, in this particular article, we shall focus on the provisions of the Indecent Representation of Women Prohibition Act, 1986 as well as the objective for which the particular Act was introduced.

Basically mere passing of Acts would not be adequate; there is also a need to replace the mindset of the contemporary society. For this, women themselves will have to come forward to declare a big NO to the cheap commercials in the mass media.

Women and the media is a subject that serves as a mirror of women's empowerment. There is a strong link between women-centred media and women's empowerment. The status of women in the Indian media has undergone a tectonic shift. Gradually, the prejudice against women in newspapers has weakened. Newspapers in India have started hiring women as reporters and subeditors. With the growing commercialisation of the mass media, there has been an increasing commodification of women in the mass media. On the other hand, the progressive discourse is often co-opted in the mass media and reconstructed again to establish the hegemony of dominant social classes and reproduce gender relations, women's groups and media professionals continue to challenge them in the context of a larger system of patriarchy and capitalism that controls the mass media and subordinate women. Hence, the task of changing media images of women has become far more difficult in today's context. It is now some sort of dubious concern, whether we might treat women as subject that might be talked over, described as well as addressed rather than object that may be viewed and touched.

Review of Literature

Margaret Gallagher (1983) rightly commented that,

> The mass media function in the larger system of patriarchy and capitalism that controls media structures and organisations and represents women as subordinates. The recent debate of mass media vis-à-vis gender produces much more complex understandings of the cultural dimensions of power and equality, and more specifically feminist analyses of the media, culture and society.

Women have emerged as an important consumer of mass entertainment with the rise of 'women's genres' includes soap operas, melodramas, women's magazines and so on. The mass media set the agenda for public opinion by selecting themes, items and points of views to reinforce the patriarchal culture. But, it simply does not reflect the social reality and conditions. It only constitutes one side, i.e. women's marginality in culture.

The relation between reality and the media is however, dialectical. Raymond Williams in his book *Marxism and Literature* (1977) stated that,

> Culture is not a static system, but an ever evolving process that constantly changes to accommodate emergent alternative and oppositional meanings, values and practices.

Although academicians, social activists, especially feminist activists, and educationists have shown their concern with the women's related questions and also critically evaluated the negative as well the positive representation of women in media. Though various mass media such as print media (newspapers and magazines), electronic media (radio and television), and films, are not very different in transmitting different types of messages so it would be worthwhile to examine the specificity of mass media in reinforcing existing gender ideology and try to shudder that ideology which is not good for the development and growth of our country.

In this portrayal, the most often criticised aspect is of the representation of the women in advertising which is usually an objectification of females. In contrary to that women should be given profoundest regard and honour while they carry out lot more important roles than males in all societies. One of the most important provisions besides other provisions in the Indecent Representation of Women (Prohibition) Act, 1986 is that,

> No person shall publish, or cause to be published, or arrange or take part in the publication or exhibition of, any advertisement which contains indecent representation of women in any form.

The Union Ministry of Women and Child Development have constituted a panel to decide few points for the media campaign against the indecent representation of women in the mass media, to have a constant media campaign to focus on positive aspects of women empowerment and try to raise voice against unfavourable, indecent and typecast projection of women in cinemas, television shows, magazines, newspapers and advertisements, etc. The members of committee are likely to recommend alterations keeping in mind the advancements in the technological system and through these mediums the systematic representation of women and children in electronic media, internet and advertising.

Clothing stylist Calvin Klein as a reviewer of the use of women in advertising stated that,

> There is a need to persuade the establishment of media watch groups that can observe the media and check with the media to make certain that woman's needs and apprehensions are properly reflected.

It is in high demand for the media and the government as well, to amend and also to find out different solutions to recuperate the conditions of women. This could be possible only with the radical changes in the system when individual women could get due respect and safety in the society as well as in group instead of treating them as objects.

The broad scope and perspective of the act is to make sure that it is adapted to newer concerns and it requires to be restructured so that the treatment towards women is to be as subject that can be discussed, portrayed or dealt with, instead of object which can be seen or felt only.

It will suggest an innovative campaign and policy to project women in a more positive, practical and authorised manner, which can have utmost impact on the society and bring about an attitudinal and behavioural modification of people towards women.

Initiated by UNESCO, the first international review of research and action drew our attention towards the striking similarities in the negative portrayal of women in mass media (Ceulemans and Fauconnier, 1979; Gallagher, 1983), and women's lack of decision-making power in media organisations throughout the world (Gallagher, 1981).

In developing countries, feminist communication research on media content, images and representation has grown since the early 1980s. It was the United Nations International Decade for Women (1975–85) that provided political impetus worldwide to initiate research and action for changing women's portrayal and participation in the mass media. In comparison to the Western feminist scholarship in the field of communication, however, communication research on Third World women has remained fragmentary and descriptive. Today, the way media is portraying the women will have a great bearing on young girls on how they perceive it. Common female stereotypes found in the media have a powerful influence over how society views women and how women view themselves. Media's unrealistic depiction of females has negative effects on the way women view themselves. Number of television programmes, advertisements, movies and magazines and other forms of popular media are using women's sexuality to brand their products. But this all depends on the women on how they wanted to get themselves portrayed in media. The programmes like The Bachelor, Flavor of love have shown dozens of women trying to attract the attention of a man through their sexuality. Even a number of magazines display half naked female body to attract readers. All this is creating the image of the women just as sexual objects and thus undervaluing the women as a whole.

Moreover the women adopting this as a profession also have a great bearing on their health. From the perspective of the mass media, thinness is idealised and expected for women to be considered attractive. While the facts show a majority of the models displayed on television and in advertisements are well below what is considered healthy body weight, the Images in advertisements, television, and music usually portray the 'ideal woman' as tall, white, and thin, with a tubular body, and blonde hair (Dittmar and Howard, 2004; Lin and Kulik, 2002; Polivy and Herman, 2004; Sands and Wardle, 2003; Schooler, et al., 2004; Tiggemann and Slater, 2003). Models shown in all forms of popular media are often under what is considered healthy body weight, which sends a powerful message that women must sacrifice their health to be considered attractive by societal standards.

In a recent study 10,000 girls aged 8–12, 17 per cent induced vomiting or used laxatives or diet pills to lose weight. By the time girls reach adolescence, eating disorders are the third most common illnesses afflicting them.

Twenty years ago the average model weighed 8 per cent less than the average woman, but today's model's weight is 23 per cent less than the average women. The messages that the media sends to women about thinness, dieting, and beauty tell 'ordinary' women that they are always in need of adjustment, and that the female body is an object to be perfected.

Schooler rightly stated,

> Consistent representations on television construct a specific portrait of reality, and repeated exposure to this content leads viewers to adopt this alternative reality as valid. Accordingly, because the representations of women's bodies shown on television are so skewed, adopting this reality for young women are believed to lead to decreased satisfaction with their own bodies, a strong desire to be thinner, and disordered eating behaviour. (Schooler et al., 2004: 38)

Images in the media today project an unrealistic and even dangerous standard of feminine beauty that can have a powerful influence on the way women view themselves. The media is littered with images of females who fulfill these unrealistic standards, making it seem as if it is normal for women to live up to this ideal. Dittmar and Howard (2004: 478) made this statement regarding the prevalence of unrealistic media images, 'Ultra-thin models are so prominent that exposure to them becomes unavoidable and 'chronic', constantly reinforcing a discrepancy for most women and girls between their actual size and the ideal body.'

Continuity and Changes in Portrayal of Women in Mass Media

The ways in which women are portrayed in media has emerged as an important area of research and action among feminist researchers and activists in developing countries since the 1980s. It was the comprehensive study of Gallagher (1983) on the portrayal of women in the mass media that drew our attention to demeaning and derogatory media images of women across the world.

It is assumed that despite apparent differences in media development and content in divergent societal context, the Indian situation throws light on how media reinforces gender and social relations, while at times challenging them.

Representation of women in the new wave cinema is also constrained by dominant ideological discourses on women that perceive the women's question as only a gender war within the framework of liberal feminism (Mazumdar, 1991).

Until recently, commercial and new wave cinema in India has been the exclusive domain of male directors and writers. However, now a few women have entered the field as directors and writers. The question arises as to what extent they have succeeded in shifting the perspective on women and related topics in films. At one level, women directors have created a much-awaited constructive space in the films for promoting feminist ethos and views. But, the terrain opened up by women directors is still uneven and patchy. In the prevailing economic and cultural context of commercial films, women directors are mostly allowed to deal with women-oriented issues such as, the family, romantic relations, maternal relations, etc. which are thought to be traditionally the domain of women (Gupta, 1994). Some of the women directors reflect more sympathetic understanding of women characters. However, there has not been a significant shift in the roles assigned to women in the films of women directors who operate within the boundaries of gender stereotypes in the commercial cinema.

Television is a medium of entertainment as well as education and information. The penetration of new communication technologies in the 1980s has widened the access to television in developing countries. With the growing awareness among development planners and media professionals about the women, there has been a significant increase over the years in the number of television programmes focusing on women and women's issues regarding how the women and their concerns are reflected on television.

On the basis of a comprehensive analysis of portrayals of women in the mass media across many countries of the world, Gallagher (1983) has shown that women and their concerns are not only misrepresented and under-represented on television, but women's images on television consistently follow traditional stereotypical patterns and are very often derogatory.

In general, a wide range of programmes is shown on television for entertainment, education and information. Very seldom the total output of television is studied in order to understand gender portrayal and the treatment of women's concerns. A pioneering study of the content of television programmes on Indian television revealed that the state-controlled television reflected common sex-role stereotypes, embedded in Indian cultural, religious and political traditions (Krishnan and Dighe, 1990).

In general, the content of women-centred fictional tele-serials centred around women's life, various forms of women's oppression along with the body, beauty and consumerism. At one level, the increasing space for women's programmes' and women's issues on television gives us an impression that the media has at least responded to women's demands for better representation in television programmes. However, a closer look at the medium suggests that although women's movement has succeeded to some extent in pushing women's issues onto the media agenda; they are accommodated within the existing patriarchal discourse.

With increasing commercialisation of television broadcasting, there has been considerable spurt in television commercials. Many of the gender differences that appear in television programmes also get reflected in television advertising. The impact of advertisements is not just due to their verbal content, but their use of sexual symbols and images. It is the images that we see in advertisements. Although women's groups and feminists have often raised their voices against images of women in television advertising, systematic research in this area is very limited.

In India, content analysis of roughly 186 television commercials, repeated several times during July 1986 on the public television network, reveals that women were utilised in advertising to sell products to both, male and female consumers through their two dimensional role: as caretakers of the household and the family and at the same time as decorative sex objects (Krishnan and Dighe, 1990: 58–62). Although women are featured in various categories of commercials, they tend to be prominent figures in the commercials on grooming aids, household goods, and food. The activities of male and female characters in advertisements varied according to the type of product being advertised. Women were shown as engaged in cooking, feeding children, serving, caring, etc. Men's activities, on the other hand, were either of an outdoor nature or related to their occupations. On the whole, the latent messages of the commercials were more demeaning than the manifest messages.

Feminist media professionals have attempted to use the space within the mainstream television to create new representations of women and project their experiences, struggles and hopes, and voice their concerns. However, such voices are limited and constrained by the existing media structures.

Print media plays an important role in influencing public opinions and setting agenda for what is constructed as news. With the increasing feminist critique of the print media and participation of feminist professionals in the print media, the situation has somewhat changed. In the 1980s, the general apathy among newspapers and periodicals towards women's issues has given way to some awareness and better coverage.

Earlier, women and their issues or problems never figured on the front page of a newspaper and women were predominantly depicted as victims of atrocities but today women are more 'visible' in the mainstream print media, where they figure side by side with the old stereotyped sexist images and the back page pin-ups. Over the years, feminist pressures on the media have led to a gradual increase in the space devoted to the selected women's issues and noticeable decline in the anti-women items and articles. Nevertheless, there is considerable ambiguity in representation of women and women's issues in the newspapers and magazines. Media still continues to emphasise events rather than processes. Newspapers give selective coverage of women's issues and often present distorted feminist views (Balasubrahmanyan, 1988).

However, the press coverage of women's issues over the years has changed significantly with noticeable changes in the presentation of news and views in the context of expansion of electronic media and new consumer-orientations of Indian economy, increasing participation of media women in 'hard' news areas of politics and economic, and changing strategy of the women's movement (Joseph and Sharma, 1994). Research studies compiled by Joseph and Sharma (1994) demonstrate that women's issues are usually given significant coverage only when they fit dominant norms of what constitutes news. With the shift in the strategy of women's movement from single issue-oriented, highly visible public campaigns centred on atrocities against women to low-key grassroots activism, there has been some dilution in the media's coverage of women.

Changing Strategies

The contemporary women's movement has played an important role in challenging the demeaning images of women in the mass media by creating alternatives and by intervening in and negotiating with the mainstream media.

In the mainstream media women are generally depicted as victims of atrocities or as protagonists in their traditional gender roles. In alternative media, there have been some efforts by individuals and organisations in India and elsewhere to evolve successful communication that makes people subjects and participants rather than objects or targets of communication. Several experiments are undertaken in India to demystify communication technology and to empower women at the grass roots with the tools to project their issues and problems in their own voices.

The alternative media has made a significant contribution in demystifying the mainstream media and in creating a space and environment for women to voice their views and concerns in their own words and images. The built-in interactivity of the alternative media allows a 'privileged communication' with the audience. However, the reach of the alternative media is limited. Audio-visual and print material developed in the alternative media is not for mass distribution or the mass market. The alternative media is used primarily by progressive groups and individuals who are already sympathetic to women's issues. It has not yet succeeded in bringing profound changes in media policies or altering drastically existing gender bias in the mainstream mass media.

Interventions in the Mainstream Media

Left to itself the mainstream media will continue to pay lip service to women's issues and reinforce gender stereotypes. For a gender perspective to permeate through the mainstream media, it is also crucial to negotiate a space within the existing media system. Women, collectively and individually, have used various strategies to intervene in the mainstream media.

Unit of the Self-Employed Women's Association (SEWA) in India also trains women workers of the urban informal sector in video production, and uses their programmes to educate, organise and train other women workers and mobilise public opinion.

Nevertheless, the women's groups, activists and academicians have played an important role in challenging the existing media policies that reinforce gender stereotypes, and pressuring the government to formulate regulations concerning the portrayal of women in the mass media.

In the early 1980s, efforts to change the portrayal of women in the mainstream media in India were in the form of direct protest actions against specific instances of sexism and obscenity in the mainstream media (print, films and television), and public consciousness raising through the general media critique (Bhasin and Agarwal, 1984; Balasubrahmanyan, 1988: 64–70). In response to the growing volume of criticism directed at sexism in the mass media, the Government of India enacted the Indecent Representation of Women (Prohibition) Act 1986. Subsequently, it formulated a bill, based on this Act that prohibits indecent portrayal of women in any form through commercial advertisements, publications, writings, or any other manner.

Over the years, more women media professionals have entered the mainstream mass media, particularly print, films and television. Women's entry into the media industry and organisations by itself does not mean that they succeed in changing mainstream media's approach and treatment of gender issues and concerns. Nevertheless, the task of the women's groups and activists in the 1990s is made much more difficult and challenging by the subtle and sophisticated ways in which images of, 'new' modern women are re-packaged in the films, television and print media. At one level, mainstream media has devoted some space for the selected women's issues and promoted the images of working women, single women and high achievers along with the traditional images of women as caretakers in the family. However, the underlying perspective on women has remained sensational, superficial and simplistic.

In summary, the long struggle by women's groups and concerned media professionals inside and outside the mainstream media system has been successful to some extent in elevating public awareness about the negative portrayal of women in the mass media and in promoting enlightened perspective on the women's question. The challenge facing the women's movement is not about choosing to work for alternative media or mainstream media, but devising appropriate strategies to explore the political space available in alternative and mainstream media for making a difference.

Conclusion

Women and their concerns are no longer invisible in the mass media. In summary, there is some visible space in the coverage of women and women's issues in the print media. However, beyond the count of the words, stories, and column spaces, the underlying perspective is often superficial, simplistic and sensational. Nevertheless, progressive media professionals continue to work within these spaces to change the mainstream media. Changes taking place in the portrayal of women in the mass media in developing countries are simply cosmetic or part of a substantial transformation at the level of consciousness. The sustained projection of negative and mortifying images of women in media communications, electronic, print, visual and audio must be changed.

References

Agarwal, Bina and Kamala Bhasin. 'Action for Change'. *Seminar*, Special Issue: *The Sexist Media*, 300 (August): 38–42, 45, 1984.

Anand, Anita. 'Mainstreaming Women's Concerns'. *Voices*, Special Issue: *Women and Communication: The Power to Change*, 2.1: 6–8, 1994.

——. 'Moving from the Alternative to the Mainstream for a New Gender Perspective'. *Intermedia,* 21.1 (June–July): 54–56, 1993.

Balasubrahmanyan, Vimal. *Mirror Image: The Media and the Women's Question.* Bombay: Centre for Education and Documentation, 1988.

Bhasin, Kamala and Bina Agarwal (eds). *Women and Media: Analysis, Alternatives and Action.* New Delhi: Kali for Women, 1984.

Brown, William J. and Michael J. Cody. 'Effects of a Pro-social Television Soap Opera in Promoting Women's Status'. *Human Communication Research,* 18.1: 114–142, 1991.

Ceulemans, Mieke and Guido Fauconnier. *Mass Media: The Image, Role and Social Conditions of Women.* Paris: UNESCO, 1979.

Department of Women and Child Development, Ministry of Human Resource Development. National Perspective Plan for Women 1985–2000 A.D. New Delhi, 1988.

Dittmar, H. and S. Howard. 'Professional Hazards? The Impact of Models' Body Size on Advertising Effectiveness and Women's Body-focused Anxiety in Professions that Do and Do Not Emphasize the Cultural Ideal of Thinness'. *British Journal of Social Psychology,* 43.4: 477–497, 2004.

Frey-Vor, Gerlinde. 'Soap Opera'. *Communication Research Trends,* 10.1: 1–16, 1990.

Gallagher, Margaret. *Unequal Opportunities: The Case of Women and the Media.* Paris: UNESCO, 1981.

——. *The Portrayal and Participation of Women in the Media.* Paris: UNESCO, 1983.

——. 'Women and Men in the Media'. *Communication Research Trends,* 12: 1–15, 1992.

Gupta, Shubhra. 'Women Film Makers: Changing Course?' *Voices,* Special Issue: *Women and Communication: The Power to Change,* 2.1: 27–29, 1994.

Joseph, Ammu and Kalpana Sharma (eds). *Whose News? The Media and Women's Issues.* New Delhi: Sage Publications, 1994.

Kapoor, Sushma and Anuradha. *Women and Media in Development.* A Report of the South Asian Regional Workshop, New Delhi: Centre for the Development of Instructional Technology, 11–24 March 1986.

Kasey, S. *Female Body Image and the Mass Media: Perspectives on How Women Internalize the Ideal Beauty Standard.* 2008. https://www.westminstercollege.edu/myriad/index.cfm?parent=2514&detai=4475&content=4795

Kishwar, Madhu and Ruth Vanita. 'The Labouring Woman in Hindi Films'. *Manushi*, 42–43 (September–December) 62–74, 1987.

Krishnan, P. and A. Dighe, *Affirmation and Denial: Construction of Femininity on Indian Television*. New Delhi: Sage, 1990.

Laxmi, C.S. 'Feminism and Cinema of Realism'. *Economic and Political Weekly*, XX (18 January) 113–115, 1986.

Mazumdar, Ranjani. 'Dialectic of Public and Private Representation of Women in Bhoomika and Mirch Masala'. *Economic and Political Weekly*, XXVI (26 October) WS81–WS84, 1991.

Media Advocacy Group. *Women and Man in New and Current Affairs Programmes*. New Delhi, 1994.

National Commission on Self Employed Women and Women in the Informal Sector. 'Communication Network Systems'. *Shramshakti*. New Delhi, 1988.

Prasad, Nandini. *A Pressing Matter: Women in Press*. New Delhi: Friedrich Ebert Stiftung, 1992.

Rao, Leela. 'Women in Indian Films: A Paradigm of Continuity and Change'. *Media, Culture and Society*, 11: 443–458, 1989.

Schooler, D., L.M. Ward, A. Merriwether and A. Caruthers. 'Who's That Girl: Television's Role in the Body Image Development of Young White and Black Women'. *Psychology of Women Quarterly*, 28.1: 38–47, 2004.

Steeves, Leslie H. 'Creating Imagined Communities: Development Communication and the Challenge of Feminism'. *Journal of Communication*, 43.3 (Summer) 218–229, 1993.

Williams, Raymond. *Marxism and Literature*. Oxford: Oxford University Press, 1977.

CHAPTER 5

Women's Indecent Portrayal in Media

CHANCHAL SINHA AND PRATEEKSHA TYAGI

The introduction of new communication technologies has led the mass media to acquire a global dimension. It only chooses some aspects of reality and represents these to us such that we become recipients of media's selective interpretation of the social reality. By highlighting only selected aspects of reality in a particular context, by projecting them as larger than life, and by continuous repetition of media images and messages, the media influences reality and shape our perception of reality. The mass media function in the larger system of patriarchy and capitalism that controls media structures and organisations and represents women as subordinates. The recent debate of mass media vis-à-vis gender produces much more complex understandings of the cultural dimensions of power and equality, and more specifically feminist analyses of the media, culture and society (Gallagher, 1992). With the proliferation of 'women's genres' – soap operas, melodramas, women's magazines and so on – women have emerged as important consumers of mass entertainment. The mass media also set the agenda for public opinion by selecting themes, items and points of views that tend to reinforce the patriarchal culture. But, the media simply does not reflect only the social reality and conditions but our values, attitudes and behaviours. They constitute only one side of the construction of women's marginality in culture.

The mass media also plays a vital role in representing women as the super mom, the guileless daughter, the eloquent lawyer, the nasty corporate climber, the austere judge, the super model and what not. Whatever the role, television, film and popular magazines are full of images of women and girls who are typically white, desperately thin, and made up to the hilt. Over the years, and especially during the last decade, India has developed a fairly extensive communication infrastructure. The subject of portrayal of women in Indian media has drawn the attention of media critiques in the present times. It arises especially when our society is going through a period of social change. Women have been portrayed as men would like to see them – beautiful creatures, submissive mothers of their children, efficient housekeepers, but nothing else.

In fact, mainstream media has failed to portray the true image of women despite the fact women have made entries into areas which were once treated as male dominated bastion. Mainstream media have been reinforcing the traditional stereotype image of submissive, sacrificing women, perpetuating the status-quo. Women are mostly shown as housewives, or even if they are working, as secretaries, stenographers, air hostess, school teachers, receptionists, etc. Despite the fact in 2009 as many as five women got the Nobel Prize.

On the other hand an aggressive, passionate, 'all body–no soul' image of women also finds space, especially in pop culture and advertisement. There is rampant commoditisation of women's bodies, where they are actually being reduced to less than the sum of their body parts. A number of studies show that this description, which appear in a proliferation of advertising that dominates the space of magazines and newspapers in much of the world, is quite literally apt: many of today's adverts display women's bodies parts, as 'buttocks, thighs, legs, breasts, facial skin'. As seen in pop culture, depictions of females is chock full of the predominately white, desperately thin, and scantily clad. And the most terrible part is women are shown enjoying their status as 'show pieces'.

Theories of Media

Media Framing

The concept of media framing exhibits a reporter and editor's choice as to what aspects of a story in the news are emphasised the most, what characteristics of individuals are highlighted. It should not be thought of as a way for reporters and editors to be subjective in their sharing of news, but rather a means for them to stress certain aspects over others – ones they believe are either more important to the desired audience, or more appealing (Palmeri, 2001). For a journalist to frame an issue or individual, it means he or she puts that issue or individual into a certain light and designs the presentation so the reader interprets it the way the practitioner feels it needs to be read. Some see the effects of framing as journalists manipulating the ideas of the audiences. Framing results in a doctored view of an issue, but these individuals in the journalism field are trained to develop ideas in a manner which should have a positive effect. This is not always the case, but it is the goal of media professionals (Palmeri, 2001). In regard to sports, journalists tend to emphasise masculinity over femininity, and, because of this, framing is used to explain why so few women are depicted in the media.

Critical Studies

Critical studies are another appropriate theory to relate to the issue at hand. Communication-based critical theory is concerned with how media and messages are connected to power relations in society. In regards to the portrayal of women in the media, one must examine the idea of male hegemony – the process of domination by the males in society. Mass media tend to reflect dominant ideologies, such as the dominance of males in the world of sport. Other ideas are considered only from that perspective and as a result become marginalised. These ideas are a reflection of the feminine studies segment of critical theory – that social structure mirrors male hegemonic beliefs (Littlejohn, 1999).

Portrayal of Stereotyped Ideologies

Since television represents mainstream ideology, the construction of gender stereotypes on television reinforces the stereotypical definitions of Indian womanhood.

Most serials are found to be reinforcing and strengthening the gender stereotypes already present in Indian society. Most themes centre on a strong sense of good and bad, right and wrong, and are mostly painted in white and black with no grey shades.

Women are mostly portrayed in the light of approval or disapproval. These role stereotypes reflect the typical patriarchal mindset; where the housewife is favoured while the women in power (power hungry and full of vices) are often depicted as villains.

Men are showing going to office while women stay at home (not that anyone ever does any work). The vamp is the antithesis of the protagonist; portrayed as ultra modern, mostly working (the boardroom woman), with a plunging neckline, short hair, bold, conniving, heartless, ruthless, and perfect in the art of seduction. Here again 'Modernity', or 'Westernisation' as it is commonly called, is co-related and confused with debasement of morals and ideals.

The attitude of women towards societal norms and values, her perception towards life, her consequent position and status in the family and broadly in society are shaped and moulded by the 'models' of womanly conduct inherited from the past. A prominent image of Indian womanhood that has dominated for long in the Indian ideology, creating an indelible impact on the Indian mindset is that of a *pativrata* woman. The central protagonists of most popular prime-time soap operas are typical prototype of the *pativrata* and the 'glorious motherhood' images. Woman is an archetype of feminine perfection and is popularly held up as a model to be emulated. The idealisation of motherhood puts serious physical and emotional pressures on women and this vision of motherhood is highly romanticised and yet its standards for success remain forever out of reach, no matter how hard women may try to 'have it all'. The question that author would like to raise is if these are the values, characters and standards that we are trying to project for our young generation to emulate. Do we expect our youngsters to follow the traditional stereotypes?

Another prominent observation is that all women in the serials appear on screen with heavy makeup, wearing expensive jewellery and attire, ready to attend a marriage party any minute. All married women are shown wearing mangalsutras. Moreover, it seems that all serials are replica of each other, because all characters look, dress and behave the same. Indian soaps show women as the primary target for drama while male characters are shown by and large, secondary and inconsequential. Men are shown hanging around impishly, clutching at the saree pallus of their aggressive wives. Few men who are shown villainous, also hang impishly around the 'real villains' wearing spaghetti straps (the women).

Indecent Representation of Women in Mass Media

In recent years it has been observed that the media has emerged in a big way as the major exploiter of woman. With changing times new ways of expressing social power have been fashioned which target the weaker components of society. The most vulnerable target are women. In last few years, a large section of the media and particularly the leading ones have taken liberty to flout all norms related to obscenity. A systematic overdose of nudity and vulgarity is being forced into the brain of common viewer through newspapers, television, films, magazines, hoardings and posters. Cable and satellite television have grown rapidly throughout the developing world. Of all the popular means of mass media, television has the greatest mass appeal and acceptance. The portrayal of gender as a product and the accompanying body politic in the media is well documented. The impact of visual media as a very powerful vehicle for communicating idea and images is known to be tremendous. Television creates a world which seems very real and viewers are unable to differentiate between the contrived world and the real one. The impact of television is more on the young children and adolescents, who sit in front of the television and for hours, the succession of pictures become imprinted on minds and are still impressionable. However, a major share of the space in the media is today occupied by advertisement. That is also one of the problem areas for women because advertisements are, by their very nature meant, to attract the attention of the consumer to the product advertised. If an attractive woman does this job of attracting attention, then she is going to be used for that purpose. With the emergence of women as consumers of products, there has been a subtle change in the nature of advertisements that are put out which appeal to women as consumers, rather than showing women for the purpose of attracting customers to the product. Women play a very significant role in advertising today both as consumer and as influencers. The depiction of women in Indian advertising has been a topic of debate for a while now. The experts against the indecent representation of women in advertising strongly believe that the women's moral and social status is mainly determined on the basis of the degree of exposure of her physical form to public view. Women advertising redefine women attractiveness as something that is away from natural. There are advertisements where the females are shown in bad light. They are clad in skimpy clothes even when their presence in the advertisements has no relevance with the brand.

There has been advertising campaigns where there is very decent portrayal of women and they have been very successful too, like Titan, Raymond's, jewellery advertisements, cosmetic advertisements like L'Oreal, etc. On the other hand, few advertising *gurus* believe that in some of the brands the so-called indecent representation of women plays an important role in brand recognition. For example condom, innerwears have more impact on the audience when such representation is done, as it is provocative. Advertising frequently commodifies women by exploiting their sexuality or by fragmenting the female body into eroticised zones such as hair, face, legs and breasts. Thus, in the exchange between the 'commodity' and 'woman' in advertisements, a woman becomes a commodity, too.

Women in Films

Cinema is a complex medium of communication that combines sight, sound, motion, drama and messages to capture audience attention. Popular cinema is an extremely potent medium since it influences us at the subliminal level through powerful images and various successful genres, such as family and social dramas, romance, vendetta sagas, mythological stories, etc.

In cinema a woman is presented as what she represents for men, not in terms of what she actually signifies. The films reinforce myths about women that exist in society. While tracing down the changing versions of idealised femininity over 75 years in mainstream films and since the 1960s in the 'new wave' (art) cinema, Rao (1989) shows that although images of women in films have changed from Goddesses to dream girls to the 'new' women, the heroines are still depicted to project patriarchal norms and values. Women are continued to be depicted in the roles of caretakers (mothers and wives) in the family.

Women are increasingly represented as sex objects and there is growing trend towards pornographic films. Rhetoric of such representation is far more important than the immediate connotation. The body of a woman is constructed on the screen from the eyes of the male 'gaze' that objectifies her as a commodity. The depiction of violence against women have moved away from psychological and subtle forms of violence against women in denial and negation of women's individuality and identity to the use of direct physical force. Rape or attempted rape scenes are becoming increasingly common in the films narratives, projected to serve as a voyeur's delight rather than enrage and invite public debate. Thus, illustrating female victimisation has become a new form of exploitation of female body.

The representation of women in cinema has been a major issue of debate among the western feminist scholars in communication. The feminist film theory has made a significant contribution to understand how the mass media construct definitions of femininity and masculinity (Gallagher, 1992: 4). Semiotic analysis of films by feminists show that in cinema, a woman is presented as what she – represents for men, not in terms of what she actually signifies. Thus, films reinforce myths about women that exist in society. In developing countries, there has been hardly any similar efforts to build a feminist film theory or examine the question of women in cinema through systematic research. In general, analysis is related too closely with specific film narratives. Nevertheless, a closer look at media images of women in Indian films will give us some insights in understanding how the powerful medium of films has attempted to redefine femininity and masculinity in the changing context of modernity.

Women in Serials

Television is a medium of entertainment as well as education and information. The penetration of new communication technologies in the 1980s has widened the access to television in developing countries. With the growing awareness among development planners and media professionals about the women's question, there has been a significant increase over the years in the number of television programmes focusing on women and women's issues.

In many serials such as *Kasauti Zindagi Ki, Kyonki Saas Bhi Kabhi Bahu Thi, Kahaani Ghar Ghar Ki, Punarvivah, Meri Bhabhi: Ek Nanad Ki Khushiyon Ki Chabi, Sapne Suhane Ladakpan Ke,* etc. theme is centered on women with primary concern on family relationships. In this context, women's achievement is valued in terms of their responsibility for running a successful household, settling down in matrimonial bliss, bearing children and making them 'ideal' human beings.

Ekta Kapoor's teleserials gave Indian television a new genre of women characters and the success of these characters calls for questioning our changing idols. Women if not shown portraying stereotyped, superhuman characters; are shown as schemers, manipulators, home-breakers or as vamps, e.g. Kamolika in *Kasuati Zindagi Ki* and Anu in *Des Mein Nikala Hoga Chand,* Mahamanga in *Jodha Akbar,* Tanveer in *Qubool Hai,* etc. Kidnappings, killings, creating family dispute and marital disharmony are some of the role attributes that are essayed by such female characters in one episode after the other. Practically each of these negative characters exhibits revenge, greed, deceit and diabolical plots. These characters are often in contrast and pitted against the ideal ones mentioned earlier.

In general, the content of women-centred fictional tele-serials centred around women's life, various forms of women's oppression along with the body, beauty and consumerism. At one level, the increasing space for women's programmes' and women's issues on television gives us an impression that the media has at least responded to women's demands for better representation in television programmes. However, a closer look at the medium suggests that although women's movement has succeeded to some extent in pushing women's issues onto the media agenda, they are accommodated within the existing patriarchal discourse. For example, an analysis of the portrayal of women in Pakistan television plays by a Lahore-based Simorgh collective shows that many teledramas had replaced the traditional vamp of the cinema with the single working women, who is depicted as a 'monster' who could, due to her lack of the qualities of submission and obedience, threaten 'male virtue' and the 'sanctity of the home'. A critique of the content of women-centred tele-serials in India by feminist activists suggests that despite liberal ideology of these programmes, they generally treat the women's question in a superficial manner and fail to challenge unequal power relations in the society.

The Idealistic: 'Superwoman'

Another feature commonly portrayed is the unrealistic 'superwoman': the super wife, the super daughter-in-law and the supermother. This 'superwoman' has multifarious qualities – loyalty, compassion, devotion, her domain is her home and her family justifies her very existence. Her greatness lies in the obliteration of her individuality and selfworth; she is more of an ideal, a superlative rather than a personality. In the role of a mother she sacrifices her happiness for her children and family, she is the panacea for all ills that might plague the family. Kumkum, Sudha in *Meri Awaaz Ko Mil Gayi Roshni,* and *Bhabhi* are some such examples. Protagonists Prerna, Parvati, Tulsi, now Renuka Shahane in *Jeena Issi Ka Naam* goes to jail or the mental asylum for crimes they never committed. In the end, they always win of course but not before going through hell, tears and physical violence. The impact of such larger than life characters is so strong that it is nearly impossible to demean their effect.

Women in Music Videos

There is yet another side to television, which is the trend of the music videos to promote music albums. When we think of a music video, one visualises image of a woman who is titillating, sensuous and whose sole purpose is to arouse men with the show of the bare breasts and half naked bodies. With so many music videos entering the television every week and becoming hugely popular among the viewers, one can analyse the intensity of its viewership and its impact on the minds of the audiences thereafter. The music industry has begun a new onslaught on women's dignity and right to privacy with the lyrics, dialogues, scenes touching dangerously low levels of degradation and sexual abuse. They can, to some extent be said as soft porn, which may mislead our youth and teenagers. It seems that music companies are using woman's body as an object to maximise their profits and promoting obscenity. This is something that is of grave concern. Such music albums and their videos that have become so popular with the youth can easily mislead them on sexual relations and encourage them to indulge in casual sex and intimate relationships. These music videos that often have skimpily dressed girls are a blur of porn and tantalising choreography.

Women in Advertisements

Advertising seems to be obsessed with gender and sexuality, e.g. the Amul Underwear advertisement, relates to man, woman and underwear. In this advertisement, a woman flourishes a pair of briefs and then washes the said garment. This ad shows exciting bosom heaves and finger wags where the woman is shown imagining about the man and his body parts. An unrealistic, obscene advertisement that created ripples and evoked strong responses from women's group since it 'showcased' woman to sell a product used by men in a 'cheap' way. Similar other examples are advertisements of VIP Frenchie, McDowell's.

Advertising frequently commodifies women by exploiting their sexuality or by fragmenting the female body into eroticised zones such as hair, face, legs, breasts, etc. Thus, in the exchange between the commodity and 'woman' in advertisements, a woman becomes a commodity, too. Women are portrayed as sex objects who are probably casted to titillate the viewers by exposing their body parts. Women are shown wearing revealing clothes and take leaning and yearning postures – signs of incompleteness or lack of security. Women and their body parts sell everything – food, clothing, cars, computers, men's shaving lotions and underwear. Even in commercials of the products consumed mostly by men-alcohol, tobacco, cigarettes, briefs; women are used as models exposing their bodies. Glamour dolls in front of cameras and ace photographers do the same behind the lenses, trapping thousands of teenagers believe in the miracle of the product.

Women in Print Media

Print media plays an important role in influencing public opinions and setting agenda for what is constructed as news. In general, newspapers and magazines reinforce sex stereotypes. On one hand, a few newspapers that carry a women's page, popular magazines and women's magazines continue the tradition of defining the 'women's world' in terms of beauty tips, fashion, recipes, home decoration, etc. Occasionally, some serious articles on the status of women or specific issues are thrown in, but often they are sacrificed due to encroachment of space by advertisements or due to emphasis on 'light' articles to attract readers. On the other hand, women are featured in articles as film celebrities or as successful urban professionals. This coverage of high profile women is done such that they are depicted as successful individuals within the existing structures, while keeping their 'femininity' intact. Furthermore, women's magazines through stories, jokes and trivial headings for serious articles contribute to negative representation of feminists and women's movement. The indecent women is often portrayed as an angry woman disruptive to the patriarchal order and projected as anti-family and anti-male. Such negative portrayal marginalises her demands and her viewpoints.

The Gallagher's study in the early 1980s pointed out that women and women's issues find comparatively little space in newspapers. In general, newspapers and magazines reinforce sex stereotypes. With the increasing feminist critique of the print media and participation of feminist professionals in the print media, the situation has somewhat changed.

Women as Athletes

The exaggerated female characteristics found in these publications focus on physical attractiveness. For example, although beach volleyball player Gabrielle Reese, figure skater Katrina Witt, and golfer Jan Stephenson are exceptionally talented athletes, the media often focuses on their attractiveness. This is a problem that is much less common for male athletes (Knight and Giuliano, 2001). Not only are individual images being subjected to ridicule but also major sports publications. Because of its prominence in sports journalism,

Sports Illustrated's coverage of female athletes faces criticisms (Salwen and Wood, 1994). According to Janet S. Fink's article, 'Female Athletes and the Media,' more coverage has been given to women in the post-Title IX era, but this coverage has been in 'sex appropriate' sports, as previously mentioned (1998). If a female athlete is not being portrayed as participating in golf or tennis, she is usually depicted in a sexualised pose, or more commonly, not found on the front of the magazine at all. Not only does this inadequate portrayal affects the media but also society as a whole. For years, female athletes have been searching for social acceptance. According to an article found in the *Media Report to Women*, 'Studies regarding the coverage and depiction of female athletes suggest that the media have not advanced the image and concomitant societal acceptance of female athletes' (2002). Since women began participating in athletics hundreds of years ago, there has been a stigma surrounding them. This stigma is known as 'the image problem' (Knight and Giuliano, 2003).

Video Games are Another Subject of Concern

- Children now find that the majority of female characters in video games were scantily clad and highly sexualised.
- Some popular video games even portray, and some glorify, violence against women. The Grand Theft Auto series featuring prostitutes is a commonly cited example.

Specific Acts to Safeguard Indecent Portrayal of Women

The Indecent Representation of Women (Prohibition) Act

This Act was passed by Indian Parliament in 1986. It extends to the whole of India, except the State of Jammu and Kashmir. This Act also punishes the indecent representation of women, which means 'the depiction in any manner of the figure of a woman; her form or body or any part thereof in such way as to have the effect of being indecent, or derogatory to, or denigrating women, or is likely to deprave, corrupt or injure the public morality or morals'. It states that no person shall publish or cause to publish or cause to be published or arrange to take part in the publication or exhibition of any advertisement which contains indecent representation of women in any form. The main objective of this Act is nonobservance. As per the above explanation, depiction in any manner of the figure of a woman, her form or her body or any part thereof would amount to indecent or derogatory representation if it has: the tendency to present a woman as a sexual object; the tendency to present a woman as a sexual commodity for man's pleasure, or the tendency to glorify woman's subordination to man as an attribute to womanhood, or the tendency to glorify ignoble servility to man as an attribute to womanhood, or the effect of being indecent or being derogatory to, or denigrating women; or it is likely to deprave, corrupt or injure the public morality or morals.

The Information Technology Act, 2000

Section 67 of the IT Act is the most serious legislative measure against pornography. The Information Technology Act 2000 (also known as ITA-2000, or the IT Act) is an Act of the Indian Parliament (No 21 of 2000) notified on 17 October 2000. Information Technology Act 2000 addressed the following issues:

1. Legal Recognition of Electronic Documents
2. Legal Recognition of Digital Signatures
3. Offenses and Contraventions
4. Justice Dispensation Systems for Cybercrimes

Cable Television Networks (Regulation) Act, 1995

It prohibits the transmission of advertisements on the cable network which are not in conformity with the Advertisement Code. The Advertisement Code is set out under Rule 7 of the Cable Television Network Rules. In Rule 7 (2) (vi) it states that no advertisement shall be permitted which, 'in its depiction of women violates Constitutional guarantee to all citizens. In particular, no advertisement shall be permitted which portrays a derogatory image of women. The cable operator shall ensure that the portrayal of the female form, in programmes carried in his cable service is tasteful and aesthetic and is with well-established norms of good taste and decency.' In spite of these provisions (and there are more), the indecent representation of women continues. The problem is with implementation of the laws.

Statutory Bodies

In India there are at least two statutory bodies, which can go into these issues.

Human Rights Commission

The National Human Rights Commission and the State Human Rights Commission can look into violations of dignity of women, even in advertisements. S. 2 (d) of the Protection Of Human Rights Act, 1993, defines human rights as the rights relating to life, liberty, equality, and dignity of an individual guaranteed in the Constitution or embodied in the international Covenants and enforceable by Courts in India. The NHRC has taken cognizance of certain infringements of dignity of women in advertisements.

The Press Council of India

The Press Council of India is a statutory body established by the Press Council of India Act, 1978, for the purpose of preserving the freedom of the Press and of maintaining and improving the standards of newspapers and news agencies in India. Sec. 14 of the Act provides the power to censure.

Civil Society Organisations

Other organisations and bodies including National and State Women Commissions, women groups and NGOs can play an important role in curbing the menace of indecent representation of women in advertisements. As a result of a collaborative effort between the National Commission for Women, the various State Commissions in different parts of the country and several non-government organisations working for the empowerment of women, media watch groups are being set up in various cities for continuous and sustained monitoring of portrayal of women in the media.

News Media

Mainstream news media is gradually waking up to the fact that women's' issues need sensitive handling. The Reuters General Style Guide emphasises on use of right kind of language while reporting on gender related issues. IFJ (International Federation of Journalists) guideline for reporting violence against women also urges journalists to use accurate, non-judgmental language. It says that sensitive reporting means ensuring that contact for media interview meets the needs of the survivor and urges the journalists to treat the survivor with respect and maintain confidentiality.

Suggestions

- The continued projection of negative and degrading images of women in media communications – electronic, print, visual and audio – must be changed.
- Women should be empowered by enhancing their skills, knowledge and access to information technology. This will strengthen their ability to combat negative portrayals of women internationally and to challenge instances of abuse of the power of an increasingly important industry.
- Women therefore need to be involved in decision-making regarding the development of the new technologies in order to participate fully in their growth and impact.
- A mechanism should be developed to ensure viewer's feedback, not only on performance but also on expectations, reservations and objections. The media authorities should therefore, assume equal responsibilities with parents in creating conditions that enable projection of women in a decent, dignified way and promote violence-free programmes.
- It is essential to enlist the support of policy makers, parliamentarians on the appropriate policy and guidelines for the media to ensure that there is no negative portrayal of women.
- Television can be used as a forum for advocacy, challenging stereotypes, provoking thoughts on sensitive issues, information dissemination that will enable in taking necessary legal action, enactment of appropriate laws, sensitising the authorities and creating public dialogue.
- The media professionals need to be sensitised on gender issues and a system of rewards may be developed for those who are able to portray women in positive manner.
- Likewise, stringent punitive action should be taken against those who defy the norms.

- A multipronged strategy for sensitisation, creating awareness and mobilisation of public opinion is needed for developing a positive image of women in media.
- It is also necessary to draw a fine line between what constitutes morality and what define boundaries of obscenity.
- Since Media is considered as the Fourth Estate, its function is to act as a guardian of the public interest and as a watchdog. As an important agent of socialisation, besides family and school, contributing to the shaping of gender roles, its mechanisms for checks and balances with respect to gender need to be strengthened.
- The media authorities should therefore, assume equal responsibilities with parents in creating conditions that enable projection of women in a decent, dignified way and promote violence-free programmes.
- It is essential to enlist the support of policy makers and Parliamentarians on the appropriate policy and guidelines for the media to ensure that there is no negative portrayal of women.
- The media professionals need to be sensitised on gender issues and a system of rewards may be developed for those who are able to portray women in positive manner. Likewise, stringent punitive action should be taken against those who defy the norms.
- New innovative decent presentation of women, based on Indian distinct culture and society through media must be introduced. Simultaneously, western culture should not be imitated despite accepting dynamic globalisation process.
- Depiction of women, when a product or advertisement does not warrant it should be avoided by all concerned like the advertisers, advertising agencies and the media. The depiction should be relevant to the products, message, layout, i.e. in general to the advertisement.
- The advertisers, advertising agencies and the media should consider it as their corporate social responsibility to be truthful and honest in advertising. They should avoid indecency and vulgarity in the advertisements and should follow norms of fair competition. The models posing for advertisements should also be sensitive to what the public would consider indecent and avoid such portrayal. It is also necessary to draw up

guidelines for policy makers regarding advertising agencies and commercial production houses to encourage positive and realistic portrayal of women.

- The last but not the least is the dire need to control T.V. programmes. The children should be encouraged to see T.V. serials like Mahabharat, Ramayan, Lord Krishna, Jai Hanuman, Shiva Mahapuran and as such as to aware them that ours is a Karam Bhumi and not a Bhog Bhumi. Sabadvani and Veda Mantra through transformed music can create peaceful environment. It will all create an atmosphere where basic needs and basic values will become a target in life and our rich heritage will be reviewed with decency and morality. Though it is very difficult task yet it is not impossible.

Conclusion

This is not a plea of literary writing for women to be scoured but to redress the enormous harm done by existing portrayals and images in print media. Women must resist being sold in this manner and it is time they took the power of this medium in their own hands to create truth in their idiom or the pressures of the mass market will make their struggle for change increasingly difficult because when girls change, everything changes. As we unite to struggle against sex oppression, we must struggle too for equal space in the media. We must make media work for us and not against us. Every human being is to be respected. The media which actually should guide us towards making this world a better place to live in, should not go against the ethics.

References

Anand, Meenu. 'Women in Television: Depiction and Distortions'. Women's Studies and Development Centre (WSDC), Academic Research Centre, University of Delhi, 2013. Retrieved from http://www.du.ac.in/fileadmin/du/academics/course_material/hrge_10.pdf

Bhardwaj, Prachi. 'Improper Portrayal of Women by Media'. 2011. Retrieved from http://www.mightylaws.in/803/improper-portrayal-women-media

Chatterjee, Mrinal. 'Dot or Dash: Stereotypes of Women in Media'. Indian Institute of Mass Communication (IIMC), Sanchar Marg, Dhenkanal 759 001, Orissa, 2009. Retrieved from http://www.angelfire.com/nd/nirmaldasan/journalismonline/dod.html

Gallagher, Margaret. 'Women and Men in Media'. *Communication Research Trends*, 12.1: 1–15, 1992.

http://admis.hp.nic.in/himpol/citizen/lawlib/c135.htm

http://en.wikipedia.org/wiki/information_technology_act_2000

http://en.wikipedia.org/wiki/the_indecent_representation_of_women_%28prohibition%29_at

http://www.legalserviceindia.com/article/l210-law-women-and-advertisements.html

Khare, Sumi, Neha Srivastava and Sankalp Srivastava. 'Changing Role of Women in Indian Advertising'. *International Journal of Transformations in Business Management*, 1.1 (January–March) 1–17, 2011.

Panda, Tanuja. 'Role of Media on Indecent Representation of Women'. *Odisha Review*, (October) 88–91, 2013.

Patel, Ila. *Representation of Women in Media*, Gujarat: Institute of Rural Management, Anand, December, 1–30, 1995. Retrieved from https://www.irma.ac.in/pdf/randp/1020_53632.pdf

Rao, Leela. 'Woman in Indian Films: A Paradigm of Continuity and Change', *Media, Culture and Society*, 11.1: 443–458, 1989.

Shaller, Jessica. 'Female Athletes in the Media: Under Representation and Inadequacy'. *Undergraduate Review: A Journal of Undergraduate Student Research*, 8.1: 50–55, 2006.

CHAPTER 6

Child Sexual Abuse

Unearthing the Quiet Corners of 'Home'

RITU SEN

The United Nations defines child sexual abuse (CSA) as contacts or interactions between a child and an older or more knowledgeable child or adult (a stranger, sibling or person in position of authority, a parent or a caretaker) when the child is being used as an object of gratification for the older child's or adult's sexual needs (UNICEF, 2003).

Women and Child Development Minister Krishna Tirath states that according to a study conducted by her ministry in 13 states, 53 per cent of children accepted that they have been sexually exploited. Though a Lok Sabha Bill (2011) exists to protect children, the cases of CSA are highly prevalent in India where the notion of 'honour' and 'purity' which stigmatise abused children, assure that most CSA offenders go unpunished.

The paper seeks to examine the representation of the above problem in mainstream media (books/films) and unearth reasons for the gross under-addressal of the issue. Moreover, the paper shall focus on two significant depictions of the above said concern, Pinki Virani's non-fictional recounting *Bitter Chocolate* (2000) and Mira Nair's film *Monsoon Wedding* (2001) and explore that how the two mediums further the above said cause, in diverse ways. The research shall analyse *Bitter Chocolate* which exposes the nexus between patriarchal systems and sexual offenders which allow extensive proliferation of CSA in India. Moreover, the book offers an insight into the socio-psychological repercussions on the life of an abused child.

Additionally, the paper shall analyse *Monsoon Wedding* as a poignant take on CSA, which destabilises the construct of 'home' as 'safe haven'.

While great awareness has been raised about sexual violence against women in India, much less is known about the problem of sexual abuse of children. India saw an alarming increase of 336 per cent in child rape cases from 2001 to 2011 – from 2,113 recorded cases in 2001, to a startling figure of 7,112 cases in 2011, says Asian Center for Human Rights in its report titled *India's Hell Holes: Child Sexual Assault in Juvenile Justice Homes.*

Though a total of 48,338 cases were recorded in the said time period, the report warns that these are only the tip of the iceberg as the majority of child rape cases are not reported and that children regularly become victims of other forms of sexual assault too. CRY sponsored studies suggest that more than 7,200 children, including infants, are raped every year; experts believe that many more cases go unreported. As recent research has shown, it is not just within institutions that Indian children suffer from sexual abuse. *The Times of India* reports that a 2007 Indian government-sponsored survey, based on interviews with 12,500 children in 13 different states, reported serious and widespread sexual abuse, thereby putting the government on notice about the gravity of the problem. Smaller surveys conducted by non-governmental organisations (NGOs) have also painted a disturbing picture. Children are sexually abused by relatives at home, by people in their neighbourhoods, at school, and in residential facilities for orphans and other at-risk children. Most such cases are not reported. Many are mistreated a second time by a criminal justice system that often does not want to hear or believe their accounts, or take serious action against perpetrators.

A wide swathe of authorities in India, including political leaders, bureaucrats, police, and judges, have publicly condemned the sexual abuse of children. Yet, poor awareness, social stigma, and negligence have facilitated the continued perpetuation of such crimes which is still largely a hidden problem. Fear of social stigma or lack of faith in government institutions prevents many people from reporting child sexual abuse. The 2007 government survey found that, among abused children, only 25 per cent had told anyone, and only in 3 per cent of the cases had the police been informed. As in many other countries, deep-rooted cultural norms discourage the open discussion of sex and make it hard for a child to complain about an older relative or a person in a position of authority. Writing in the introduction to the government survey, the then women and child development minister, Renuka Chowdhury, said that child sexual abuse in India, 'is shrouded in secrecy and there is a conspiracy of silence around the entire subject'.

In recent years this 'conspiracy of silence' has finally begun to break down, thanks to activists working on the rights of women and children, the small but growing number of NGOs that counsel survivors and raise awareness, and to the central government's Ministry of Women and Child Development, which has taken a leadership role on the issue. However, it is a grossly under-addressed issue in the media, and this marginalisation super-imposes another layer of silence on the already shrouded problem.

One attempt to shatter the conspiracy of silence around Child Sexual Abuse (CSA) in Indian homes is Pinki Virani's non-fictional recounting, *Bitter Chocolate* (2000). This path-breaking book, the first of its kind in the country, attempts to give a well researched representation of the process of child sexual abuse as well as the socio-psychological and emotional state of the sexually-abused child.

The book provides damning disclosures about case studies from middle and upper middle class families, where children are abused and then silenced into submission. Based on live interviews, studies, reports and investigation, the research reveals that a minimum of twenty per cent of girls and boys, under the age of sixteen, are regularly being sexually abused; half of them in their own homes, by adults who have the child's trust (*Bitter Chocolate* 77).

In *Bitter Chocolate,* the journalist travels across the country to record the testimonies of the police, doctors, child psychologists, mental health professionals, social workers, lawyers and the traumatised victims themselves. The book opens with an account, brave and devoid of self-pity, of the author's own experience. It is pertinent that Virani offers her journey through abuse for analysis, almost a cathartic retelling, which as Virani says is 'the first step to counter child sexual abuse, to admit that it has happened to me' (*Bitter Chocolate* 7). Going beyond blaming, Pinki Virani then proceeds with her insightful analysis of the issue in three Notebooks. The first spells out what constitutes CSA, causes and processes of subversion and the devastating and far-reaching consequences of the same.

Notebook 1 starts with an account of the author's own childhood experience. It then touches upon scores of instances of CSA from all across the country, cutting across social strata (both of the victim and the perpetrator) and age of the victim. There are some instances where the abused is too young to even know she has been abused. The author makes categorical assessments of the research and produces it in succinct terms. To summarise the findings of the first notebook:

1. Perpetrators of CSA are often people within the family, who the child is actually dependent upon for security.
2. Boys are the target of the abusers too.
3. There have been cases of women being perpetrators (although this forms a small percentage)
4. In many cases the abuse goes unnoticed by the family members of the child. However, in the instance that it is discovered, it is generally quietly overlooked due to the social mores of 'honour' and 'purity' which the girl child symbolises. For instance, in the recent Asaram Bapu CSA case, the godman's statement: 'voh ladki pavitra hai' (*TOI*, 29 August 2013) focuses on the 'purity' of the molested child, instead of the depravity of the accused.
5. In a vast majority of the cases, the victim feels guilty that (s)he was responsible for what happened and generally the family/society does nothing to dispel this guilt.

Having oriented the reader towards the enormity of the problem, Notebook II undertakes a long-term study of a couple of real-life stories, thereby examining the effects of CSA on a victim. It explains the short-term and long-term effects of CSA, and how it has the potential to destroy a healthy notion of 'self'. Some of the effects mentioned include:

1. Physical scars and emotional insecurity.
2. Confused sexuality, promiscuous behaviour on part of the victim (this is a long-term effect where the victim might experiment with homosexuality/multiple partners in an attempt to 'erase' the memory of the abuse). Psychologists state that most victims of CSA fall into chronic patterns such as theft/lying/aggression.
3. Problems in family life, including emotional and sexual problems.
4. Most destructive of all, the abused may turn predator in the long run, and when the child grows up, (s)he may end up abusing a child.
5. Virani cites studies from the US State Prison records, which reveal that close to 30 per cent of the convicts accused of aggressive crimes were sexually abused as children. It is imperative to notice that such socio-psychological profiling and analysis of serial sex offenders does not occur in India.

The book goes on to cite the opinions of several counselors, doctors, child psychologists on this matter. The bottom line is: CSA devastates a child and this devastation can manifest itself much later in the life of the victim.

The third Notebook provides closure through practical solutions on how to counter CSA, including a framework involving the law, the parent and the child. A special chapter addresses adults who have never before disclosed their sexual abuse as children.

Virani's account of the effects of CSA, when taken into temporal perspective provides an interesting analysis. It seems to offer a connect between rising cases of sexual violence against women and the 'silent corners' of abuse at 'home' which goes largely unpunished and unaddressed. The notion of guilt, which the abused child wears, especially the female child, works in a dual fashion. Firstly, it accustoms the child to abuse, at all levels, from lewd comments on the road to serious molestation. The repeated abuse tends to allow the child an episodic acceptance of the same. The 'silence' around abuse at home, structures the psyche of the victim to convict herself in the process of abuse and therefore allows it to proliferate. Secondly, the abuser, who remains unpunished, is emboldened to perpetrate further actions of abuse, at home and outside. The absence of resistance/punishment encourages the offender to abuse multiple children.

Pinki Virani goes on to provide several practical approaches to tackle the menace. These revolve around the idea that if the perpetrators of CSA are brought to book, then it could help partly in discouraging such despicable acts in the future. The approaches include:

1. Tougher, and clearer laws dealing with CSA – starting with the proper definition, to increasing the punishment. This has been addressed by the Child Sexual Abuse Bill 2012, but it is the implementation which needs to be effective.
2. Child-friendly process to deal with the case (for example, the child not having to be repeatedly cross-examined and explain the harrowing experience several times, in graphic detail, to complete strangers).
3. Child Protection Units (to counsel the victim of abuse) and Child Protection Courts (to handle all cases where the victim is a child).

Though Virani's research is compelling and intensive, it fails to reach out to the masses. An issue, which suffers most due to suppression of voices, Virani's effort, though commendable, does not fill the lacunae of expressions. The newspapers, magazines and other sources of infotainment do not approach the issue at the grassroots level, nor is the reporting on the issue a consistent practice. The reporting is sensational and topical, and therefore becomes irrelevant as soon as the date changes. CSA is a largely under-addressed issue and requires to be explored through mass mediums of infotainment like television and films besides the coverage through newspapers and news channels. It requires a persuasive, consistent and constant voice which allows the issue to be addressed without inhibition.

Mira Nair's film *Monsoon Wedding* is one such attempt. Nair's film provides a creative dimension to Virani's scholarly research and extends the above inquiry into the domain of the 'family', deconstructing the myth of secure homes.

Mira Nair's *Monsoon Wedding* (she calls it the realistic version of *Hum Aapke Hain Kaun*) is the coming of age of the wedding micro-genre narrated from the point of view of the 'modern' Indian family. The film is a complex narrative and talks at multiple levels. The primary plot is about Lalit Verma who is trying to get his daughter Aditi married to Hemant Rai, an Indian engineer settled in Texas. The subplots revolve around the wedding planner (P.K. Dubey) who is smitten with the maid servant (Alice) in the Verma household, Aditi's secret married lover Vikram and Aditi's unmarried older cousin Rhea who has a history of child sexual abuse at the hands of the patriarch of the Verma clan.

Screenwriter Sabrina Dhawan feels the film's child sexual abuse story is the most important single thing in the script-even as she knew her hometown audience would find it so shocking. In an interview to film researcher David S. Cohen, Dhawan states:

In America, the issue of CSA is totally open for discussion. In India, we prefer to believe that these things do not exist. And if they do exist, they happen to other families, not like ours. The assumption is that if people do it at all, servants do it; respectable people don't do it. I have seen so much of that growing up in India. We never, never had a film about sexual abuse of a child by a family member in India.

Dhawan had to fight to retain the sex abuse sub plot, 'the most important part of the story' according to Dhawan. The subplot juxtaposes the narrative of Rhea, the older unmarried cousin, who has been sexually abused as a child by her uncle, with Rhea's eleven year old niece, who is being abused by the same uncle, during a family wedding.

The innocence of the child and her vulnerability in the commotion of the wedding are underlined in the film. The ease with which child sexual abuse can happen when a trusted member of the household is the perpetrator of the crime, is also clearly defined through the subplot. The unease of the abused child, the uncomprehending parents and the guile of the abuser are focused upon with startling and subtle reflection. The subplot climaxes with Rhea's outburst at her ex-abuser where she accuses him of jeopardising her childhood through CSA and further accuses him of attempting to do the same with her little niece. The symbolic absence of protection through the untimely death of her father, the innate depression that underlines Rhea's character and the refusal to get married on her part, all posit the psychological aftermath of child sexual abuse in a person's life.

Nair's film takes on an exceedingly challenging representation of sexual abuse, especially when it is embedded into the wedding genre. Dhawan states in her interview to Cohen that she had to really fight with the producers, HNA, for the inclusion of the above subplot. Most of the team members felt that it was incongruous with the otherwise feel-good, Bollywoodised melodrama the film was charted to be.

As difficult as it was to structure an abuse story into the wedding genre, it was equally challenging to circle the difficult problem of how the father of the bride, Lalit, would handle the revelation. Dhawan states, 'In real life, the head of an Indian household would probably sweep the whole thing under the rug; it would be too painful to address even in private, and it would be unthinkable to take the issue outside the family. But that would have been too hopeless'. Dhawan wanted Lalit to find a solution that would serve as an example for Indian families to follow in real life. The solution, as seen in the film, has indeed had a profound impact on Indian viewers. 'When the film opened in India, people told me it was just wonderful, because where their own fathers in that situation didn't know how to deal with it, (the film showed them that) there was a way'.

Thus, through Rhea, the film jeopardises the notion of patriarchy by breaking the image of 'honour' and 'security' which the patriarch projects. Simultaneously, it exposes the dark underbelly of the normative notion of the 'joint family' by exposing the highly prevalent instances of child sexual abuse at the hands of a trusted family member. More concretely, it metaphorically rejects patriarchy through the expulsion of the patriarch of the family at the behest of the 'marginalised' orphaned, unmarried, female member of the family, thereby jeopardising the 'fantasy' of the joint family. Finally, the narrative brings peace and closure to Rhea's character after she opens up about her violation as a child. Thus, the film emphatically proclaims the need to voice one's revolt against sexual abuse, even if it has happened in the distant past.

To conclude, the paper focuses on two contemporary, though formulaically divergent studies which arrive at the important conclusion, that child sexual abuse can only be effectively countered by expression, on the part of the abused, the family and society. The narratives, both fictional and real, comment on the need to de-closet the rampant cases of abuse and treat the 'victim' as a 'survivor' thereby removing the stigma attached to the crime. Moreover, the need to segregate the idea of 'shame' from the psyche of the abused child and its imposition, instead, on the abuser, is the definitive message of the research undertaken. Ultimately, the research concludes, there is a dire need to shun complacency and observe our 'homes' and truly examine if they are 'safe havens' for the child or for the abuser.

References

Nair, Mira. *Monsoon Wedding* (Film), 2001.

Protection of Children from Sexual Offence Bill, 2011.

Times of India, 29 August 2013.

UNICEF. *The State of World's Children, 2003.*

Virani, Pinki. *Bitter Chololate.* New Delhi: Penguin India, 2000.

CHAPTER 7

Indian Fiction

(W)Righting the Wrongs of Women's Word and World

RUCHI SHARMA

The possibilities of women's lives in today's world provide us with the vision of various social movements that have endorsed women-specific activism. Women play distinctive roles in the families contesting and rectifying the presumptions about them being naturally subordinate to men. The main tendency of providing role-sets to women set them to discuss social, political and cultural dimensions that have been subservient in nature. The idea to create a work representing reality has been emphatically utilised by fiction writers. This chapter attempts to recognise literary writings that create a fictional world in accord with the real world. The authors represent a worldwide view of and about women to readers as they relate to various cultural concepts that are faithfully portrayed in their writings. Both male and female authors have particularly considered emerging concerns of women in their works that are reflective of potential threat to the society and culture. These writings are productive spaces of women characters whose word and world together interrogate existing boundaries of their encounters, ruptures and subversion.

The characters reflect upon the struggle of women as portrayed by emerging writers belonging to the literary canon. The writings present a range of issues like oppression, significance of bodily existence, female foeticide, sex, gender bias, desires. Consequently, fiction becomes a particular mode of representing the feminine world in its versions. The conventions of feminist sensibility are challenged in these writings that usher a new movement within their narrative structures. The complex web of the narrative helps readers consider the oppressive state of women, which is often associated with social norms. The significant thing to note in the literary works is the depiction of female with various social judgments that often outcast female protagonists.

This chapter attempts to compare the works of literature with the world it represents. To analyse too many literary works would have been exhaustive and therefore attempt has been to examine the writings from Indian Literature in English that present a collage of various women characters in the novels, monologues and articles throwing light upon women-specific struggles. The primary text that would be studied is Raj Kamal Jha's first novel *The Blue Bedspread* (2000). The other writings would be discussed around the contours of various themes discussed by Jha in his novel. It would be interesting for readers to note women's plight as has been represented by distinct male and female authors.

The immersed creation of female protagonists not only in literary writings, but also in films and advertisements has opened a new trajectory for women of our country. These mediums provide an alternative way through which women have succeeded in giving a voice to their marginalised sect. The consequent reconstruction phase in the present society provides women a centre-stage. *Femina* magazine in its March 2014 edition emphasises on how Vidya Balan has turned a hero-crazy industry on its head. To make matters better traditional forms of special attention given to man has been thwarted in possible avenues that trigger change at a social level. The advertisements like ICICI bank's *Par Bande Ache Hai* (2013) and films like *English Vinglish* (2012), *Gulab Gang* (2014) and *Highway* (2014) have definitely emerged as the collective efforts of the society that must be given credit for accepting the challenge of rebuilding women's strength and confidence. However, it would be too soon to take position and find women readers identifying with the few who have become key figures either in literary history or in social-media platforms through their writings or speeches. The stories of women who have suffered, succumbed, survived and recovered suggest that people are now open to receive and listen to their experiences, concerns and opinions. Media's representation of women has fairly brought awareness yet important stories are still missing from the mainstream discussion. Writing and reading have, therefore, become a trend not only to showcase the relative knowledge of reading at social networking sites like *Goodreads*, but has also turned reader towards an opportunity to face a future. The delusion quickly transports readers into the fictional world as he returns to the centre once and for all becoming aware of reality after finishing the novel. Clearly, the cognitive process of reader recognises the inevitable social consequences, but the fact that these fictional stories also include autofiction serves a valuable purpose of literature.

Mary Ellmann in the preface to her book *Thinking About Women* (1968) states – 'I am most interested in women as words' (xv). Toril Moi took on from this line to define 'Images of women' criticism in her book *Sexual/Textual Politics* (2002). She emphasises on the study of female stereotypes in the works produced by male writers. Interestingly, writings produced by men have been studied and interpreted with the formative influences that essentially set their works as agents of patriarchy. The fact that male authors have created opportunities for women in their writings by removing obstacles in women's progress has largely been ignored. Indian fiction has provided avenues by writing openly about passion, love, deceit, betrayal, rejection, violence and many such themes. Jainendra Kumar, a prominent Hindi novelist, created a new perspective of women in his novel *The Resignation* (*Tyagpatra*) written in 1937. The adventures of female protagonist Mrinal help one retrospect an Indian woman's relationship with society. Dharamvir Bharati's *The Sun's Seventh Horse* (1952) is another prominent novel that provides a range of female characters that invariably questions their subordination. Indian literature has had a history where women's consciousness has played a significant role. Bankim Chandra Chatterjee's *Rajmohan's Wife* (1864) appreciates an independent woman who launches herself separately from society that discriminates and oppresses women. Feminist ideas, therefore, had been rooted in the social set up society which has often been the target for writers and activists.

Society in various ways imposes restrictions on woman within social boundaries. The social phenomenon of the given values as an essential intake to attain success in the social set up often intervenes with the personal principles. Unfortunately, the woman is left alone in the clusters of critical and increasingly powerful laws that are both visible and hidden. On the periphery these laws are able to take hold of her life so much so that one cannot deny her character in the incisive model of a society to which she belongs. It is predominantly for this reason that studying male writer's portrayal of women in contemporary times is necessary.

The civil codes and strident calls of a section of society have been clubbed in Raj Kamal Jha's writings. Jha (2002) is one of these prominent writers who present stark realities of women's lives through their novels. In his much acclaimed first novel *The Blue Bedspread* Jha eloquently presents journey of an Indian woman from 'womb to tomb'. The novel presents a divide between the two sentences – 'I am sorry, sir, your sister is dead' (7) and 'The baby is alive' ... 'It's a baby girl' (8). It is a result of short stories written by a man for a one-day-old baby who comes 'unseen and unheard' about the recollected events of narrator's sister's life who is dead. The novel presents traumas and secrets of woman, which she often says 'not in words, but in gestures and glances'. The stories emerge and re-emerge with the narrative technique and language of the novelist that pertinently reflect upon the social construct. This chapter is a feminist study of the novel as it explores and identifies the malaise in women's life around a common terrain of restrictions imposed by the society. The prevailing attitudes and social arrangements presented in the novel further pin down their sense of need and potential in life with limited social opportunities to be grabbed at the mercy of a patriarchal set up of society.

Jha at the onset of his novel *The Blue Bedspread* introduces the question often asked by 'fine woman' – 'Who am I?' he presents women's trouble highlighting the operation that is usually associated with their feminist strivings. Laxmi Murthy in the chapter 'Women, Men and Emerging Other' unravels social stigmatisation with the question what makes a woman. She asserts – 'We make up our minds based on certain markers: clothes, mannerisms, and of course outward anatomy. All of us know, however, that a woman who has small breasts is a woman, as also a woman who has had her breasts removed (mastectomy) during surgery for breast cancer, for example. A woman who has had her uterus removed (hysterectomy) continues to be regarded as a woman' (33). Jha's novel also presents such oppressive constraints of sex, self expression and autonomy. The narrative echoes 'some stories' that characteristically reflects and radically extend wider picture of society that includes much more than 'the black and yellow Boroline banners catching the wind on Durga Puja day ... the maternity ward ... a red handkerchief floating down'(6).

It reflects upon the dilemmas of the adolescent girl who is at the threshold of adulthood. She has to come to grips with her sexuality and responsibility with little support from the outside world. The novel exposes the new interests which the brother and sister begin to develop when sexual maturation is complete. The interests are not only romantic in nature, but are also accompanied by a strong desire to cope with the physical changes that are usually perplexing. Darshan K. Narang states in his book *Adolescent Girls: Awareness, Rights and Reproductive Health* (2010) – 'A majority of adolescents have their first sexual experiences during the adolescent years.' As a result the expected social and gender norms are broken in the novel only to mark the norms that confront girls with specific challenges including the restrictions imposed on their independence and mobility. The first sexual experience for the brother and sister was not forced. But in the due course of the novel the novelist presents how their secret harms their sexual health once their 'secret was laid bare'. It becomes difficult for the brother to remain alone in the house as he feels like 'a rabbit with an ear missing, a dog after its tail' after his father had molested him. The only way to escape the destroyed confidence in adults was found lying still in the darkness with his sister:

> She was fourteen, I was ten, and it was on our ninety square feet of fabric sky that we first kissed and, later, touched each other in what then we thought were the wrong places. And it was this daily theatre of pleasure and fear, played out on our blue bedspread, that carried us as if on a wave from one night to the next. (56–57)

It is the desire to stimulate the other through physical touch that involves their emotions and mental restrictions throughout the novel. The readers witness changing sexual identities of the characters as they realise that they cannot engage in a socially unacceptable relation. However, novelists presents the limits, boundaries and flexibility of a person's sexual identity specially that of a woman which are fluid and ever-changing. Interestingly, Girish Karnad also focuses on clearly identifiable boundaries set for women in his play *Wedding Album* (2009). Vidula's attempt to maintain her social position against her uncovering appearance in Internet Café underpins the textual strategy in the play to reconstruct a character with distinct female authority.

Moreover, we find that being a girl one has to be conscious about her appearance so much so that this consciousness is much affected by the stereotypes given by society about one's beauty. Indian society has an obsession for the fair skin, which has drastically affected the psychology of people. Jha chooses to write about the conditioning as a result of which the markets have been stacked by numerous whitening creams.

> ... this one's for Fair and Lovely, the cream which dissolves the brown and keeps the skin fair and glowing. She'd bought it once, Mother threw it out, 'You are dark and you are beautiful', she had said. (112)

The consistence strain to which women have been subjected has lead to the massive movement *Dark is Beautiful Campaign* by Nandita Das. She says, 'Indians are very racist. It's deeply ingrained. But there is so much pressure from peer groups, magazines, billboards and TV adverts that perpetuate this idea that the fair is the ideal'. Women often feel unhappy, anxious and confused as the expected social norms reinforce the idea of beauty that makes them conscious of their outer appearance. The distorted personality is an outcome of the oppression which merely transports women in the world where they compensate and compromise by rejecting them. The suggested measures offered by the family members in the novel also reflect the conditioned mindset that hampers women's psychology.

> 'Let's get the scar on the forehead removed,' he said. Doesn't look nice. Why don't you paint your eyebrows thicker so that it can't be seen? (127)

Father's concern for the daughter in the novel when she rests her face against the grille confirms the difference that appearance makes in the world:

> 'Don't sit like this, the iron will leave marks on your face, spoil your skin.' (115)

Representation of women in the novel through *The Statesman Newspaper* shows that there is a long history behind the obsession of skin colour that further expresses the idea of a pretty woman. The novelist chooses the most popular image of Indian Goddess to present the commonly believed notions of beauty:

> They have a picture of the Goddess on the front page, a Goddess with dark lipstick, high cheekbones and a blouse that glitters. (114)

The complex relationship between contemporary parameters set for women against the traditional parameters of being a woman are forced together in the novel. Jha leaves behind in his work the purported picture of society marking the expression of the alleged inferiority of woman as a daughter, sister, wife, sister in law, and mother. It presents diverse experiences of women characters within different political, economic, social and cultural realities that they face in their community. Yet the common thread of projected self, running through their lives is what makes them women. The sense of their needs and potential in life is restricted by the feminine roles of daughter, wife, and mother consigned by the society. The question of woman's obedience to men is presented in the conversation between the nurse and the mother:

> 'Doesn't your husband complain?'
>
> 'What husband? I left him long ago.'(130)

The need for the positive dialogue is inevitably seen in the marital relationships of various couples. Yet the idea of women as wives to have been subordinate being smudges their identity. However, the novel examines the changing family structures and living conditions where women become the central figure who suffers. The rapidly changing norms and social behaviour thrusts upon woman's hopes and concerns that are demanded by the supportive relationship out of the institution of marriage. However the very institution and idea of marriage becomes impassive in passing time. Eventually there comes a situation where a woman has to limit her control over her sexual and reproductive life, for she is merely seen as a procreation machine by the family whose expectation jostle her existence.

Marriage in the novel becomes the turning point in the sexual and reproductive behaviour of women. The far reaching consequences of fertility, child rearing can be noticed after 'miscarriage' that casts aside women's right over her body. Gloria Steinem in the Foreword to *The Choices We Made* (1991) emphasises that 'It was men's need to own children that had made some 'legitimate' and some 'illegitimate ... it was women's bodies as the most basic means of production, the means of reproduction, that had always been the object of this deep political game' (xi–xii). Tracing the time one finds that this argument was compelling not only in the past, but is also relevant to the present times where the husband mistreats his wife on the stake of the child she couldn't give him':

> 'I am a former student so they treated me as a special case. I told them I wanted my child admitted there.' ... 'Where do you think you are going?' he says. 'Didn't you hear what I said, that's where I wanted to send my child. And now what do I tell the Principal?' (136)

Jha makes his women characters stand as evidence of the complex and personal factors that surround the reproductive choice. The suffering that results when choice is denied gets converted to guilt strained by the social stigma – guilt about what 'miscarriage' had left her with. To have lost the baby becomes the cruelest form of punishment as one feels as if one has been stripped of an identity. The result is that after her miscarriage woman protagonist 'dreamt of pregnant women, young and old, their white gown billowing in the night, dancing in the sky' (128). The patriarchal set up of society where males dominate over females have set norms for women as the social structure often obstructs women in overcoming the problems of oppression and exploitation. Pateman describes patriarchy as a distinctive character of sexual inequality that 'rests on the appeal to nature and the claim that women's natural function is child-bearing prescribes their domestic and subordinate place in the order of things' (1989: 124). Tied up in the chains of patriarchy, women are left with ideas of femininity which are frequently used to measure the negligent value of women.

The cultural upbringing of women is such that they are 'trained' not to inconvenience men. The dismal picture of keeping man before woman, you before me is what exposes women to collide with their self. Fleeting responses to women's health, particularly reflect the fear that is associated with their bodies. The trouble in the modern world is that young girls are giving in their choices to retain their relationships with their partner. The physical intimacy is not what bothers social activists, it is rather the unknown consequences of having too many contraceptive pills that worries doctors. Most gynecologists have witnessed a high increase in the number of patients suffering from thyroid and polycystic ovaries. Eventually, when women discover about their infertility, warning lurks only to add to their misery. They are too frightened to deal with the situation as it is too late for them to call for help. The bitterest irony is that women themselves become violators of the rules that were designed for their good. The crestfallen woman with disintegrating body further entices potential harm from society.

The social practices presented in the novel are such that fuse gender inequalities. Ammu Joseph points out in her work 'The Battle of the Sexes and Other Myths' (2010) how 'A whole web of customs, norms and mechanisms subsequently came into being to deprive women of autonomy, free movement and economic independence, and to minimise any chances of rebellion' (15). Women characters are often shown in the light where men are exercising control over every aspect of their lives. Ironing the clothes becomes a significant symbol in the novel to escape the miseries of life for the female protagonist as it was for Allison's character in John Osborne's play *Look Back in Anger* (2007). Both the characters are trying to remove kinks of their lives, but in making such an attempt their act of resistance reflects them in the light of oppression where women are shown to be submissive in nature as to fit in the society. Various instances in the novel reflect upon the everyday world of these women where they struggle each day against the sustaining patriarchal and hierarchical social structures. Consequently, husband and his family are shown to apply considerable pressure on the wife to fulfill their conditions as shown in the chapter *Girl Talk*:

> It better be a son, says One's mother-in-law. ... All two's mother-in-law wants is a boy.

> Three says her husband beats her up and mother-in-law watches. Not real bad as in documentaries, just pulls at her hair or slaps her hard on the cheek .... Mother in law 'Young women don't take care of their husbands any more' ... 'Take care of his son inside you' (142–143)

The imperative contemporary issue of violence against women has also been emphasised by the novelist for his woman characters are often juggling between employment and family responsibilities. It is a workplace that provides powerful evidence of stories that 'are pillars on which they build ... their dream house where for an hour every day, to the sound of lunch boxes being opened and closed, they live in peace, away from their mothers-in-laws' (144). These events underpin a series of feminist endeavours to counter their oppressions. Jha metaphorically presents these avenues and efforts through the poster where 'a small woman in a tight-fitting shining dress balancing herself on a rhino's back' (8–9) is exposed in the novel. In an attempt to balance the life and to fit in the acceptable frame of society women often act in ways that harm their bodies. Rajashri Dasgupta illustrates how 'Readers, including women, are assured there is a pill for every conceivable condition, whether it is hair loss, obesity, menstruation cramps, infertility, menopause, osteoporosis and even sexual dysfunction. The media is replete with headlines, making people 'victims' of diseases ...' (189).

Jha deliberately brings in his novel the analogy of Durga – 'Goddess who comes down from the hills, with her children, to her father's place. For ten days every year (112)'. He uses the mythological reference of the most impressive and formidable goddesses of the Hindu pantheon. The parallel celebration of *Durga Pooja* in the chapter with the aforementioned title reflects the role of mother taken up by the goddess. Kinsley unravels the significance of blood offerings at the festival in his book *Hindu Goddesses* (1988) which suggest the renourishment of her powers of fertility. Sudeshna Banerjee illustrates in her book *Durga Puja: Yesterday, Today and Tomorrow* (2004) that today it 'is a socio-cultural event that has long transcended religious contours. ... It is in fact, a state of mind on the one hand and on the other a living, breathing physical reality, to which the city wakes up every autumn' (61). The writer conceives the faith associated with the rituals and beliefs that provide him a setting for his novel that equates the strength that the female protagonist manifests and in due course to which the readers might awake. The systematic formulation of myth and belief provide shape to the novel's structure to a large extent.

The novelist, not only provides his take on the mythology, but also symbolically reveals the obvious alternative ideas that formulated women's roles. The sister's character is depicted to primarily function in her life by taking its reign in her own hands like the goddess who is to combat demons who threaten the stability of the cosmos. The husband had further failed to play the role of God Shiva who was a caring husband. Consequently, the female protagonist sheds off her role of Durga which assumes domestic characteristics when identified with the goddess Parvati. Notably, Toril Moi presents the dilemma of the authors in presenting female role-models in literature. She quotes Cheri Register from her essay published in 1975 – 'A literary work should provide role-models, instill a positive sense of feminine identity by portraying women who are self-actualising, whose identities are not dependent on men (46)'. Jha's portrayal of female characters and the choice of issues in the novel reflect strong normative aspects of literature.

Moreover, the narrative technique used by the novelist presents his readers with the choice of the end they want for the story – 'How should we end this story? ... Or we could end it like this' (137). He fills his women characters with enormous strength like the goddess associated with power, blood and battle and provides them with the alternative of fighting against the oppression by investing heavily into their suppressed desires which makes them avenge their perpetrators through the attainment of power to kill them to overcome the battle of years of oppression.

> I could end the story here but that would leave it forever trapped in past, incomplete and purposeless.
>
> So let's imagine that the child grows up, leaves this city, ... (53)

The novel helps readers perceive women's desire to challenge or escape the miseries that limit their existence. It shapes the most important insight concerning the possibility of women's life where the novelist tries to reform the oppressive social conditions through his writing. It presents the efforts of the writer to understand the limits and opportunities that would help women overcome the oppression. It is the impending challenge of society that is demonstrated in the novel. The narrative structure unpacks the structures of oppression that remains multifaceted, even in today's world. The novel *The Blue Bedspread* celebrates women's sexual freedom and provides them free choice to contend the given values of the world creating a utopian world of words for them.

The academic output of the authors as witnessed above provides a scope for the study of fictional devices in the portrayal of women characters. This article emphasises on the way in which writers select elements in their texts to convey to the reader that the power structure in our society is highly questionable even in the present day world. With the advent of new writings from emerging writers like Kalki Koechlin one can only expect articulation of relentless authorship of many more masterpieces in the future. Kalki's monologue entitled 'Just Another Rant' was performance narrative that was published in India Today Conclave. The problems and tensions hovering around the monologue help readers study women's silences that are broken to present the tradition of the oppressed across the ages and continents:

> You remember Draupadi?
> Draupadi married off to all five Pandavas.
> She garlanded only Arjun
> But they told her you got to marry all of us.
> Five husbands! That can't be fun.
> God knows I have enough trouble with one.

Often writers choose to provide an imaginary identity to the female characters only to let them enjoy specific female values. Bulbul Sharma in her book *Now That I'm Fifty* (2011) presents her character with her extolling support towards ideologies that repress and suppress a woman. The character says, 'I like being told what to do. My father, then my husband, and now my sons always laid out my day for me. I nodded and pretended to go along. Though sometimes, soon after they told me what to do, they forgot and I could slip through the crevices and do what I wanted to (3).' The writer distinguishes between the imaginary world of the female and the real world as the instructions remain out of the framework of their existence. The duality contended with words and created world's rejects past hegemonic structure of society. The context further demonstrates how the reader wrangles over the conceptual words female, feminism and femininity. To understand the accurate picture of the reader's position we must read S.K. Cornillon's *Images of Women in Fiction: Feminist Perspectives* (1972) which is a collection of essays published in 1972. These essays establish connection between the reader and his life experience. According to Toril Moi 'new field of feminist literary studies is here presented as one essentially concerned with nurturing personal growth and raising the individual consciousness by linking literature to life, particularly to the lived experience of the reader' (42).

The characters presented in Indian fiction create a dense web that can be studied analytically by young scholars. The texts produce resistance narratives that abundantly present female efforts of rejecting the given roles not only in literary writings but also their position in cultural debates. The fact that many writers continue to portray women as the subversive all sacrificing characters can be looked into the light of satirical writing today by critics. New writings, however, map the feminine struggle within the rigid mould of society and further proclaim to establish supremacy of the counter narratives thus produced. Ever changing parameters of judging a literary writing will relatively lead to lack of interest in studying works that are often forgotten in the resonance of acclaimed or popular works. Although, each work produced by an authoritative female voice is suffused with strength yet not many of them derive directly to present characters that might induce changes in society.

The narrative of the novel significantly providers symbolic expression outlining women's utopian world. The symbiotic relationship of the writer and reader adds to the benefit of novel as a genre that consciously allows a glimpse of the debates that could rise by asserting and revealing various forms of agitation that redress women's grievances. It is through the narratives that the writer creates a fantastic utopian world where women is free from male interventions in her life and can choose her mode of resistance. This seeks an understanding of various forms of resistance that are symbolically presented in Indian fiction. This article provides an insightful analysis of women's subjectivity that is immediately controlled not only in the setting but is also constantly fractured in the writer's struggle towards creating a new social history. The narratives of Indian fiction shuttle backwards and forward between female concern with burden of the past and anxieties about future. There is little doubt that literature discusses these imposed timelines in the context of social structures that make a society.

The drawback in the coverage of themes induced in literary writings and their studies have been that they are concerned with dramatic events instead of the effect they leave on a character's psychology. The consistency in the crime inflicted upon women in news stories have pushed them towards an edge from where they choose to either stay silent in retaliation or to sacrifice everything they have in their never ending struggle for their rights. The inordinate focus on raising the individual consciousness by changing syllabus in our education system is not enough. Rather, everyday events that often go unnoticed on roadside must become a part of our consciousness that will remind us of questions raised by thousands of women like Ruchika, Damini, and Jessica Lal who could not be provided specific social and political stance. Reading these special stories through the cinematic adaptations seems to be an easy option for people. But over a past couple of years, most people have begun to read woman's stories in a different light. The retaliatory acts of writing have led to movements like *V-Day*. Eve Ensler's book *The Vagina Monologues* (2001) has led to this massive movement against violence done to women. Now she celebrates 14 February, Valentine day as V-day where V stands for vagina, violence and victory. Writers and activists have both tried to inject a perspective that excludes women from contemporary politics that often misses out the objective that it had set to do in the first place.

Women must attempt to position themselves in a location where power and domination confronts various modes of resistance. The social, economic, political and legal relations of society inhabited by women must be deeply entrenched in the writings. It is imperative that with new models presented in frameworks of new writings very soon women would be able to set the wrongs done to their community right. (W)righting the wrongs helps readers examine collective rites of females. The ceaseless efforts made to break the patriarchal norms to continue with woman's location in a subaltern world are apparently debarred from the analysis that such works call for. Hoping that this chapter would lit up the lives of women readers, at the disposal of the readers, I would like to end it with few lines from Kalki's monologue that undercut certain strains which sharply point towards the feminine concerns in contemporary writings.

> Here we are,
> We've survived this far,
> Thanks to seduction, perhaps some manipulation,
> But mostly thanks to Mother Nature and ovulation.
>
> Now look at all the queens and goddesses of history,
> No prince came to the rescue,
> No king ever went down on one knee,
> No deity was even that trustworthy,
> Yet all we've be told since we were three,
> Are fairytales, adverts, and pretty stories,
> Telling us to pray, hope,
> And wait to be saved.
>
> Here we are today,
> Here we are,
> On International Women's Day,
> With some minor disappointments,
> And a few little things to say.

References

Addlakha, Renu. *Deconstructing Mental Illness: An Ethnography of Psychiatry, Women, and the Family*. New Delhi: Zubaan, an imprint of Kali for Women, 2008.

Ajneya (trans. and ed.). *The Resignation* and *The Sun's Seventh Horse*. New Delhi: Rupa Publications India Pvt. Ltd., 2011.

Ali, Imtiaz. Dir. *Highway*. Prod. Sajid Nadiawala. Perf. Alia Bhatt and Randeep Hooda. UTV Motion Pictures, 2014.

Arora, Deepa. *Women's Writing*. Jaipur: RBSA Publishers, 2010.

Banerjee, Sudeshna. *Durga Puja: Yesterday, Today and Tomorrow*. New Delhi: Rupa, 2004.

Bharati, Dharamvir. *The Sun's Seventh Horse*. Bombay: National Book Trust, 1952.

Bonavoglia, Angela (ed.). *The Choices We Made: Twenty-Five Women and Men Speak Out About Abortion*. New York: Random House, 1991.

Chakravarti, Uma. *Gendering Caste: Through a Feminist Lens*. Calcutta: Stree, 2009.

Chandiramani, Radhika. *Good Times for Everyone: Sexuality Questions, Feminist Answers*. New Delhi: Raj Press, 2008.

Chatterjee, Bankim Chandra. *Rajmohan's Wife*. Calcutta: Rupa, 1864.

Cornillon, Susan Koppelman (ed.). *Images of Women in Fiction: Feminist Perspectives*. Bowling Green, Ohio: Bowling Green University Press, 1972.

Ellman, Mary. *Thinking About Women*. New York: Harcourt Brace Jovanovich, 1968.

Ensler, E. *The Vagina Monologues*. London: Virago Press, 2001.

Geetha, V. *Patriarchy: Theorizing Feminism*. Calcutta: Stree, 2007.

Greer, Germaine. *The Female Eunuch*. Great Britain: MacGibbon & Kee Ltd., 1970.

Guerin, Wilfred L., Earle Labor, Lee Morgan, Jeanne C. Reesman and John R. Willingham. *A Handbook of Critical Approaches to Literature*, 5th ed. New York: Oxford University Press, 2005.

Jain, Jasbir (comp. and ed.). *Women's Writing: Text and Context*. Jaipur and New Delhi: Rawat Publications, 1996.

Jha, Raj Kamal. *The Blue Bedspread: A Novel*. London: Picador, an imprint of Macmillan Publishers Ltd., 2000.

Joseph, Ammu. 'The Battle of the Sexes and Other Myths'. In Kalpana Sharma (ed.), *Missing Half the Story: Journalism as If Gender Matters*. New Delhi: Zubaan, 2010.

Karnad, Girish. *Wedding Album*. New Delhi: Oxford University Press, 2009.

Kumar, Jainendra. *The Resignation (Tyagpatra)*. Bombay: Hindi Granth Ratnakar, 1956.

Lal, Malashri, Shormishtha Panja and Sumanyu Satpathy (eds). *Signifying the Self: Women and Literature*. New Delhi: Macmillan India Ltd., 2007.

'Five Husbands! That Can't be Fun, God Knows I Have Enough Trouble with One', Kalki Koechlin writes a monologue on Women's Day. Kalki Koechlin. IBNLive Specials. 12:26 PM. 10 March 2014. Web. 11 March 2014.

Kinsley, David R., *Hindu Goddesses: Visions of the Divine Feminine in the Hindu Religious Tradition*. Berkeley and Los Angeles, CA: University of California Press, 1988.

Moi, Toril. *Sexual/Texual Politics*. London: Routledge, 2002.

Mummery, Jane and Peta Bowden. *Understanding Feminism*. Jaipur: Rawat Publications, 2012.

Murthy, Laxmi. 'Women, Men and the Emerging Other'. In Kalpana Sharma (ed.), Missing *Half the Story: Journalism as If Gender Matters*. New Delhi: Zubaan, 2010.

Narang, Darshan K., Neeru Chhabra and Kavita Koradia. *Adolescent Girls: Awareness, Rights and Reproductive Health*. Jaipur: Pointer Publishers, 2010.

Nawale, Arvind M., *Indian Writing in English: Speculations and Observations*. New Delhi: Authors Press, 2011.

Osborne, John., *Look Back in Anger*. Westport, CT: Greenwood Publishing Group, 2007.

Par Bande Ache Hain. Lyrics by Swanand Kirkire, ICICI Prudential Life. Lowe Lintas & Partners. 23 February 2013.

Panikkar, K.N. *Culture and Consciousness in Modern India: A Historical Perspective*. New Delhi: People's Publishing House (P) Ltd., 2003.

Pateman, Carole. 'Feminist Critiques of the Public/Private Dichotomy'. In her *The Disorder of Women*. Palo Alto, CA: Stanford University Press, 1989, 118–140.

Prasad, Amar Nath and Kanupriya. *Indian Writing in English: Tradition and Modernity*. New Delhi: Sarup & Sons, 2010.

Rajesh, Monisha. 'India's Unfair Obsession with Lighter Skin'. *The Guardian*. Web. 14 August 2013.

Sanga, Jaina C. (ed.). *South Asian Novelists in English: An A-to-Z Guide*. Westport, CT and London: Greenwood Press, 2005.

Russell, Bertrand. *Marriage and Morals*. Great Britain: Routledge, 1996.

Sen, Soumik. Dir. *Gulab Gang*. Prod. Anubhav Sinha. Perf. Madhuri Dixit and Juhi Chawla. Alumbra Entertainment, 2014.

Sharma, Bulbul. *Now That I'm Fifty: Short Stories*. New Delhi: Women Unlimited, an imprint of Kali for Women, 2011.

Shinde, Gauri. Dir. *English Vinglish*. Perf. Sridevi, Adil Hussain, Amit Trivedi and Priya Anand. Eros International, 2012.

Singh, Pramod Kumar (ed.). *Indian Fiction in English*. New Delhi: Atlantic Publishers, 2001.

Steinem, Gloria. Foreword. *The Choices We Made: Twenty-Five Women and Men Speak Out About Abortion*. New York: Random House, 1991.

CHAPTER 8

Emotional Abuse

The Invisible Wounds of Women

PRIYANKA SHARMA

The marginalisation of women and the cultural pressure to accept this secondary status has been a global phenomenon in human history. Women across the world have struggled for ages to live a life of dignity. They have been victims of crimes like female infanticide, abduction, molestation, sexual exploitation, domestic violence, eve-teasing and rape. Their aspirations and dreams are further squashed by child marriage, physical mutilation and casual or planned trafficking. Though, the legislative bodies all over the world ensure an equal access to women to socio-economic participation and opportunities the same as their male counterparts enjoy, the socio-psychological discrimination, malice and violence continue to play havoc with their lives. However, the apparent exploitation of women through physical violence is only the tip of the iceberg. The emotional trauma caused to women at the hands of hostile patriarchal attitudes is often overlooked. The wound of emotional abuse is generally deeper than the physical or external causative and continues to haunt the woman long after the physical injury heals. As Loring, a clinical-social worker suggests that like any other form of abuse, emotional abuse is 'an ongoing process in which one individual systematically diminishes and destroys the inner self of another through belittling his/her essential feelings, perceptions and ideas' (1994: 1). Emotional abuse against women is exerted through withdrawal of affection; denial of her right to emotions; putdowns or constant criticism; name calling; isolating her to control her activities; denial of personal pleasures or satisfying interests; threats to harm friends or family; making her account for every moment and every action; and controlling her through fear.

Women, in both developed and developing countries are the victims of this abuse. In India women are exposed to the pangs of this emotional abuse from the cradle to the grave. Parents are the unchallenged stakeholders in the lives of girls. They bear the responsibility of socialising the girls in compliance of 'culture' and 'religion' and passing on typical life skills. In the process of this socialisation, the parents supply all the physical and material needs of girls but completely neglect (whether knowingly or unknowingly) their emotional needs. And thus they introduce themselves in girls' life as passive abusers. Their passive abuse includes restricting a girl's movements in the name of protection, denigration of her self-confidence, intimidation to follow the social and gender specific norms, discrimination and rejection, etc. Being the repository of the family's social honour, a girl is rendered an object of restrictions. She is supposed to be more sensitive, gentle, submissive, modest, emotional and people-oriented in order to be an effective *homemaker*. In order to be socially fit, once entering adulthood, a girl's sitting; standing, talking and interacting gestures are also under observation and restriction. She should not talk loudly; her body movement should not be like a male. If she is too meek and obedient to perform household duties she will be called *Lakshmibanti*, i.e. the Hindu goddess of wealth. If her body postures are boyish or similar she is called *chandi*. The parents perceive that if the girl is not trained well during her adolescence, there will be a problem in arranging her marriage.

The failure of parents to provide an appropriate and supportive environment has an adverse effect on a girl's self-motivation, self-confidence and self-worth. These effects are detrimental and long-lasting in her life. When a girl grows up with this constant sense of being weak or in need of protection and insistence on submission, dependence and respect for authority on her part, she takes her subjugation and oppression as an inevitable destiny. This subjugation and oppression becomes more complex and diplomatic when a girl gets married and becomes subject to the spousal abuse.

Though, women are destined to face discrimination even before birth, which continues through their childhood, adolescence and adulthood, the strongest bias towards women and their inferiority is palpable in conjugal relationships. Under the existing socio-cultural dogma a married woman is supposed to be submissive and devoted to her husband and his family. The ideal wife is one whose single aim in life is to satisfy her husband. She is judged on the basis of how properly she performs the services demanded by her husband. *'Patrivrata'* with full devotion to the husband, is identified as wifely ideal by Hindu scriptures (Lebra, 1984: 26). These traditional and ideal role expectations to offer a selfless nurturance endorse the husband to misuse the power, intimacy, commitment and dependency to make the woman unequal, powerless and unsafe through emotional abuse.

In order to address this concealed yet extremely damaging facet of women's victimisation, firstly it would be pertinent to analyse the complex hegemony of masculinity maintained by structural control, i.e. emotional abuse. The social problem of emotional abuse against women, by their husband, is a greatly unrecognised crime which should receive proper attention. Emotional abuse is a shrewd power strategy to maintain dominance over women by shifting their attention away from their victimisation. Though the emotional bruises are more devastating, deeper and lasting than physical assault yet few of us recognise it or identify it because emotional abuse leaves few physical scars. It's victims suffer no broken bones, torn flesh or spilled blood. Thus the abuser wins in 'control and power' game without any criminal liability. In this case women's awareness of emotional abuse often does not occur until it damages their sense of self completely. Therefore it is very essential to discuss and explain the entire continuum of emotional abuse that is equally harmful and more deliberate and strategic.

Continuum of Emotional Abuse to Wife

The concept of emotional abuse was introduced and explored by the clinical psychologist and feminist researcher Lenore Walker in 1979. Before it, only the physical violence or abuse was emphasised as a means of women victimisation in intimate relationships. Eventually researchers and sociologists found that except physical abuse there are several kinds of maltreatment to women in any abusive relationship which were more detrimental and long-lasting than physical abuse and also difficult to enumerate. In the series of later researchers of emotional abuse Chang, Loring and Patrick-Hoffman expanded complex phenomenon of emotional abuse to women. Several terminologies, for example psychological abuse, psychological aggression, emotional abuse, etc. had been interchangeably employed to label women's complex experiences of emotional abuse. At first Lenore Walker, in 1979, used the term psychological abuse identifying four types of demeanor: (a) verbal abuse; (b) isolation; (c) jealousy and/or possessiveness of one's partner; and (d) threats of abuse. Later on, Patrick-Hoffman acknowledged some twenty behaviours like: denial of the women's perceptions, overt aggression, disregard for the women's desires or feelings, possessiveness and isolation, use of verbally disparaging language in public and private places, and refusal to acknowledge any responsibility for problems in the relationship. In the last decade, in his efforts to distinguish emotional abuse from psychological abuse, along with all other psychologists like Follingstad and Tolman, Loring made an accurate remark 'I use the term emotional abuse rather than psychological abuse or maltreatment in an attempt to encompass the relational and societal components of this process ...' (1994: vii–viii).

Concluding these theoretical stances, Emotional abuse perpetrated by husband against his wife is a continuous, systematic, pattern which can occur in a covert to overt abuse continuum. In an emotionally abusive relationship, a husband intentionally chooses the tactics to diminish his wife's selfhood in all aspects. Three or more of the following tactics are used by a husband to transform his wife into a passive and silent dupe. In order to monopolise her time and energy, he makes all the big decisions and determines how, when and what she gets communicated. He determines to have his own way to decide her rights, beliefs, and desires. For this purpose he puts inappropriate restrictions including to refuse the wife to go out for job, discourages her from any interest that he is not part of. The abusive husband goes to the extent of an outright prohibition to the wife from seeing family and friends. He isolates her and calls her name telling her that she cares more for her friends and family than for him.

An emotionally abusive husband takes up a passive negligence of the care, respect and support, generally expected in conjugal relationship, just to show indifference to his wife. He shows as if she has no importance for him. He makes himself busy in TV, the newspaper, friends and other individuals to ignore or belittle her and avoids her when she begins a conversation. This deep silence or passive emotional withdrawal is used to strengthen the illusion of a flaw in the wife and to put a control over her 'self' through guilt. To enjoy an intact supremacy, free from any challenge, he starts to create a double bind mystification to confuse and harass the wife. He pretexts that he wishes to be one with her but cannot do so because there is something wrong with her. Ironically the moment wife corrects herself on the recommended ground, he identifies something else that is wrong with her, and thus escapes from the liability of emotional barrenness towards the wife. This way he cannot be blamed even of badgering the wife. As a famous psychologist, Douglas has suggested 'an abusive husband uses love also as a coercive tool' (1994: 24). He threatens to divorce or abandon her if she does not get his way. Paradoxically, he warns the wife that if she leaves, he will commit suicide and she will be responsible. This double mind conveys the message that 'if you withdraw from me any manner I will punish you, but if you reach out to me, I will reject you'.

In this situation the wife cannot help blaming herself for this withdrawal because this inexpressiveness is just for the wife. The wife finds that he shares with others happily what she expects from him for herself. He either refuses to help in her requirements or pretends to forget. Gradually these mind games turn into symbolic aggressions and physical assaults like damaging property or throwing something but not at the wife. Statements like 'If you say another word I don't know what I'm going to do' are used to terrorise the wife. However, he succeeds to minimise his abusiveness using social institutions saying that this hierarchy is natural.

Here, it is essential to distinguish between the abuse in a 'normal' relationship and the emotional abuse in a relationship where the male determines to establish and maintain 'power and control'. In a 'normal relationship' the man adopting abusive behaviour is also willing to resolve the conflicts in relationship and take the responsibility for his behaviour. He gives some symptoms of being willing to adapt to equality and affinity in the conjugal relationship. But the emotional abuse as discussed in the present study is about 'power and control', a pattern of behaviours used over time. It is intended to dominate and to win at all costs.

Lenore Walker posits that this premeditated emotional abuse takes place in three phases (2000: 126). During the first phase of 'Tension Building', the husband creates an ambience of tension through withdrawal, isolation, disapproval which results into lack of opportunity of communication for the victimised wife. Subsequently, the wife feels confused, frustrated and is compelled to pacify the husband through unquestioned submission. In the second phase, i.e. 'Incident', the abuse takes on more explicitly when there are incidents of verbal and emotional abuse with symbolic aggression or outbursts like blaming, name calling, threats and bullying directed at the wife or her natal family. In the next phase of 'Reconciliation', the male suddenly reverts back to his position, seemingly softer towards the partner. He offers excuses or refuses to accept that any kind of abuse has taken place or that the abuse or his behaviour is not as ruthless as the wife claims it to be and rationalises his behaviour by reminding her of times he was sensible and she was offensive. In the fourth phase, there is a period of apparent 'Calm', as there is a brief let up in the abusiveness. The incidents are 'forgotten' and there is a temporary peace. But it proves to be a mirage only. Eventually the tension retrieves again and gradually there is the phase I of the cycle – the wheel completes a full circle and continues (Walker, 2000: 126–127).

This systematic pattern of abuse confuses the wife of what she should expect and accept. She thinks that he did not intend to hurt her as his malice is temporary and his commotions are beyond his control. In this context French psychotherapist Hirigoyen has rightly said no woman can believe 'anyone would hate her so much for no good reason' (2000: 35). But due to these continuous paradoxes of abuse, the wife gets depressed and feels that she is in a situation in which whatever she does she cannot put the things in right way. The research shows that long term emotional abuse proves to be fatal. Hoffman has advocated that the longer the abuse, the more likely women are to believe the abuser's evaluation of them (1984: 37). Chang also propounded that emotionally abused women have a decreased sense of self and less trust in their ability to make judgments and assess situations (1996: 88). As many of us undermine this deployment as a normal part of a relationship it is necessary to ascertain how fatal these evaluations by an abusive husband can result.

Scars of Emotional Abuse on Wife

Although physical abuse results in serious injuries, emotional abuse has an equal or even greater impact. Female victims experience shame, guilt and distress for something they have not done. The guilt and doubt engendered in a woman serves the abuser's ultimate intention. She loses her trust in her 'self' and its worth. Moreover, she experiences collapsing of her 'self' and feels as if she is losing her sanity. She starts to undermine her sense of power and control. She becomes self-loathing and blames herself for everything which goes wrong around her. Her subjective reality and sense of self determination gets distorted leading to a feeling of non-existence. The persistent tension, anxiety and the contradictory nature of the emotional abuse leads to greatly heightened problem, i.e. 'traumatic bonding' (Dutton and Painter, 1981: 139). Traumatic bonding refers to a kind of attachment to the abuser who swings between terroristic behaviour and kindness. This attachment stops the woman to detach from the abuser. She finds herself going crazy and confused about whether to remain with the man or get out of abusive marital relationship. She finds that she is not sure who or what to believe. Ironically the socio-cultural ethos heightens this confusion and loss of 'self' of women victims.

Emotionally Abused Wife and Social Retort

The male, whether in form of father, husband, brother or son, is known in society as nurturing, life-giving, and supportive force to women within the family. The concept of woman as subservient to man, and as man's property, is deep rooted in Indian tradition. Therefore, woman has been regarded as '*paraya dhan*' who is handed over to her rightful owner, her husband, by her previous custodians, i.e. her parents. It encourages the natal family to disown its married daughters. A happy and satisfied married daughter brings a sense of respect and appreciation from neighbours and other kinsmen, so even if a married daughter is unhappy, she is advised to adjust and please the people in her in-laws family. Due to socio-cultural imperatives of unequal power relationships between men and women, it is always the women who have to walk the tight rope to save marriage and family honour at all costs. Otherwise she is labeled as a loser or loose. The ideas inculcated in a woman ensure her submission and compliance to 'ideal womanhood'.

Indian woman's identity is always defined within the parameters of her social relationship with man – as a daughter, a wife and a mother. A woman's individual identity has never been realised positively in Indian social life. Therefore, the Indian mother teaches her daughter to sustain in a relationship even at the cost of self-sacrifice. She takes it as her pious and prime duty to enable her daughter to fit into the patriarchal image of an ideal wife and daughter-in-law; otherwise she will face rejection in the society. The burden of such societal norms practised within the society plays havoc with the psyche of emotionally abused wife. When she is subject to abuse she falls in conflict with cultural norms of authority and goes back and forth between the choices of staying with or leaving her partner.

If a woman stands up to leave the abusive partner her orthodox community fails to appreciate her spirit and sense of self-respect. Rather she is seen as falling short in notions of sex appropriate behaviours. It is ingrained in our mindset that the marriage is a woman's asset and her worth can be measured only through her marital status. Even if her natal family accepts back a divorced woman, her situation is a juicy topic for the society. The people in the surroundings are the least bothered about what has happened to the woman. They may express their lip sympathy at her discomfiture but also blame her for the shame she brings on the family through her divorce. Divorce is seen as a sign of failure in conjugal life. According to the stakeholders of the society whatever may be the situation the woman should not take divorce; she should try her best to adjust. Only in extreme cases she can go for divorce. If the husband is not ready to compromise or bend, then the woman should bend a little more to keep the marriage intact but one should never go for divorce. So without an extremely reasonable case, divorce makes her an outcast in society. Ironically, the divorce on the basis of emotional abuse does not come under these extreme cases, because the effects of emotional abuse are 'invisible wound' and are often obscured (Loring, 1994: 12). In the case of emotional abuse, wife is not hit physically but her 'soul' is bruised and her 'self' is stolen. There is no physical proof for 'bruised soul' and 'broken self-esteem'. That is why emotional abuse is often neglected in public discourse of domestic violence and spousal abuse and family or friends do not believe or understand the abused woman; even blame her for lack of adjustment.

Ultimately an emotionally abused wife has to face pressures from the natal family to reconcile with the abuser. Otherwise she is credited with the marital discord. Now disappointed and frustrated, she seeks to cope with the disgrace, and humiliation caused by an abusive husband. In Indian tradition, family matters are not even shared with individuals outside the family. To badmouth her husband is not a quality of an ideal and good wife. Because every relationship has to have some problems, it can't all be smooth. Thus the wife avoids even asking for help because she has to be seen to cope, to assume a mask of happiness and to conform to what is called ideal role of wife 'to keep the peace'. Thus to turn to the justice system for assistance is something far from their vision and mission.

Legal Inadequacy and Lineage of Wounds

Despite these socio-cultural taboos, some women do not meekly accept their plight and decide to resist and reject this diplomatic male dominance, and cross the social boundaries to have legal assistance against their abusive husbands' cold blooded torture. As it has been vested with the responsibility of deterrence of and protection against domestic violence to women, in Indian Constitution, the legal aid and support mechanisms are easily available to women; Still there are some serious impediments in providing true protection for women from emotional abuse.

Before 2005, the Indian Penal Code granted only two avenues for criminal sanctions against the domestic violence, i.e. Section 498-A and Section 304B. Section 498-A of the Indian Penal Code, i.e. 'Anti-Cruelty Act' provides that 'whoever, being the husband or the relative of the husband of a woman, subjects such woman to cruelty, shall be punished with imprisonment ... and shall also be liable to fine' (cited in Hornbeck et al., 2005: 277). Section 304B, i.e. 'Dowry Death Act' criminalises violence against a woman when it can be proved that the death of a woman was caused in conjunction with dowry demands (cited in Hornbeck et al., 2005: 277–278). The Dowry Death Act has a presumption of murder 'where the death of a woman is caused by any burns or bodily injury or occurs otherwise than under normal circumstances within seven years of her marriage and it is shown that soon before her death she was subjected to cruelty or harassment by her husband or any relative of her husband for ... any demand for dowry' (Lawyers Collective, Women's Rights Initiative, 2004: 11). The point at which a woman can demand for justice varies between these two Acts; the Anti-Cruelty Act can be called upon while a woman is still alive, while the Dowry Death Act provides punishment after the woman is dead. But in both cases criminal sanctions are available only if the abuse involves extreme cruelty or dowry related acts of violence.

Furthermore, stereotypes of women that are entrenched within a patriarchal mindset have led police and the courts to disbelieve and put allegations of misuse of the law on women. Due to these accusations and inadequate remedy, before 2005 women had only two options either to live with the violence or endure the wrath of a community that does not accept divorce. Moreover, the greatest impediment to a woman seeking recourse against a violent husband was her own fear that exposing her husband's violent behaviour would force her into homelessness and shame.

Even the new domestic violence act, i.e. The Protection of Women from Domestic Violence Act 2005 which provides an expansive definition of domestic violence including multiple forms of violence, i.e. physical, sexual, verbal, emotional, and economic abuse also fails to protect a woman in an emotionally abusive relationship. The most significant limitation to The Protection Act 2005 is its civil character. The legislatives have strategically drafted the Act's remedies as 'civil'. As a Civil Act, it proscribes any criminal punishment for men who engage in domestic violence. Therefore, even with the enactment of the Act, in order to bring criminal charges for domestic violence, the options for the women are again the

Anti-Cruelty Statute and the Dowry Death Act. As discussed above, these acts are not resourceful wide enough to provide criminal recourse for the victims of domestic violence. Furthermore, the Act does not provide a permanent relief to the victims. The Act provides only a temporary relief, in terms of Protection Orders and other temporary orders, designed to give women time to evaluate their options. Though, the Act grants the victim the right to reside in a shared household during this period. Yet despite protecting her from being thrown out of her home, it does not directly protect her from being subjected to violence. Because, while the orders of protection, which are granted under the Act, prohibit the respondent from committing any act of domestic violence and require the executor to have no contact with the victim, these orders are only temporary. After this period, the Act does not provide any protection for victims of domestic violence.

Moreover, in practice mental or emotional injury is not so easy to prove in court, simply because it is not visible (Protection of Women Act, chapter 2 and 3). There are no objective criteria or standard tests that can decide the extent of the injuries endured or even to know whether it is a part of casual conjugal life of the two individuals or the malice of an insensitive being. Therefore, only the individual judge before whom the case is filed is left to determine meticulousness of mental cruelty and mental injury. Courts in India have defined cruelty as necessarily involving a subjective element. This implies that the judge takes into account the facts of the situation and the surrounding circumstances to arrive at a finding of mental cruelty, i.e. whether a woman is justified in alleging cruelty in the particular circumstances. This requires an assessment of the facts like surrounding circumstances, educational, economic and cultural backgrounds of the wife, the physical or mental condition and the intention of the accused person and the knowledge of the actual probable effect of his conduct on the other's health.

A perusal of the judgments in this regard shows that instead of basing judgments on the perception of the woman while deciding the case the judge applies his own perceptions. This leads to the introduction of bias, often a male chauvinistic nature of the decision. In an extreme case, to prove charges of mental cruelty and injuries to mental health there has to be sufficient medical reports of the victim woman to hold the accused guilty. There is no medical report to prove mental injuries caused to the woman by the treatment of her husband. Hence the said provision of Indian Penal Code again leads the women towards re-victimisation, branding their victimisation as mere domestic disputes.

Conclusion

Thus, the patriarchal mindset affects not only the general public; it also affects the very people who are supposed to protect women from domestic violence. Home, which is considered as the safest place to dwell, occurs to be a repository of increasing crime against women and girls. Therefore, steps must be taken to promote awareness for the fact that violence against women, in any form, is unacceptable. Now, at this point of time, the need of the hour is to create public awareness, developing a better policy and legal framework and provide the necessary support system to women and girl which can enable them to uncover their unseen pain. While physical injuries can be witnessed easily by people, mental and psychological injuries are not visible and cannot be proved to the people, despite the fact they cause even greater damage. Therefore, there should be training for sensitisation of girls, right from the childhood, to shield themselves against the emotional assaults which diminish their self esteem. Since the patriarchal social structure proves even legal solution to be a failure, we should work together to dismantle the patriarchal mindset. A cheerful life, free from violence, is a fundamental human right. We should facilitate women's empowerment by trying to provide encouraging factors or take away inhibiting factors. We should assist the women in analysing their situation; encourage them for sharing their experiences and telling her that though Indian society considers a certain level of violence against women to be the norm, tolerance of nominal forms of violence is the procreation of extreme forms of violence against women. Despite the legal potentials of the constitution, violence against women cannot be reduced or eliminated in all sense unless the patriarchal mindset of the Indian society is taken apart and every girl is born and brought up with the thought that violence in any sense is unacceptable.

References

Anderson, Kim M., Lynette M. Renner and Fran S. Danis. 'Recovery, Resilience and Growth in the Aftermath of Domestic Violence'. *Violence Against Women*, 18: 1279–1299, 2012.

Basu, Asmita. 'Violence Against Women: A Statistical Overview, Challenges and Gaps in Data Collection and Methodology and Approaches for Overcoming Them, Needs of Users of Data Collection'. Paper presented in Expert Group Meeting organised by UN Division for the Advancement of Women in collaboration with Economic Commission for Europe (ECE) and World Health Organisation (WHO), 11–14 April 2005, Geneva, Switzerland. Unpublished conference paper, 2008. Web. 29 August 2013.

Catherine, A. and B. Elizabeth. 'Fear, Guilt, and Grief: Harm to Pets and the Emotional Abuse of Women'. *Journal of Emotional Abuse*, 7.1: 51–70, 2007.

Chang, V.N. *I Just Lost Myself: Psychological Abuse of Women in Marriage*. Westport, CT: Praeger, 1996.

'Domestic Violence Act: Women Can Now be Prosecuted'. *The Indian Express*, New Delhi, 4 June 2010.

Douglas, K. *Invisible Wounds: A Self-Help Guide for New Zealand Women in Destructive Relationships*. Auckland, NZ: Penguin, 24, 1994.

Dutton, D.G. and S.L. Painter. 'Traumatic Bonding: The Development of Emotional Attachments in Battered Women and Other Relationships of Intermittent Abuse'. *Victimology: An International Journal*, 7.4: 139–155, 1981.

Elizabeth, V. *Patterns and Trends of Domestic Violence in India: An Examination of Court Records*. Washington, D.C.: ICRW, 1999. Web. 18 March 2013.

Hirigoyen, M.F. *Stalking the Soul: Emotional Abuse and the Erosion of Identity*. New York: Helen Marx Books, 35, 2000.

Hoffman, P. 'Psychological Abuse of Women by Spouses and Live-In Lovers'. *Women and Therapy*, 3.1: 37–47, 1984.

Hornbeck, Amy et al. 'The Protection of Women from Domestic Violence Act: Solution or Mere Paper Tiger?' *Loyola University Chicago International Law Review*, 4.2: 273–307, 2005.

Hunnicutt, Gwen. 'Varieties of Patriarchy and Violence Against Women: Resurrecting "Patriarchy" as a Theoretical Tool'. *Violence Against Women*, 15: 553–573, 2009.

Kaukinen, Catherine. 'Status Compatibility, Physical Violence, and Emotional Abuse in Intimate Relationships'. *Journal of Marriage and Family*, 66 (May): 452–471, 2004.

Lawyers Collective Women's Rights Initiative. *Only Her Word: A National Campaign for Law on Domestic Violence*. New Delhi: Gondals Press, 2004.

Lebra, Joyce, Joy Paulson and Jane Everett. *Women and Work in India: Continuity and Change*. New Delhi: Promilla & Co. Publishers, 26, 1984.

Lobbestael, J. and A. Arntz. 'Emotional, Cognitive and Physiological Correlates of Abuse-Related Stress in Borderline Personality Disorder'. *Behaviour Research and Therapy*, 48: 116–124, 2010.

Loring, M.T. *Emotional Abuse*. New York: Lexington Books, 1994.

Mishra, Suchismita et al. 'Socialisation and Gender Bias at the Household Level Among School-Attending Girls in a Tribal Community of the Kalahandi District of Eastern India'. *Anthropological Notebooks*, 18.2: 45–53, 2012.

Morse, A. Melissa. 'An Exploration of Women's Experiences of Emotional Abuse'. Ph.D. Thesis, University of Georgia, Athens, May 2003, http://spock.fcs.uga.edu/ss/docs/morse_melissa_a_200305_phd.pdf (29 August 2013).

Murphy, Clare. 'Women Coping with Psychological Abuse: Surviving in the Secret World of Male Partner Power and Control'. M.A. Thesis, University of Waikato, New Zealand, February 2002, http://www.nzfvc.org.nz/sites/nzfvc.org.nz/files/clare%20murphy.pdf (29 August 2013).

'Psychology Today, Emotional Abuse Violates Civil Rights'. n.d., psychologytoday.com blog, http://www.psychologytoday.com/blog/anger-in-the-age-entitlement/201002/emotional-abuse-violates-civil-rights (22 August 2013).

Protection of Women Act, Chapter 2 and 3. 1 October 2006.

Roberts, Gwenneth. 'The Impact of Domestic Violence on Women's Mental Health'. *Australian and New Zealand Journal of Public Health*, 22 (1998). Web. 17 March 2013.

Schwartz, L.L. 'The Historical Dimension of Cultic Techniques of Persuasion and Control'. *Cultic Studies Journal*, 8.1: 37–45, 1991.

Simon, George. *In Sheep's Clothing: Understanding and Dealing with Manipulative People*. Little Rock: Parkhurst Brothers, pp. 111–136, 2010.

Singh, Kirti. 'Violence Against Women and the Indian Law'. In Savitri Goonesekere (ed.), *Violence, Law and Women's Rights*. London: Sage Publications, pp. 77–82, 2004.

Sweetnam, Stephanie. 'Where Do You Think Domestic Abuse Hurts Most?' *Violence Against Women*, 19: 133–138, 2013.

Tutty, Leslie M. et al. 'I Built My House of Hope: Abused Women and Pathways into Homelessness'. *Violence Against Women,* 19: 1498–1517, 2013.

'What is Emotional/Verbal Abuse?' n.d., loveisrespect.org, http://www.loveisrespect.org/is-this-abuse/types-of-abuse/what-is-emotional-verbal-abuse (22 August 2013).

Walker, L. *The Battered Women Syndrome*. New York: Springer, pp. 126–127, 2000.

Weston, R. and J. Fam. 'Insecure Attachment Mediates Effects of Partners' Emotional Abuse and Violence on Women's Relationship Quality'. *Springer Science,* 23.6: 483–493, 2008.

Section III

Violence and Security Concerns

CHAPTER 9

Traditions, Honour, and Women Security in a Global Context

RAMESH KUMAR

The context in which an ancient Hindu religious text such as *Manusmriti* answers the question of traditions, honour, and women security is essentially not similar to the context in which the 20th century Indian feminist journal such as *Manushi* does. There may be many commonalities in both the texts; however, they remain non-comparable. Even if one wants to locate commonalities, one cannot do so until one considers their contexts. It suggests that temporal human intellect is contextual; its uniform application across different historic times is beyond possibility, which in turn indicates an inevitable contextual horizon of reference characterised by temporal historicity for any sort of enquiry involving a temporal issue. In other words, the importance of temporal historicity (with all its limitations) is undeniable in the plurality of contexts.[1]

The plurality of context, however, does not reduce the significance of any issue of utmost priority and importance for human beings' collective co-existence in a given context. Paradoxically, human intellect is limited and enriched by plurality of contexts. What is relevant in one context may seem irrelevant in the other.

For instance, when it comes to the ways of ensuring human security (read women security), it will be an irrelevant view adopted from *Manusmriti* law if it suggests a way that does not maximise human security in a global context. Equally irrelevant would be an anarchist argument that does not offer a mutually sustainable idea of human security in private and public spheres of collective social existence. It follows then that temporal historicity is helpful in differentiating issues of immediate frames of reference (such as self-identity) from that of eternal quests such as the queries concerning transcendental existence beyond our immediate frames of reference or spiritual horizons of the existential self.[2]

Temporal historicity gives us scope to contextualise the idea of good. Context is important because, for instance, the issue of human security or, more specifically, women security is not a stand alone technical question of physical safety in domestic and public environment; it is rather a matter of dealing with both physical as well as mental aspects of the inconvenient truth of human anatomy in a global context. In this sense, paradoxically, it involves both the temporal and the transcendental phenomena of creativity.

Given the paradox, it would be disadvantageous to restrict our understanding of women security merely to the task of maximising the impact of the legal framework of the state on our collective behaviour. It follows that neither a rigid ideal of preservation nor an anarchist ideal of freedom would be much helpful in our attempt to maximise women security, because neither the positive laws solely nor the state alone are sufficient in maximising women security. In view of this assumption, while dealing with the issue of women security in a global context, this article looks beyond the compartmentalised frameworks of tradition and modernity. The article assumes that practices of traditions, honour, and women security are intrinsically interrelated. It argues that any attempt towards maximising women security needs to begin with by re-visioning the ideas of honour and traditions. The article does not aim to prescribe any immediate remedial measures towards maximising women security; it is rather a modest attempt towards highlighting the need for evolving a conceptual framework that could be used as a tool to minimise the problems generated due to the intricacies of traditions, honour, and women security in a global context. Keeping this approach and assumption in view, this article first discusses briefly feminist politics of women's movement. Next, it raises the issue of traditions, honour, and women security along with the problem of killings in the name of honour. Finally, it deals with the issue of women security in the context of the dilemma of the tradition of local self-governance with specific reference to Khap Panchayats (KPs) in rural areas of Haryana.

Feminist Politics

The well-popularised slogan 'personal is political' is an expression of the assumption that the politics of recognition of women and men is based on the construction of womanhood and manhood or feminity and masculinity wherein ideology of patriarchal society plays central role. Feminists argue that for women social and economic security are essential tools to gaining political security. Political security is needed to rationalise the public sphere and to minimise violence and suppression of women in the personal sphere. Most often, feminists see women security as an element of the major goal of women's liberation from subjugated social, economic, and political condition in a patriarchal society.

Many feminists argue that women security will remain an incomplete task until we disown patriarchal society, and for this, we need to demasculanise legal discourse on private and public relationship. In the absence of the idea of power, what would be a realistic society? Feminist movements have not been able to answer this question satisfactorily. In their attempts to demasculanise legal discourse, they have become victim of 'logic of circularity' (Ajay Gudavarthy, 2013). Does it follow from this that, so far, feminist movements have been less empowered or less effective in laying down a roadmap for women security in a global context?

Recent feminist politics draws its sustainability from a series of women's movement that began in the 1970s and 1980s. This was the period when, the women's movement started 'negotiating with the dilemma regarding the place of law and state action in relation to gender issues' by taking 'multiple, contrasting and contested approaches pulling the movement in different directions' (Gudavarthy, 2013: 128). The dilemma concerning 'the place of law and state action in gender issues' continues to remain central in the issue of women security.

One of the reasons for such a dilemma is heterogeneity of women's movement, the impact of which needs more attention in feminist research. Heterogeneity, to some extent, has kept the women's movement fragmented. For instance, in the Indian context, the gap between rural and urban basis of the movement has given rise to the phenomenon of 'professionalisation of feminism, and NGO-isation of the autonomous women organisations' (Gudavarthy, 2013: 146). Divisions among feminist across the lines of caste, class, and race along with the so-called ideological inclinations such as liberal, radical, socialists have kept the movement away from effectively handling issues of women security.

Despite all these drawbacks, feminist politics has consistently registered a critique of law and state action, and has tried to create a situation of awareness that could positively affect the making and implementation of public policies in terms of securing women's lives in domestic and public spheres. Seen from this perspective, women's movement has been the backbone of the feminist discourse on gender and society in 21st century. Partly against the backdrop of women's movement and partly due to the National Policy for the Empowerment of Women (2001), the number of legal measures to maximise women security has increased substantially during the last decade of 20th century and the 1st decade of 21st century. Ironically, the impact of various state led plans, policies, and programs has been partial and slow. Legal protection is necessary but these are continuously being proved insufficient for maximising women security. The incidents of crime against women have not come down. Against such a backdrop of feminist politics of women's movement, we now move on to discuss traditions and honour in women's lives.

Traditions and Honour

Many of us invoke phrases like 'times immemorial', 'a thousand years old', and so on while authenticating an idea or its practice in a given socio-political and cultural context. It sometimes goes well, if an idea or a practice is compatible with the larger collective interest of our society. However, not all ideas and practices can remain beyond dispute, and, in the process of looking for a way out, we tend to judge and subsequently either adopt or abandon them. The ideas of traditions and honour are not something that we can easily adopt or abandon.

Human history reminds us repeatedly that these ideas have caused innumerable battles ranging from individuals to groups to feudal empires to nation states. One of the outcomes of human struggle with these ideas is ever increasing level of awareness about many irrelevant aspects of these ideas. For feminists, relating honour with human anatomy is objectionable if it minimises women's physical security.

Feminists argue that by putting the idea of honour into the domain of sexism, women are first constructed as lovable, beautiful, complex, fathomless, all mysterious, and then they are treated by virtue of all these features as only emotional individuals who cannot act rationally and are subsequently labeled as fickle minded human beings hence incomplete individuals.[3] Such an idea of authenticating women's honour is a direct denial of women as rational and holder of mind and intellect. Here also, context matters. The way we look at a human activity depends on the context within which we infer its meaning and interpret it. This is where we tend to observe some repetition of our behaviour and try to adjust such behaviour in the light of changing context. Our activities are diverse and may take multiple forms.

An activity may appear to one group of human beings as a tradition and a coercive practice or a symbol of authenticating dominant practices to other groups. When it comes to tradition, it can be an invented phenomenon also.[4] In the context of India, for example, there was a time when the contentious notion of sati was treated as a religious or spiritual act of a woman. As of now, there is none to buy such interpretations. Even a simple attempt towards examination of the very psychology of Sati is also addressed by feminists with strong criticism.[5] The reason for this shift of understanding about an act done by a woman is the context of an increased awareness of human being and contextual utilisation of human intellect.[6] Almost same is the case with the idea of honour.

There has been substantial change in the meaning of honour during past few hundred years. The change was more prominent in the enlightenment age and is clearly visible in our times.[7] How various codes of honour effectively determine our interactive relations is an issue that has close linkage with women security.

Feminists cutting across regional boundaries have tried to trace the genesis of such codes in the origin of private and public relations between men and women with a focus on violence in the name of honour. If so, honour then emerges as a problem and a solution.[8] It is so because honour is a complex expression of human behaviour involving the questions of life and death. For example, resistance to certain codes of honour may become unacceptable to so-called protectors of these notions, which may motivate them to kill an individual or a group of individual. Violence in the name of honour is thus not restricted to a region or a religion; it goes beyond a given context also. Though found in various contexts, the nature of violence in the name of honour is contextual.

Violence in the Name of Honour*

Killings in the name of honour have been one of the most serious problems concerning women security. Such killings are commonly, though mistakenly, called as 'honour killings', because these killings are not simply 'emotional murders'; in their standard form, they may be viewed as taking away the right to life of an individual by physically making it impossible to continue the mechanism of bodily existence.[9] General trend in the literature on killings in the name of honour have been preoccupied with the assumption that it is chiefly a problem of Mediterranean societies. However, this assumption has lost support because of new findings that tell us that crimes of honour are found in other societies also.[10]

Family honour and shame are roots of killings in the name of honour, which is often a form of gender violence; despite substantial resistance campaigns, killings in the name of honour

---

* I have drawn this discussion from my unpublished M.Phil. Dissertation, 'Tradition, Honour, and Authenticity: A Critique of Khap Panchayats', submitted to Department of Political Science, University of Hyderabad, India. I am thankful to Professor Vasanthi Srinivasan for offering scholarly inputs on this topic during my M.Phil. days. However, I am solely responsible for the views expressed in this article.

still occur in parts of the Middle East and South Asia.[11] For example, Pakistan's independent Human Rights Commission said in its latest report that nearly 650 women were killed in that way in 2009.[12] Ironically, India too is not free from violence in the name of honour.[13] It is in this context of controversial killings in the name of honour that a variant of a tradition of local self-governance in Haryana namely, Khap Panchayats (KPs) has been suffering from a sort of democratic dilemma, which we shall discuss now.

The Dilemma of a Tradition

Recently, peasant community of Haryana was criticised for not being sensitive to women's right to domestic security-with-dignity.[14] It was also criticised for not being able to regulate and monitor functions of KPs while dealing with controversies surrounding contentious matrimonial alliances and misuse of modern technology against the backdrop of rapidly falling sex ratio.[15] In this vein, experiences of peasant community in post-colonial Haryana attracted attention of many newspapers, journals, magazines, television-talk-shows and film industry, etc. Though the prime phase of media trial is over, it has left some issues unresolved which include women security in social, economic, and cultural life at village level.

One of the most important questions concerning these issues has been the problem of synchronising various practices of self-governance, which involve conflicting norms and virtues of peaceful and harmonious collective life. The question has emerged partly because of the widening gap between 'modern' principles of law and conventional wisdom of peasant community in the wake of global impact of human intellect demonstrated through unprecedented technological advancement. The question is about the four interrelated issues of right to domestic security-with-dignity, contentious matrimonial relations, conflicting ethics of collective life, and competing claims of self-governance. It is apt to discuss briefly these issues in the light of feminist literature.

Right to Domestic Security-with-Dignity: Radical advocates of women's rights allege that even while ensuring physical and economic security for women within the patriarchal family institution ignore and undermine their dignity as equal partners in the making of the primary unit of human society. They often trace the root cause of such undignified security to daughters' act of voluntarily sacrificing a share in paternal properties.[16] They allege that patriarchal society does not recognise such sort of sacrifices. As part of diluting such sacrifices, patriarchal society designs daughters' education at home and at public institutions in discriminatory ways, which deny them basic rights such as freedom of choice in terms of livelihood and matrimonial socialisation. This very process of educating daughters substantially affect their status as capable human beings thereby blocking the prospect of dignified space – after marriage – within the prospective family where they are sent for the rest of their life. Such a discriminatory treatment, results into unequal and problematic matrimonial relations.

Contentious Matrimonial Relations: This issue became central to feminist discourse in India in the context of increasing violence in matrimonial relations in Haryana. Radical advocates of women's rights have expressed strong discontentment about the status of women's security in the contentious matrimonial relations in rural Haryana.[17] While highlighting the problem of merciless killings of youngsters in the name of preserving traditions and honour, they have criticised various traditions of matrimonial relations, which, according to them, reflect the psychology of patriarchal social structure behind daughters' status within family system.

They allege that matrimonial relations in rural Haryana are decided in the light of an assumption according to which daughter-givers' status is treated secondary to daughter-takers' status. Such a secondary treatment of daughter-givers negatively affects the niceties of matrimonial relations.[18] One of the negative impacts of such treatments often surfaces in the claims of gotra-superiority within a caste and the claims of caste-superiority within religious communities; both the claims directly contribute for daughters' status as inferior to that of son's status and thereby deny them right to equality among members of family system. This sort of treatment reduces their status down to the level of disclaimed daughters or someone else's wealth. Radicals extend such criticism to the domain of ethical concerns of collective co-existence.

Conflicting Ethics of Collective Life: These ethics involve those norms and practices of collective life that are crucial in maintaining peaceful and harmonious coexistence of different groups at village level. One of such norms is idea of *bhaichara* (brotherhood), a core of ethical codes of collective village life. There are a variety of traditions and notions of honour based on *bhaichara* in rural areas of many districts of Haryana such as Bhiwani, Karnal and Rohtak. Feminists argue that the idea of *bhaichara* needs to be reinterpreted in the light of both modern principles of law and conventional wisdom of peasant community because many norms and practices of *bhaichara* are dated now and therefore irrelevant to the changed social, economic, and political context in rural areas.

The need for reinterpretation has gained importance in the wake of an increase in media reports describing controversial cases of marriage alliances and the resultant troubles experienced by the members of peasant community at local, state, national, and international level.[19] The main controversy in this regard has been that of conflicting interpretations of honour and traditions concerning same-gotra marriage alliances. The controversy has posed serious questions before peasant community regarding traditions of self-governance in Haryana. Institutions of both formal and informal self-governance in post-colonial rural Haryana have addressed such controversies surrounding social life of peasant community from time to time.

To refresh, the Constitution of India provides for a formal institution of state controlled-and-regulated self-governance at village level, namely, Gram Panchayat. Gram Panchayat is composed of the village people, by the village people, and for the village people. It does not have the privilege of being at the highest level in the hierarchy of state institutions; therefore, it becomes one of the horizontally organised institutional mechanisms at village level. Against such a backdrop, self-governance becomes an arena of competing claims.

Competing Claims of Self-Governance: A general review of local government at village level suggests that Gram Panchayat is the lowest hierarchical institution representing modern nation-state.[20] However, apart from the formal institution of Gram Panchayat, informal institutions such as customary village councils, caste councils, Khap Panchayats (KPs) etc still find their existence relevant to many people in India.[21] As far as institutions of informal self-governance in Haryana is concerned, their roots can be traced back to pre-colonial times when traditional panchayats used to deal with disputes at village level while functioning as justice delivery mechanism on ad hoc basis. One variant of such panchayats was the tradition of KPs, which are still considered useful in rural areas.[22]

During colonial times, modern judiciary had little impact on the process of justice in rural areas;[23] therefore, institutions such as KPs used to function independently. According to oral tales, the central areas of KPs' activities ranged from present Hisar to Bharatpur and Bijnor to Aligarh during colonial times.[24] KPs were named according to *numberdari*, which was a system of numbers of a particular gotra/clan/caste in a village or khap area. Membership of KPs was both territorial (khap area) and ascriptive (clan and caste). Representation in KPs was hereditary and there was no direct participation of women. M.C. Pradhan (1966) has extensively dealt with KPs organisational units.[25]

The founding principle of KPs was the idea of collective protection of peasants' interests against exploitative feudal and colonial rulers. Therefore, the primary objective of KPs was to protect the khap areas (a geographical territory, comprising of some villages – ranging from twelve to 84) against cultural and territorial invasion during pre-colonial and colonial times. In order to fulfill the objective, KPs used to practice military activities. Since KPs were helpful to peasants in terms of safeguarding their collective local interests against the atrocities of Mughal and colonial rulers, they became popular among rural masses, and eventually traditions of *bhaichara* (brotherhood) was internalised in order to resolve intra-khap and inter-khap disputes concerning land rights. However, with the demise of feudal and colonial rule, military functions of KPs also became irrelevant.

In our times, when rural Haryana is experiencing a number of changes in its social, economic, and political spheres in the wake of rapidly declining jajmani system, and when the gap between various interpretations of law and self-governance is widening, peasant community is being exposed to the danger of being misunderstood and misinterpreted. In order to avoid such a danger, one needs to look into the dilemma of peasant community from a broad perspective. Such a perspective should focus on land relations, impact of changing nature of technology and its culture, etc.

Land Reforms and the Dilemma of Peasant Self: In rural Haryana, an important source of peasant self is often traced to the Vedic ideal of 'Arya', which has occupied central space in the epical stories and figures revolving around Kurukshetra region of Haryana and in our times in reform movements such as Arya Samaj Movement. For our understanding, we can interpret the term 'Arya' as an ideal human being, not necessarily belonging to a particular breed of human race.

In our times, however, many radical critics dispute institutionalisation of human being in the light of the ideal of Vedic self as an authentic source of reference point for collective life; the conflict emerges here. For example, many radical advocates of women's rights dispute the patriarchal system, which was integral to Vedic life; they hold such system responsible for the crisis of women's right to security-with-dignity and troubled matrimonial alliances. On the other hand, those who treat themselves as the guardians of good society make allegations of social irresponsibility or social anarchism on such advocates. Some others want to take a central position while interpreting the crisis of falling number of women. The real issue lies somewhere else.

As discussed earlier, radicals argue that the tradition of daughters' voluntary act of giving up right to paternal properties after their marriage needs to be revisited in the context of changing socio-economic and political status of girl child – partly due to the impact of human excellence demonstrated through technological advancement at global level.[26] On the other hand, critics of recently enacted land reforms act, which include women's right to paternal property, have expressed strong disappointment over the provision that enables daughters to claim a share in their paternal property. They argue that this provision has turned land into a 'travelling commodity' which comes to a family with daughter-in-law and goes to another family with daughter. Such a provision is in sharp contradiction to 'the age-old conventional wisdom of peasant community'.[27]

For radicals, such traditions are the vehicle of patriarchal system. However, some argue that these types of traditions have been evolved scientifically and therefore they do not pose serious ethical dilemmas before a community. The argument here is that contemporary lawmakers' tendency to ignore and reject everything associated with 'conventional wisdom of peasant community' in the name of dated traditions shows their lack of comprehensive understanding of various dimensions of a social group for which they have drafted various laws. Critics of radical approach to women security argue that one needs to keep in view the fact that human relationship in terms of family system and civic associations in rural areas differs substantially from that of urban areas in many parts of India. It is important to note that the presence of modern institutions of justice delivery has not enabled the peasant community in avoiding the crisis of contentious matrimonial relations, misuse of modern technology, etc.

Culture of Technology and Conventional Wisdom: Peasant community in rural Haryana has remained skeptical observer as far as internalisation or traditionalisation of the cultural contents of technological advancements is concerned. The reasons may be many. First, cultural contents of technological revolution are coextensive with the mode of technological advancement and therefore the life span of these contents is restricted to a temporary cultural trend emerging out of a particular mode of technology. Second, technological advancement and human relations are not coextensive; therefore, mere technological advancement and material richness are no guarantee to sustaining human virtues. Third, human virtues and cultural contents of a particular mode of technology are not identical in their intent and scope. The reluctance of peasant community regarding traditionalisation of cultural contents of technological advancement points once again to the communication gap between the lawmakers and policy makers who are born, brought up, and trained in urban areas to make laws for their counter parts in the rural areas.[28]

Such a reluctant response to the newly unfolding culture of technology suggests that technology and conventional wisdom are not the poles apart and that neither of the two can be a substitute to each other. Perhaps, this seems to be the referential horizon of temporal human self in village life. The reality of human relationship in village life is not identical to urban life. The ethical codes therefore are likely to differ as far as social relations are concerned. In village life, the meaning of freedom, honour, and responsibility practiced in a particular context is likely to differ according to the geographical settlement and local practices of that peasant community. If it is so then the task of ensuring women's security-with-dignity, harmonious matrimonial relations, and peaceful coexistence at village level is not as easy as suggested by the media trial of the controversies surrounding these issues.

The task of balancing radical elements of human efforts aimed at betterment of material and spiritual life involves building capability of peasant community in terms of legal awareness, rethinking the scope of cultural contents of a particular mode of technology, reorienting civic associations and so on. However, the task will remain a partial attempt if we ignore the gap between a peasant community guided by the geographical limitations of rural areas and the lawmakers and implementers who are socialised and trained in urban areas.

Conclusion

It becomes clear from the above discussion on the dilemma of peasant community regarding the tradition of KPs in rural Haryana that the two most important aspects of women security namely, social and economic security, need to be taken seriously. In both these aspects, one of the central issues here is to contextualise modern principles of law and 'conventional wisdom'. Though both are part of temporal human self, they seem to be paradoxical. On one hand, the fact that peasant self is guided by conventional wisdom even while reluctantly adopting to modern principles of law makes the former an immediate frame of reference. The changing nature of technology and the resultant culture highlights the limitations of conventional wisdom on the other. Apparently, both the changing contents of technology and the conventional wisdom are collectively determining the nature of peasant self. Orientation of such a two dimensional peasant self cannot be restricted to either modern principles of law or conventional wisdom alone. This is why, women security in rural areas needs to be seen in the context of this newly emerging historic peasant self. Such a perspective demands an innovative approach to women security that goes beyond the one discussed and debated by stereotype feminist politics. The need for a post-stereo type feminist politics emerges against the backdrop of the unprecedented impact of globalisation on the existential aspects of peasant community in rural areas. This is in part due to shifting emphasis from community oriented agricultural practices to market oriented agricultural practices that are contributing for the growing discontentment in peasant self thereby giving rise to various dilemmas. The dilemma of the tradition of self-governance is one of them. The dilemma points to the need for innovative reforms in formal and informal institutions of self-governance. Such a task should involve re-visioning of traditions and honour that should fit the newly emerging peasant self in the temporal historicity of human existence.

Notes

1. For more on contextual political analysis see, Robert E. Goodin and Charles Tilly (eds). *The Oxford Handbook of Contextual Political Analysis*. New York: Oxford University Press, 2006.
2. For an engaging analysis of how we as human beings are limited by our own horizons of referential frameworks in the temporal and the transcendental see, Charles Taylor. *Sources of the Self*. Cambridge: Cambridge University Press, 1989.
3. One can trace the issue of incompleteness to Vedic literature and in the philosophy of other religious belief systems such as Jainism, which finds women lacking anatomical capabilities that are required for higher levels of deep meditations.
4. One can define an invented tradition, according to Eric Hobsbawm, as a 'set of practices' which seek to inculcate certain values and norms of behaviour by repetition. He argues that accepted rules or a ritual of a symbolic nature governs these practices during their attempts of establishing continuity with a 'suitable past' through inculcation and repetition. Hobsbawm assumes that the process of inventing a tradition essentially involves formalisation and ritualisation, which is characterised by reference to the past. Accordingly, 'invented traditions', being the products of time line, have their own age (which is often deceptive in appearance), because traditions that seem to be 'ancient, and linked to an immemorial past ... are often quite recent in origin and sometimes invented' (*The Invention of Tradition*. Cambridge: Cambridge University Press, 1983, 1–13).
5. For example, Ashis Nandy, while examining the psychology of sati, attracted harsh criticism from many sections of feminists ('Sati in Kaliyuga'. *Economic and Political Weekly*, XXIII.38: 17 September 1988).

6. For more on the colonial discourse on sati and its critique see, Lata Mani. *Contentious Traditions: The Debate on Sati in Colonial India*. Berkeley: University of California Press, 1998.
7. Kwame Anthony Appiah has foregrounded this shift in the meanings of honour while narrating various traditions of honour across the world covering many centuries. For Appiah, the idea of honour is intrinsically related to the idea of respect. Therefore, the existence of honour in any society must precede the existence of someone having the right to be 'entitled to respect' or 'to be treated with respect'. This entitlement or treatment must adhere to 'a set of norms, a code'. By suggesting the idea of honour as broadly about entitlement and treatment to something that is worth practising, Appiah implicitly declares 'entitlement as a qualification' – in the form of 'expected obedience' to a code, and 'treatment as a consequence' – of successfully obeying that code (*The Honor Code: How Moral Revolutions Happen*. New York: W.W. Norton, 2011).
8. Ibid., xvii, 170.
9. In other words, it is a murder done by any person or persons acting in concert with or, at the command of a member of the family or a member of a body or group of the caste or clan or community or caste panchayat (by whatever name called). This activity of murder is based on the belief that the victim has brought dishonour or perceived to have brought dishonour on the family or caste or clan or community or caste panchayat (T.K. Rajalaxmi. 'Bill of Honour'. *Frontline*, 27.17, 14–27 August 2010).
10. Diane Baxter. 'Honor Thy Sister: Selfhood, Gender, and Agency in Palestinian Culture'. *Anthropological Quarterly*, 80.3 (2007): 742.
11. Diane E. King. 'The Personal is Patrilineal: Namus as Sovereignty'. *Identities: Global Studies in Culture and Power*, 15.3 (2008): 318.
12. Based on a report published in an online edition of *Dawn* (http://www.dawn.com), accessed on 19 May 2011.
13. For more on the ideology of honour and contentious marriage alliances see, Prem Chowdhry. 'Redeeming "Honour" Through Violence: Unraveling the Concept and Its Application'. Centre for Equity and Inclusion, 2010, 8–10 (http://cequinindia.org), accessed on 20 August 2011.
14. Prem Chowdhry. *The Veiled Women: Shifting Gender Equations in Rural Haryana*. Delhi: Oxford University Press, 1994 and *Contentious Marriages, Eloping Couples: Gender, Caste and Patriarchy in Northern India*. Delhi: Oxford University Press, 2007.

15. According to Census 2011, sex ratio (females per 1000 males) in Haryana is 877, which is the lowest among rest of the states of India (http://www.censusindia.gov.in/2011–provresults/datafiles/india/final%20ppt%202011chapter5.pdf) accessed on 28 March 2011.
16. The political economy of land rights, specially the question of social and economic rights of women in paternal property as well as in their husbands' property is a well-debated issue in feminist literature in India. See, for example, Bina Agarwal. *A Field of One's Own: Gender and Land Rights in South Asia*. Cambridge: Cambridge University Press, 1994 and Prem Chowdhry (ed.). *Gender Discrimination in Land Ownership*. Delhi: Sage Publications, 2010. For the question of women in development discourse see, Devaki Jain. *Women, Development and the UN: A Sixty-year Quest for Equality and Justice*. Bloomington, Indiana: Indiana University Press, 2005.
17. Personal interview with Jagmati Sangwan (Rohtak), June 2011.
18. For example see, Stig Toft Madsen 'Clan, Kinship, and Panchayat Justice Among the Jats of Western Uttar Pradesh'. *Anthropologists* (1991): 355–361.
19. Most of these reports are centered on the troubled matrimonial relations due to *gotra* controversy. For example, one of the most frequently reported issue has been that of Manoj-Babli killing case.
20. Under the constitutional scheme of local governance, in most states of India, there exists three-tier system of Panchayati Raj institutions – a council at district, block and village level with varied names. Village councils (here statutory panchayats) are at the lowest levels of institutions of local self-governance (*The Constitution of India*, Part IX, Articles 243).
21. Customary village councils in Karnataka, for example, as Kripa Ananthpur and Mick Moore argue, 'enjoy considerable local authority because the opportunities for them to abuse these powers for personal or small-group gain are limited' as their clients have options to exit the domain of this authority. Seen from this angle, instead of exercising control over access to land or other valuable assets, these informal institutions in India, face a competitive, pluralist, institutional environment in relation to their judicial functions in particular. Besides, they have 'significant roles as gatekeepers between their populations and the higher-level electoral and bureaucratic institutions that offer access to growing volumes of public money' ('Ambiguous Institutions: Traditional Governance and Local Democracy in Rural South India'. *Journal of Development Studies*, 46.4, 2010: 605–606).

22. According to a survey conducted by a sub-committee headed by K.S. Sangwan under the guidance of the Haryana Backward Class Commission, most people in Haryana prefer khap panchayats for various reasons (*The Times of India*, 16 December 2012). Support for khap panchayats comes also from a writer such as Sompal who, inspired by the ancient and medieval Indian context of self-governance, considers khap panchayats as institutions of community governance ('A Paradigm of Self-Reliant Village India: The Modern Context'. In Y.P. Singh (ed.), *Indian Villages 2020: Vision and Mission*. Vol. 1, New Delhi: Concept Publishing Company, 2006, 94). On the other hand, while acknowledging historical importance of these 'old institutions' a critic of khap panchayats such as Prem Chowdhry argues, they should take 'reformist agenda' [*Khaps Have to Reform*, outlookindia.com, 12 July 2010 (http://www.outlookindia.com/article.aspx?266072), retrieved on 13 January 2011]. For more on Khap Panchayats see, K.S. Sangwan. 'Khap Panchayats in Haryana'. In Kalpana Kannabiran and Ranbir Singh (eds), *Challenging the Rule(s) of Law: Colonialism, Criminology and Human Rights in India*. New Delhi: Sage Publication India Pvt. Ltd., 2008, 331–350.
23. It was partly because of the fact that the British model of administration of justice was non-participatory, extremely formal, and alien to Indians (114th Report of the Eleventh Law Commission of India, 1986, 7).
24. Personal interviews with K.S. Sangwan (Rohtak), Hawa Singh Sangwan (Bhiwani), Bhaleram Beniwal (Dupedi, Karnal) and Col. Risal Singh Sangwan (Charkhi Dadri, Rohtak), April–June 2011.
25. These units are *khandans* (networks of nuclear and joint families belonging to common ancestor), *thoks* (a number of *khandans*), clan (consists of *khandans* and *thoks*), village panchayat, *ganwand* (informal political unit of the khap area), *thamba* (consists of neighbouring villages ranging from five to twenty), khap (inhabitation area of people organised into different clans and castes in nearly placed villages).
26. Personal interview with Jagmati Sangwan (Rohtak), June 2011.
27. Some suggest, instead of drafting 'self-destructive provisions', lawmakers should focus on land rights of the girl children who have no brothers. For example, according to 'conventional wisdom of peasant community' if a family has no son, then one of the daughters of that family can be given land rights to paternal property. According to this traditional wisdom, instead of daughter being sent

to her in-laws, a man is brought to the girl's house as legitimate candidate to become the girl's husband and at later stages the custodian-cum-owner of her parents' property. Such a husband is called *ghar-jamai*. This tradition has been practised widely in many parts of rural northern India. Such a tradition provides social and economic security not only to the girl child but also to her parents. Such a tradition does not disturb niceties of matrimonial relations and retains the sustainability of family institution. Another tradition is to adopt formally a boy of one's brothers, in case the person does not have a male child.

28. This gap and the resultant problems were highlighted by S.S. Rana, Vir Singh and Jaipal Vidyalankar during the author's group discussion with them (June 2011, Delhi). I am thankful to Professor K.C. Suri for clearing my doubts on paradoxes of local democracy and peasant communities in India.

References

Agarwal, Bina. *A Field of One's Own: Gender and Land Rights in South Asia*. New Delhi: Cambridge University Press, 1994.

Ananthpur, Kripa and Mick Moore. 'Ambiguous Institutions: Traditional Governance and Local Democracy in Rural South India'. *Journal of Development Studies*, 46: 4, 2010, pp. 605–606.

Appiah, Kwame Anthony. *The Honor Code: How Moral Revolutions Happen*. New York: W.W. Norton, 2011.

Baxter, Diane. 'Honor Thy Sister: Selfhood, Gender, and Agency in Palestinian Culture'. *Anthropological Quarterly*, Vol. 80, No. 3, p. 742, 2007.

Chowdhary, Prem. *The Veiled Women: Shifting Gender Equations in Rural Haryana*. New Delhi: Oxford University Press, 1994.

——. *Contentious Marriages, Eloping Couples; Gender, Caste and Patriarchy in Northern India*. New Delhi: Oxford University Press, 2007.

——. *'Khaps Have to Reform'*, Interview to *Outlookindia.com*, July 12, http://www. outlookindia.com/article.aspx?266072, retrieved on 13 January 2011.

——. 'Redeeming "Honour' Through Violence: Unraveling the Concept and Its Application', *Centre for Equity and Inclusion*, (2010) pp. 8–10 (http://cequinindia.org), retrieved on, 20 August 2011.

Chowdhry, Prem (ed.). *Gender Discrimination in Land Ownership*. New Delhi: Sage Publications, 2010.

Goodin, Robert E. and Charles Tilly (eds). *The Oxford Handbook of Contextual Political Analysis*. Oxford: Oxford University Press, 2006.

Gudavarthy, Ajay. *Politics of Post-Civil Society: Contemporary History of Political Movements in India*. New Delhi: Sage Publications, 2013.

http://www.censusindia.gov.in

Hobsbawm, Eric and Terence Ranger (ed.), *The Invention of Tradition*. Cambridge University Press, 1983, pp. 1–13.

Jain, Devaki. *Women, Development and the UN: A Sixty-year Quest for Equality and Justice*. Bloomington Indiana University Press, 2005

King, Diane. 'The Personal is Patrilineal: Namus as Sovereignty'. *Identities: Global Studies in Culture and Power*, p. 318, 2008.

Kothari, Rajni. *Politics in India*. Hyderabad: Orient Longman Pvt. Ltd., p. 23, 1970.

Mani, Lata. *Contentious Traditions: The Debate on Sati in Colonial India*. Berkeley: University of California Press, 1998.

Nandy, Ashis. 'Sati in Kaliyuga'. *Economic and Political Weekly*, Vol. XXIII No. 38, 17 September 1988.

One Hundred Fourteenth Report of the Eleventh Law Commission of India, p. 7, 1986.

Pradhan, M.C. *The Political System of Jats of Northern India*. London: Oxford University Press, 1966.

Rajalaxmi, T.K. 'Bill of Honour: A Draft prepared by AIDWA for the proposed Bill to deal with honour crimes includes a comprehensive definition of honour killing'. *Frontline*, Volume 27, Issue 17, 14–27 August 2010.

Rudolph, Lloyd I. and Susanne Hoeber Rudolph. *Modernity of Traditions: Political Development in India*. Chicago: University of Chicago Press, 1984.

Sangwan, K.S. 'Khap Panchayats in Haryana' in Kalpana Kannabiran and Ranbir Singh ed., *Challenging the Rule(s) of Law: Colonialism, Criminology and Human Rights in India*. New Delhi: Sage, pp. 331–350, 2008.

Sompal. 'A Paradigm of Self-Reliant Village India: The Modern Context'. in Y.P. Singh (ed.) *Indian Villages 2020, Vision and Mission*, Vol. 1. New Delhi: Concept Publishing Company, p. 94, 2006.

Stig Tof-Madsen. 'Clan, Kinship, and Panchayat Justice among the Jats of Western Uttar Pradesh'. *Anthropologists*, pp. 355–361, 1991.

Taylor, Charles. *Sources of the Self*, Cambridge University Press, 1989.

The Constitution of India, Part *IX*.

CHAPTER 10

Gender Inequality and Women's Empowerment

A Comparative Analysis of Kerala and Rajasthan

RAMESHWAR JAT AND RINKU BALA

Discrimination against women is found in every culture and society in varying degrees. It is manifested in economic, social, political and religious domains of life and activity. Despite many international agreements affirming their human rights, women are still much more likely than men to be poor and illiterate. The status of women is subordinate to men and they have little access to education, food, nutrition, health care, property ownership, credit, training, employment and wages due to gender discrimination. In addition, women are far less likely than men to be politically active and far more likely to be victims of domestic violence. Women's empowerment is a multi-faceted, multi-dimensional and multi-layered concept. Actually, it is a process in which women gain greater share of control over resources, knowledge, information, decision-making and power. The ability of women to control their own fertility is absolutely fundamental to women's empowerment and equality. If reproductive rights of woman are promoted and protected without any discrimination, coercion and violence, then she will be capable to participate more freely, fully and equally in society. When women are empowered then whole families get benefit, and these benefits often have ripple effects to future generations. The roles that men and women play in society are not biologically determined – they are socially determined and are also changing and changeable. Although they may be justified as being required by culture or religion and vary widely by locality and over time.

Over the past decade, gender equality and women's empowerment have been explicitly recognised as key not only to the health of nations, but also to social and economic development. UNDP also focused on gender equality and women's empowerment not only as human rights, but also identified as a goal in the Millennium Declaration, which recognises the need 'to promote gender equality and the empowerment of women as effective ways to combat poverty, hunger and disease and to stimulate development that is truly sustainable'.

Since, the pairing of the two concepts of women's empowerment and gender equality into one MDGs implicitly recognise that gender equality and women's empowerment are two sides of the same coin: progress toward gender equality requires women's empowerment and women's empowerment requires increases in gender equality. Further, socio-economic development of any economy, to a large extent, is being affected by the demographic changes that have been taken place. Taking into consideration this fact, over the period of time, more attention has been made worldwide to attain demographic goals. Despite the fact that India has made tremendous progress to attain its demographic goals, still, India has lag behind to developed countries at the front of various demographic indicators. Given the poor socio-economic background, the demographic indicators are lower in Bihar, Madhya Pradesh, Assam, Rajasthan and Uttar Pradesh (BIMARU states) than the southern states.

Review of Literature

Naila Kabeer (2005) in the article entitled 'Gender Equality and Women's Empowerment: A Critical Analysis of the Third Millennium Development Goal' has discussed the third Millennium Development Goal (MDG), on gender equality and women's empowerment. The author explored the concept of women's empowerment and highlighted ways in which the indicators associated with this Goal – on education, employment, and political participation can contribute to it. The study revealed that multi-dimensional gender inequalities cannot be reduced by single and universally agreed set of priorities. Therefore it is argued that each of the three indicators embodied in the third Millennium Development Goal has the potential to make a difference.

Each can bring about immediate changes with longer term consequences. Indeed, the same could be said of any set of policies that seeks to improve women's access to resources. Further, it has also argued that unless provision is made to ensure that policy changes are implemented in ways that allow women themselves to participate, to monitor, and to hold policy makers, corporations, and other relevant actors accountable for their actions, this potential is unlikely to be realised. Therefore, to what extent the international community is prepared to provide support to women at the grassroots – support which will ensure that they have the collective capabilities necessary to play this role.

Augusto Lopez-Claros and Saadia Zahidi (2005) in the study entitled *Women's Empowerment: Measuring the Global Gender Gap* assessed the current size of the gender gap by measuring the extent to which women in 58 countries have achieved equality with men in five critical areas: economic participation, economic opportunity, political empowerment, educational attainment, and health and well-being. Undertaking data from international organisations, national statistics and unique survey data from the World Economic Forum's Executive Opinion Survey, the study assessed the status accorded to women in a broad range of countries.

The study revealed that even in light of heightened international awareness of gender issues, it is a disturbing reality that no country has yet managed to eliminate the gender gap. Those that have succeeded best in narrowing the gap are the Nordic countries, with Sweden standing out as the most advanced in the world. These are followed by New Zealand (6), Canada (7), United Kingdom (8), Germany (9) and Australia (10), countries that have made considerable progress in recent decades in removing obstacles to the full participation of women in their respective societies. France (13) ranked ahead of the United States (17) among the 58 nations. Seven

East European nations hold places among the top 25, with Latvia (11), Lithuania (12) and Estonia (15) the highest ranking in that group. Switzerland (34), Italy (45) and Greece (50) perform poorly, lower in rank than many of the East European group, and below Latin American nations such as Costa Rica (18), Colombia (30) and Uruguay (32). Brazil (51), Mexico (52), India (53), Korea (54), Jordan (55), Pakistan (56), Turkey (57) and Egypt (58) occupy the lowest ranks.

These country comparisons are meant to serve a dual purpose: as a benchmark to identify existing strengths and weaknesses, and as a useful guide for policy, based on learning from the experiences of those countries that have had greater success in promoting the equality of women and men. Further, the study suggested concrete measures to reduce the gender gap within the five categories identified above by providing an unambiguous framework for future policy-making in each of the countries. Moreover, by quantifying the size of the gap in each of five key categories, the study also highlighted the priority areas for reform.

Kamla Gupta and P. Princy Yesudian (2006) in the paper entitled 'Evidence of Women's Empowerment in India: A Study of socio-spatial Disparities', reviewed that various national and international communities have addressed women's issues and taken various efforts to empower them so as to enhance their social and health status and involve them in developmental activities. Utilising the data sets from the Indian DHS survey (National Family Health Survey, 1998–1999), four indices – household autonomy index, mobility index, attitude towards gender index and attitude towards domestic violence index – are constructed to measure the different dimensions of empowerment. Using these indices, the spatial and socio-economic and cultural disparities that exist within India are analysed.

Finally, an attempt is made to identify some important determinants for women's empowerment using multiple logistic regression analysis. The results of this analysis revealed that at the national level, 43 per cent of the women have high household autonomy; 23 per cent of the women have high freedom to move outside their home; 40 per cent of the women have no gender preference attitude; and only 43 per cent of the women defy domestic violence. But there are significant divergences in these indices of women's empowerment across the different states and socio-economic and cultural settings within India. Women's educational levels emerged as an important predictor for all the four dimensions of women's empowerment. Additionally, media exposure and age have emerged as the important predictors for some dimensions of woman's empowerment.

C.M. Lakshmana (2007) in the working paper entitled 'Demographic Change and Gender Inequality: A Comparative Study of Madhya Pradesh and Karnataka', has made an attempt to understand the demographic changes and gender inequality in the States of Madhya Pradesh and Karnataka. The analysis is based on secondary data collected from Census of India reports and other published documents. The analysis of this paper revealed that the gender gap in index of deprivation (IOD) is lower in Karnataka than Madhya Pradesh, implying that Karnataka has better position compared to Madhya Pradesh on women empowerment.

Ethiopian Society of Population Studies (2008) studied on gender inequality and women's empowerment and assessed the gender gap in socio-economic and demographic characteristics that included literacy, educational attainment, work status, access to media, marital status and age at first marriage, and desire for children. It further examined women's empowerment at household level by using a set of direct and evidence-based indicators included in the Ethiopian Demographic and Health Survey (EDHS). The study was primarily based on data from the 2005 EDHS and the sample comprises 14,070 women and 6,033 men of reproductive age (women in 15 to 49 and men 15 to 59 age group). In the analysis of the DHS data both bivariate and multivariate tests were employed to ascertain the statistical significance of differences and associations.

Based on the results of the study, it is suggested that although appropriate policies and institutions pertaining to women's development are in place, existing programmes and strategies should be reviewed and new ones should be designed to make the effort more innovative and effective. Further, priority should be given to programmes that improving girls' education focusing on retaining girls in schools, creating opportunities to marginalised women by means of alternative schooling (neighbourhood mobile classes);

fighting early marriage and creating opportunities for women to work for earning an income; intensifying family planning programmes and services; focusing on gender sensitive rural development programmes; and more importantly, working to bring a cultural revolution towards gender equality in all aspects.

David de la Croix and Marie Vander Donckt (2010) in their article entitled 'Would Empowering Women Initiate the Demographic Transition in Least Developed Countries?' examined the pathways by which several dimensions of gender inequality affect fertility. The study revealed that reducing the social and institutional gender gap is of no immediate help to escape the high-fertility regime in low-income countries; nevertheless, we do not discard the importance of achieving gender parity.

Manisha Desai (2010) in the paper entitled 'Hope in Hard Times: Women's Empowerment and Human Development' addressed the conceptual and methodological issues related to women's empowerment, the trends in women's empowerment over the last 20 years in key areas such as education, health, economic and political participation, and finally the best practices of state and non-state actors in empowering women. Following a brief critique of human development, it began with a discussion of the growing conceptual consensus around empowerment, i.e. empowerment being control over resources, women's agency, a process and outcomes, to the methodological issues involved in its measurement, specifically focusing on the gender empowerment measure and arguing that minimally the measure needs to move away from its urban, elite, and formal employment bias.

The trends in women's empowerment over the past 20 years showed that while there have been gains in primary and secondary education, in political representation at the national level, in waged labour and in fertility and maternal mortality decline, but still, violence against women and HIV/AIDS continue to be endemic. Further, these trends vary across regions, within countries, urban and rural poor, ethnic minorities, and older and disabled women fare. Furthermore, a decrease in gender gap does not translate into gender equality and positive trends are often accompanied by negative trends resulting from unintended consequences of development. Finally, it was suggested by the author that the world's governments will need to undertake a stimulus plan for women's equality and empowerment.

Schuler et al. (2010) in the article entitled 'Women's Empowerment Revisited: A Case Study from Bangladesh' explored the changing dimensions of women's empowerment over time in three Bangladesh villages. Authors discussed theoretical issues related to the measurement of women's empowerment and also examined the types of social, economic, and political change that affect the measurement of women's empowerment. The findings from this study suggested that social, political, and economic changes at the micro level, many of which reflect macro-level changes, can have substantial implications for the measurement of women's empowerment. Since, empowerment is typically conceptualised as a process, and therefore change is at its very essence. Once a resource, capacity, or form of agency becomes commonplace, it no longer distinguishes more empowered women from less empowered women. Therefore, it would be argued that the measurement of empowerment must change and a new set of indicators to measure women empowerment in the rural Bangladesh must be adopted.

Objectives

In the context of background of the study, following are the major objectives of the present study:

- To analyse demographic changes particularly in education, health and employment in the states of Kerala and Rajasthan.
- To investigate the relationship between the gender inequality and women's empowerment and
- Some policy measures and suggestions are also given in order to reduce gender inequality and empower women.

Data Source and Research Methodology

The study is based on secondary data collected from Census of India, Statistical Abstract of India and other published documents. The comparative analysis has been carried out for the decades 1991–2001 and 2001–2011 to understand the demographic changes and gender inequality particularly on education, health and employment for the States of Kerala and Rajasthan. In order to interpret and analyse the data, simple statistical tools are used.

Results and Discussion

Variation in Demographic Indicators

This section deals with analysis of population growth and variation in crude birth rate, sex ratio, crude death rate, infant mortality rate and life expectancy rate. Percentage decadal population growth of India and the states of Kerala and Rajasthan for the period of two decades as from 1991 to 2001 and 2001 to 2011 are shown in Table 1. During the decade 1991 to 2001, percentage decal growth of India's total population was measured 21.54 per cent; thereafter it decreased to 17.64 per cent during 2001–2011. Further, Rajasthan has always ahead above to national-level in percentage decal growth of population in all categories – persons, male and female. On the other hand, Kerala has below national level percentage decal growth in all the categories cited above. However, percentage decal growth of population has observed declining trends over the period.

Table 1

Percentage Decadal Population Growth

(In %)

	India			*Kerala*			*Rajasthan*		
	1991–2001	*2001–2011*	*Decadal variation*	*1991–2001*	*2001–2011*	*Decadal variation*	*1991–2001*	*2001–2011*	*Decadal variation*
Male	17.41	17.01	–0.31	08.25	3.57	–4.65	27.67	20.08	-6.87
Female	18.02	18.03	0.28	10.53	6.01	–4.43	29.21	21.08	-7.41
Persons	21.54	17.64	–3.9	09.43	4.86	–4.57	28.41	21.44	-6.97

Source: Census of India 2001, 2011

Table 2(a) shows variations in crude birth rate, sex ratio and crude death rates for India as well for the states of Kerala and Rajasthan. The average birth rate in India was registered 25.4 in 2001 which has decreased to 21.8 by 2011. A similar decreasing pattern is also observed both in rural and urban birth rates in India. The birth rate for the state of Kerala in all categories was registered below the national average in both the years 2001 and 2011. While, the same rates in all categories found above the national-average in the state of Rajasthan.

The Sex-ratio of population, i.e. the ratio of females to males in India is a significant variable. The number of females per 1000 males is not equal across the country; actually, it is varying from one region to another or one state to another state.

Table 2(a)

Variation in Demographic Indicators

	India		*Kerala*		*Rajasthan*	
Crude Birth Rate	*2001*	*2011*	*2001*	*2011*	*2001*	*2011*
Total	25.4	21.8	17.2	15.2	31	26.2
Rural	27.1	23.3	17.4	15.4	32.3	27.4
Urban	20.2	17.6	16.6	14.4	24.7	22.5
Sex Ratio						
	933	940	1058	1084	922	928
Crude Death Rate by Sex						
Total	8.5	7.1	6.4	7.0	8.5	6.7
Male	8.9	7.8	7.4	8.3	8.4	7.3
Female	8.1	6.3	5.5	5.8	8.6	6.0

Source: Census of India, 2001, 2011

For instance, as per 2001 Census, the sex ratio of India, Kerala and Rajasthan was registered 933, 1058 and 922 respectively. This sex ratio has increased to 940, 1084 and 928 respectively for India, Kerala and Rajasthan in Census 2011. This variation shows that sex ratio in Rajasthan remained consistently low and below the national average. Actually, this trend of sex ratio is a matter of serious concern. On the other hand, Kerala has relatively a better status as compared to the other states in the country. The sex ratio of 1084 per 1000 males in Kerala shows higher by 156 over that of Rajasthan. From this point of view, it is revealed that Kerala has a better status in sex ratio as compared to the other states of the country.

The average death rates in India decreased from 8.5 in 2001 to 7.1 by 2011. Further, crude death rate for male and females of India also decreased from 8.9 and 8.1 to 7.8 and 6.3 respectively during the same period under analysis. The similar pattern of reduction in death rates in all categories is also registered for the state of

Rajasthan. But surprisingly, this pattern is found reverse in the state of Kerala. The average death rates in Kerala slightly increased from 6.4 in 2001 to 7.0 by 2011 and the similar pattern is also reported for both male and females.

Table 2(b)

Variation in Demographic Indicators

	India		*Kerala*		*Rajasthan*	
	2000	*2011*	*2000*	*2011*	*2000*	*2011*
Infant Mortality Rate by Sex						
Total	67.8	44	13.9	12	78.7	52
Male	66.8	43	14.5	11	76.4	50
Female	68.9	46	13.3	13	81.2	53
Gender Disparity in IMR	2.1	3.0	–1.2	2.0	4.8	3.0

Source: SRS Bulletins, April 2002, Volume 36, No.1 and October 2012, Volume 47, No.2, SRS, New Delhi.

Table 2(b) shows variations in infant mortality rate by sex which states that the total IMR in India was 67.8 in 2000 and it decreased significantly to 44 by 2011. The similar noteworthy reduction is also reported in both the male and females during 2000–2011. For the state of Kerala, the IMR for all the categories as total, male and females was reported 13.9, 14.5 and 13.3 respectively in the year 2000, which decreased slightly to 12, 11 and 13 respectively in Census 2011.

As evident from the Table 2(b), the IMR rate was reported much higher in Rajasthan in all categories as compared to Kerala in both the year 2000 and 2011 and it also remained above the national average, however, a significant reduction is reported in Census 2011. Further, the IMR is reported higher in females as compared to males in India as well as in both the States except Kerala in the year 2000. In addition, the IMR was reported very low in Kerala in all categories both for India and Rajasthan. This reveals that, the gender disparity in IMR is low in Kerala compared to both India and Rajasthan.

The average number of years of a new born child expected to live under current mortality conditions is called expectation of life at birth. A low life expectancy reflects poor socio-economic status of population concerned and also reveals lack of basic health care facilities needed for human development. Therefore, higher the level of socio-economic development and female literacy, the higher will be life expectancy. This in turn will improve the health status of the people. As shown in Table 2(c), the life expectancy rate of India, Rajasthan and Kerala are compared for two time periods 1993–97 and 2006–10. During both the periods, the life expectancy rate for males is reported lower compared to females in India as well as in both the states, however, the life expectancy rate for males and females in Kerala is much higher than both India and Rajasthan, implying that the progresses in socioeconomic development in Kerala are relatively better as compared to Rajasthan. Further, life expectancy in India has been contrary to normal biological expectations of life, i.e. women having a longer life than men.

Table 2(c)

Variation in Demographic Indicators

	India		*Kerala*		*Rajasthan*	
	1993–97	*2006–10*	*1993–97*	*2006–10*	*1993–97*	*2006–10*
Life Expectancy Rate at Birth by Sex (In Years)						
Male	60.0	65.8	70.4	72.0	59.1	66.1
Female	61.8	68.1	75.9	76.8	60.1	69.2

Source: Statistical Abstract of India, 2003 and National Health Profile, 2011

Education, Literacy and Gender Inequality

As shown in Table 3, the literacy rate for both male and female in Rajasthan was reported below the national average in both the Censuses 2001 and 2011, while, the literacy rate in Kerala was reported above the national average in the same period. Further, the gender gap in literacy rate in Rajasthan has decreased from 31.85 in Census 2001 to 27.85 in Census 2011.

However, it is almost seven times more in Rajasthan, when compared to Kerala, i.e. it is 4.04 in Kerala as against 27.85 in Rajasthan. It implies a wide gender gap in literacy between Rajasthan and Kerala; however, the gender gap in Kerala is much lower as compared to Rajasthan. Further, in order to understand the gender gap in education, the status of women enrolment in school education (primary and upper primary) is also given in Table 4. It is revealed from the Table 4 that, in 2011–12 about 48.4 per cent of girls were enrolled for school education in India, Whereas, the enrolment of girls in school education was 48.9 per cent in Kerala and 46.3 per cent in Rajasthan.

Table 3

Literacy Rates of India, Kerala and Rajasthan

	India		*Kerala*		*Rajasthan*	
	2001	*2011*	*2001*	*2011*	*2001*	*2011*
Persons	64.83	74.04	90.86	93.91	60.41	67.06
Male	75.26	82.14	94.24	96.02	75.70	80.51
Female	53.67	65.46	87.72	91.98	43.85	52.66
Gender gap in LR	21.59	16.68	6.52	4.04	31.85	27.85

Source: Census of India 2001, 2011

Table 4

School Enrollment in Primary and Upper Primary Education

(Girl's Enrolment in Percentage)

	2002–03		*2011–12*		*Total (2011–12)*
	Primary	*Upper primary*	*Primary*	*Upper primary*	*All schools*
India	47.6	44.5	49.3	52.1	48.4
Kerala	49.7	46.1	49.9	46.8	48.9
Rajasthan	46.5	38.8	49	74.3	46.3

Source: Department of School Education and Literacy, Department of Higher Education, Ministry of Human Resource Development, Government of India.

This implies that the school enrolment percentage in Rajasthan is still below to national level while, this percentage in Kerala is above the national average despite a considerable progress has been archived by the state of Rajasthan in the girl's enrolment percentage at both primary and upper primary level during the year 2011–12 as compared to 2002–03. This significant gender gap in girl's enrollment in school education suggests appropriate policy measures at government level in order to increase girl's enrolment in schools and decrease gender gap in literacy.

Health, Longevity and Gender Gap

Morbidity, infant mortality, maternal mortality, infanticide, and female foeticide are regarded as major issues of concern in literature which affect women's health and longevity. Strong preference for sons and adoption of small family norms lead to female foeticide and female infanticide, as a consequences of this sex ratio declines and gender gap widens. As evident from the Table 2(b), the IMR rate was reported much higher in Rajasthan in all categories as compared to Kerala in both the year 2000 and 2011 and it also remained above the national average. It also reflected in the sex ratio as it was registered 1084 in Kerala and 928 in Rajasthan as per Census 2011. As evident from Table 2(a) the gender gap in terms of sex ratio between Kerala and Rajasthan is 156 females per 1000 males. This means Rajasthan is far lagging behind to Kerala in terms of sex ratio, therefore, it may be suggested that Rajasthan has to do a lot in order to change the mind set regarding strong preference for sons and also make efforts to reduce female foeticide, female infanticide and maternal mortality, etc. in order to narrow the gap between males and females.

Further, as per Table 2(c) the life expectancy was 72 and 76.8 for males and females respectively in Kerala, while the life expectancy rate for Rajasthan was reported 66.1 for males and 69.2 for females. The figures suggested that life expectancy of females is higher compared to males in both the states as well for India as a whole, but when Rajasthan is compared to Kerala, then it is found that both males and females of Kerala have about six and seven years higher longevity to males and females of Rajasthan respectively. The empirical evidences suggest that low life expectancy reflects lack of basic amenities like safe drinking water, health care facilities besides the better nutrition. Further, as a consequences of economic development and progress in basic amenities of life increases, the living standard of people also increases, this in turn also increases the life expectancy of the people. Therefore, Rajasthan should be focused on economic development projects along with better basic amenities of life particularly by providing safe drinking water and better health care facilities.

Gender Inequality in Employment

The study of various Censuses of India revealed that the occupational status of women in India is low in both urban and rural areas.

Low proportion of women workers in total workers in India leads a wide gap in the percentage of workers between men and women. For example, as per Census 2011, the percentage of total workers in India was 39.8 per cent and the percentage of male and female workers were 53.3 per cent and 25.5 per cent respectively (Table 5). Further, the work participation rate for women in Rajasthan is almost double than Kerala in 2011.

Table 5

Percentage of Male and Female Workers

States	*2001*			*2011*		
	Total	*Male*	*Female*	*Total*	*Male*	*Female*
India	39.1	51.7	25.6	39.8	53.3	25.5
Kerala	32.3	50.2	15.4	34.8	52.7	18.2
Rajasthan	42.1	50	33.5	43.6	51.5	35.1

Source: Census of India 2001, 2011

The high work participation rate in Rajasthan may be due to the higher proportion of tribal population among workers where they are engaged in forest based primary and mining activities rather than urban based tertiary activities. Again, percentage of male and female workers in both the states of Kerala and Rajasthan are lower than national level; however, the percentage gap between male and female workers was 27.8 in India, 16.4 in Rajasthan and 34.5 in Kerala. This reflects wide gender inequality between men and women. Moreover, the percentage of male workers is more than double to that of female workers in India's total working population in 2011, implying that Indian women economically depend on men. Thus, gender inequality in work participation has adversely affected women's empowerment and their socio-economic development.

Gender Inequality in Wages

Gender disparity also exists in wages and earnings between men and women for a similar work. In order to explain this type of disparity, data of the effective (adult) wage rates reported in agricultural and non-agricultural sectors for India as well as for both Kerala and Rajasthan are undertaken in Table 6.

Table 6

Effective Wage Rate 2011 (₹ Per day)

	Agriculture Sector Wages			*Non-agriculture Wages (Rural labour wages)*		
	India	*Kerala*	*Rajasthan*	*India*	*Kerala*	*Rajasthan*
Male	22.50	58.63	24.97	29.4	63.33	33.05
Female	17.47	31.77	25.30	16.2	36.80	22.80
Disparity in Wages	5.03	26.86	0.33	13.2	26.53	10.25

Source: Labour Bureau, Government of India, New Delhi,2011.

The majority of the population (60–70%) in total population in both the states depends on agriculture, which, indicates that both the states Kerala and Rajasthan are agricultural dominant economies. It can be seen from the Table 6 that, agricultural wage for both men and females is much higher in Kerala compared to Rajasthan as well as national level. A similar wage rate pattern is also seen in Non-agriculture sector. However, the wage rate in non agricultural sector was comparatively better than in agriculture sector for men. It is evident from Table 6 that a wide gender disparity exists in the wage rates between men and women except wage rate for agriculture sector in Rajasthan. Thus, the analysis further reveals that the gender disparity in wages exists more in Kerala compared to Rajasthan.

HDI and GDI Scores and Gender Gap

Inclusive development cannot be attained unless women participate equally in the development process. Developing countries like India face huge gender inequalities, which have a direct bearing on their human development. For instance, in a patriarchal set up where gender discrimination is rampant, a female child is ignored when it comes to health or education. Females have little control over their lives and suffer a great deal from intra-household discrimination.

HDI dimensions, by themselves, do not portray a complete picture of human development therefore, in order to account for such inequalities; UNDP developed the Gender-related Development Index (GDI) in 1995. The Gender Development Index is the HDI adjusted index which measures inequalities between men and women in the same dimensions as those of HDI. Actually, it is a gender sensitive HDI – the higher the gender inequality, the lower the GDI.

Table 7

HDI and GDI Scores for Rajasthan and Kerala

States/Union Territories	*HDI Score 2006*	*HDI Score 1996*	*Difference between HDI score 2006 and HDI Score 1996*	*GDI Score 2006*	*GDI Score 1996*	*Difference between GDI score 2006 and GDI Score 1996*	*Loss in HDI due to gender inequalities (HDI–GDI) 2006*
Kerala	0.764	0.736	0.028	0.745	0.721	0.024	0.019
Rajasthan	0.541	0.472	0.069	0.526	0.448	0.078	0.015
All India	0.605	0.53	0.075	0.590	0.514	0.076	0.015

Source: Annual Report 2009–10, Ministry of Women and Child Development, GOI, New Delhi

In India, the Ministry of Women and Child Development (2009) calculated the GDI for the years 1996 and 2006 for 35 states/UTs. As shown in Table 7, the all India GDI for 2006 was 0.590 compared to 0.514 in 1996, whereas, the HDI for the same years was 0.605 and 0.530 respectively. This shows that the loss in HDI on account of gender inequalities (which is the difference between HDI and GDI) has decreased over the decade, albeit only marginally. As per MWCD report (2009), the value of GDI was much low in the Rajasthan compared to Kerala in both the years 1996 and 2006. Therefore, Kerala comes among the top performer states that did well in terms of both GDI and HDI, whereas, Rajasthan comes among poor performer states that has done worst performance on GDI and HDI.

The loss in HDI due to gender inequalities (HDI–GDI) was 0.015 for India as well as for Rajasthan in 2006. However, Kerala comes among those states in which loss on account of gender inequalities was higher than the all India level. As evident from the Table 7, the scores of HDI and GDI reflect an increase over the period, thereby implying that progress has been made over the decade both at national and state levels. However, the estimated

GDI scores for India and both the states are lower than the HDI score at both points of time due to the existence of gender based disparities. Moreover, both the HDI and GDI score are very lower in Rajasthan compared to Kerala, which implies that Rajasthan possesses low human development status and also suffers from wide gender disparities as compared to Kerala. In addition, the analysis reveals that basic social services in Rajasthan has increased over time by attaching higher priority to health and education but still the progress is far lagging behind in many states.

Conclusion

As revealed from the above analysis, both Kerala and Rajasthan are predominantly rural agrarian economies. The demographic variables like birth rate, death rate and infant mortality rate in Kerala have always been below the national average and also below to Rajasthan. Further the analysis shows that infant deaths in Rajasthan are more than four times that of infant deaths in Kerala. The analysis also revealed a wide gap in literacy rate in females of Rajasthan. The gender gap in literacy rate is almost seven times more in Rajasthan compared to Kerala. Further, the sex-ratio in Rajasthan is below the national average and it is shortage of 158 females per 1000 males compared to Kerala. Similarly, both males and females in Kerala have better longevity than in Rajasthan, since the life expectancy for both males and females in Rajasthan is more than 6 year less than that of Kerala.

The girl's enrolment in school education in Rajasthan is found lower compared to Kerala. A significant gender gap between males and females is also revealed in the work participation rate in both the states; however, work participation rate for females in Rajasthan is much higher (35.1%) than Kerala (18.2%), therefore, Rajasthan has relatively lower gender gap in work participation over that of Kerala.

Further, except wages in agricultural sector of Rajasthan, a wide gender gap in workers' wage exist between males and females in both the agriculture and non-agriculture sectors. Further, both the states have better wage rate for males and females compared to the national average, however, disparity in wages is found more in Kerala compared to Rajasthan. In addition, Moreover, both the HDI and GDI score are very lower in Rajasthan compared to Kerala, which implies that Rajasthan possesses low human development status and also suffers from wide gender disparities as compared to Kerala. However, Kerala is far better state compared to Rajasthan in terms of socio-economic, demographic indicators and human development indicators. Further, a widespread gender inequality is also found more in Rajasthan compared to Kerala in terms of socio-economic, demographic and human development indicators.

Suggestions

It is suggested that existing programmes and strategies should be reviewed, strengthened and implemented effectively so that the gender inequality may be removed and empowerment of women may be improved. Specifically, priority programmes should improve girls' education by focusing on retaining girls in schools, stopping early marriage, creating opportunities for women to work for earning, intensifying family planning programs and services and focusing on gender sensitive rural development programmes.

References

de la Croix, David and Marie Vander Donckt. 'Would Empowering Women Initiate the Demographic Transition in Least Developed Countries?' *Journal of Human Capital*, 4.2 (Summer): 85–129, 2010.

Department of Elementary Education and Literacy. *Progress towards Universal Access and Retention: Analytical Report 2001*. Ministry of Human Resource Development, Government of India, New Delhi, 2001.

Department of School Education and Literacy Department of Higher Education. *Annual Report 2012–13*. Ministry of Human Resource Development, Government of India, New Delhi, 2013.

Department of School Education and Literacy Department of Higher Education. *Elementary Education in India: Analytical Report 2003*. Ministry of Human Resource Development, Government of India, New Delhi, 2003.

Desai, Manisha. 'Hope in Hard Times: Women's Empowerment and Human Development'. United Nations Development Programme, Human Development Reports, Research Paper, July 2010.

Directorate of Economics and Statistics. *Statistical Abstract of India*. Ministry of Statistics and Programme Implementation, New Delhi, 2003.

Ethiopian Society of Population Studies. *Gender Inequality and Women's Empowerment: In-depth Analysis of the Ethiopian Demographic and Health Survey 2005*, Addis Ababa, October 2008.

Gupta, Kamla and P. Princy Yesudian. 'Evidence of Women's Empowerment in India: A Study of Socio-spatial Disparities'. *Geo Journal*, 65.4 (May): 365–380, 2006.

Kabeer, Naila. 'Gender Equality and Women's Empowerment: A Critical Analysis of the Third Millennium Development Goal'. *Journal of Gender and Development*, 13.1: 13–24, 2005.

Lakshmana, C.M. 'Demographic Change and Gender Inequality: A Comparative Study of Madhya Pradesh and Karnataka'. Working Paper 183, Institute for Social and Economic Change, 2007.

Lopez-Claros, Augusto and Saadia Zahidi. *Women's Empowerment: Measuring the Global Gender Gap*. Geneva: World Economic Forum, 2005.

Ministry of Health and Family Welfare. *National Health Profile 2011*. Government of India, New Delhi, 2011.

Ministry of Home Affairs. *Census of India 1991*. Government of India, New Delhi, 1991.

Ministry of Home Affairs. *Census of India 2001*. Government of India, New Delhi, 2001.

Ministry of Home Affairs. *Census of India 2011*. Government of India, New Delhi, 2011.

Ministry of Labour and Employment. *Report on Wages and Earnings*. Labour Bureau of India, New Delhi, 2011.

Ministry of Women and Child Development. *Annual Report 2009–10*. Government of India, New Delhi, 2010.

Registrar General of India. *SRS Bulletins*. Ministry of Home Affairs, Government of India, New Delhi, 2001–2012.

Ruth Schuler, Sidney, Farzana Islam and Elisabeth Rottach. 'Women's Empowerment Revisited: A Case Study from Bangladesh'. *Development in Practice*, 20.7 (September) 840–854, 2010.

Usami, Yoshifumi. 'Recent Trends in Wage Rates in Rural India: An Update'. *Review of Agrarian Studies*, 1.1 (January–June) 149–182, 2011.

CHAPTER 11

Social Protection of Women Workers in Informal Sector in India

Scenario and Significance

SUBRATA S. SATAPATHY

The informal economy comprises half to three-quarters of all non-agricultural employment in developing countries. Even though there lays a difficulty in generalising the work concerning the quality of informal employment, it basically signals at poor employment conditions and is linked with escalating poverty. Some of the characteristic features of informal employment are lack of protection in the event of non-payment of wages, compulsory overtime or extra shifts, lay-offs without notice or compensation, unsafe working conditions and the absence of social benefits such as pensions, sick pay and health insurance. Women, migrants and other vulnerable groups of workers who are excluded from other opportunities have little choice but to take informal low-quality jobs. During the 1970s and 1980s, the informal sector was broadly defined as unregulated economic enterprises or activities. The International Conference of Labour Statisticians (ICLS), in the year 1993, approved for an international statistical definition of the informal sector so defined: namely, all unregistered (or unincorporated) enterprises below a certain size, including:

(a) micro-enterprises owned by informal employers who hire one or more employees on a continuing basis; and
(b) own-account operations owned by individuals who may employ contributing family workers and employees on an occasional basis.

In so doing, the 1993 ICLS mentioned that an enterprise-based definition would not capture all dimensions of informal employment and suggested for additional work on the employment-based dimensions of informality. Women in Informal Employment Globalizing and Organizing (WIEGO) have worked in proximity with the Bureau of Statistics of the International Labour Office (ILO) to create and endorse an employment-based definition of the informal economy that would confine all dimensions of informal employment – i.e. employment that is not protected or regulated – both inside and outside informal enterprises.

In pushing for this expanded employment-based definition of the informal economy, the ILO Bureau of Statistics, the Delhi Group, and the WIEGO network sought to incorporate the whole of informality – including both enterprise and employment relations – as manifested in industrialised, transition, and developing economies. As such, this expanded definition helps to capture the real world dynamics in labour markets today – particularly the less visible segments of the labour force in which the working poor, especially women, are often engaged.

In 2003, the International Conference of Labour Statisticians adopted statistical guidelines concerning this expanded concept of informal employment to complement the resolution concerning statistics on the informal sector (ILO, 1993). Informal employment includes:
(a) Employment in the informal sector (as defined in 1993 by the ICLS); and
(b) Informal employment outside the informal sector.

In non-statistical terms, informal employment broadly defined, includes the following:
1. employers in informal enterprises;
2. own account workers in informal enterprises;

3. unpaid family workers (in informal and formal enterprises); and
4. members of informal producers' cooperatives (where these exist).

In addition to the aforementioned, informal economic activity could be regarded as temporal in nature. Regulations (and degrees of enforcement) alter rapidly and frequently, sometimes daily, and any instance of economic activity can shift between categories of formal and informal with even minor changes in policy. Given the complexity of the phenomenon, the simplest definition of informal economic activity might be: any exchange of goods or services involving economic value in which the act escapes regulation of similar such acts.

Informal Economy: Historical Backdrop

Governments have attempted to regulate (formalise) aspects of their economies for as long as surplus wealth has existed. Yet no such regulation has ever been wholly enforceable. Archaeological and anthropological evidence strongly suggest that people of all societies regularly adjust their activity within economic systems in attempt to evade regulations. Therefore, if informal economic activity is that which goes unregulated in an otherwise regulated system then informal economies are as old as their formal counterparts. The term itself, however, is much more recent. The optimism of the modernisation theory school of development had led most people in the 1950s and 1960s to believe that traditional forms of work and production would disappear as a result of economic progress in developing countries. As this optimism proved to be unfounded, scholars turned to study more closely what was then called the traditional sector. They found that the sector had not only remained, but in fact expanded to encompass new developments. In accepting that these forms of productions were there to stay, scholars started using the term informal sector, which was first used by the British anthropologist Keith Hart in a study on Ghana in 1971 and then taken up by the ILO in a widely read study on Kenya in 1972. The Resolution concerning decent work and the informal economy adopted by the International Labor Conference in June 2002 called for the needs of workers and economic units in the informal economy to be addressed, with emphasis on an integrated approach from a decent work perspective. The ILO has set up mechanisms to collect and share lessons from good practice and policy across the four strategic objectives and different regions with a view to improving 'know how' and 'show how'. In the second half of the 1990s the term 'informal economy' began to be used instead of 'informal sector' to refer to a wider concept that incorporates enterprises as well as employment in developing, transition, and advanced industrialised economies. The above definition debars the inclusion of certain activities including crime and domestic labour. Crime cannot be included because such acts have no regulated counterpart against which they may be compared. Domestic labour, such as childcare and cooking, cannot be included when performed in the natural course of daily living and to one's own benefit. Such activities can easily be performed for others and exchanged for goods and services with economic value and depending on broader conditions; these can be either formal or informal economic activities. However, when performed for personal benefit they have no external economic value (they cannot be exchanged).

Theories on Informal Economy

Early debates regarding the causes and characteristics of the informal sector crystallised into four dominant schools of thought. The Dualist School, popularised by the ILO in the 1970s, pledges to the idea that the informal sector encompasses marginal activities – distinct from and not related to the formal sector – that provide income for the poor and a safety net in times of crisis (ILO, 1972; Sethuraman, 1976; Tokman, 1978). According to this school, the prevalence of informal activities is caused due to inadequate modern job opportunities to absorb surplus labour, a slow rate of economic growth and/or a faster rate of population growth. Propounded by Caroline Moser and Alexandro Portes, the Structuralist School, (among others) in the late 1970s and 1980s, subscribes to the notion that the informal sector should be seen as subordinated economic units (micro-firms) and workers that serve to reduce input and labour costs and, thereby, increase the competitiveness of large capitalist firms. In the structuralist model, in marked contrast to the dualist model, different modes and forms of production are seen not only to co-exist but also to be inextricably connected and interdependent. According to this school, the nature of capitalist development (rather than a lack of growth) accounts for the persistence and growth of informal production relationships.

The Legalist School, popularised by Hernando de Soto in the 1980s and 1990s, subscribes to the notion that the informal sector is comprised of 'plucky' micro-entrepreneurs who choose to operate informally in order to avoid the costs, time and effort of formal registration. According to de Soto, micro-entrepreneurs will continue to produce informally so long as government procedures are cumbersome and costly. In this view, unreasonable government rules and regulations are stifling private enterprise. The Il-legalist School, popularised by neo-classical and neo-liberal economists across the decades, subscribes to the notion that informal entrepreneurs deliberately seek to avoid regulations and taxation and, in some cases, to deal in illegal goods and services. This perspective is associated with the notion that the informal economy is an underground or black economy. According to this school of thought, informal entrepreneurs choose to operate illegally – or even criminally – in order to avoiding taxation, commercial regulations, electricity and rental fees, and other costs of operating formally.

Current re-thinking of the informal economy suggests the need for an integrated approach that looks at which elements of dualist, structuralist, legalist, and il-legalist theories are most appropriate to which segments of informal employment in which contexts. Clearly, some poor households and individuals engage in survival activities that have – or seem to have – very few links to the formal economy and the formal regulatory environment (dualist school); some micro-entrepreneurs choose to avoid taxes (il-legalist school) and regulations (legalist school); while other informal units and workers are subordinated to larger formal firms (structuralist school).

Perspectives of Informal Economy

The following figure is a concrete substantiation of the prevalent old and new views regarding informal economy.

Figure 1

Views on Informal Economy

The Old View	*The New View*
The informal sector is the traditional economy that will wither away and die with modern, industrial growth.	The informal economy is 'here to stay' and expanding with modern, industrial growth.
It is only marginally productive.	It is a major provider of employment, goods and services for lower-income groups. It contributes a significant share of GDP.
It exists separately from the formal economy.	It is linked to the formal economy – it produces for, trades with, distributes for and provides services to the formal economy.
It represents a reserve pool of surplus labour.	Much of the recent rise in informal employment is due to the decline in formal employment or to the informalisation of previously formal employment relationships.
It is comprised mostly of street traders and very small-scale producers.	It is made up of a wide range of informal occupations – both 'resilient old forms' such as casual day labour in construction and agriculture as well as 'emerging new ones' such as temporary and part-time jobs plus homework for high tech industries.
Most of those in the sector are entrepreneurs who run illegal and unregistered enterprises in order to avoid regulation and taxation.	It is made up of non-standard wage workers as well as entrepreneurs and self-employed persons producing legal goods and services, albeit through irregular or unregulated means. Most entrepreneurs and the self-employed are amenable to, and would welcome, efforts to reduce barriers to registration and related transaction costs and to increase benefits from regulation; and most non-standard wage workers would welcome more stable jobs and workers' rights.
Work in the informal economy is comprised mostly of survival activities and thus is not a subject for economic policy.	Informal enterprises include not only survival activities but also stable enterprises and dynamic growing businesses, and informal employment includes not only self-employment but also wage employment. All forms of informal employment are affected by most (if not all) economic policies.

Source: Chen, Martha, Joann Vanek and Marilyn Carr. 2004. '*Mainstreaming Informal Employment and Gender in Poverty Reduction: A Handbook for Policy-makers and Other Stakeholders*'. London: Commonwealth Secretariat.

Thousands of informal workers in the poor nations dwell under utterly worse circumstances and remain unprotected. They receive quite low and indeterminate incomes, severe levels of threat associated with the work which is not even covered by social protections. The informal economy is diverse, with different categories of employment within the informal economy (Chen, 2008), and these have a bearing on the degree of workers control over their work and their place of work, and to their access to social protection.[1]

> According to Chen, there is a significant range of average earnings and poverty risk across employment statuses within the informal economy with a small entrepreneurial class (comprised of most informal employers and a few own account operators) and a large working class (comprised of most informal employees, most own account operators, all casual day labourers, and all industrial outworkers). There is also gender segmentation within informal labour markets resulting in a gender gap in average earnings with women over-represented in the lowest-paid segments and earning less on average than men in most segments (Chen, 2008).

It is quite apparent that there is a trivial section of high earners in the informal sector. However, incomes earned in the informal economy are lesser than those in the formal sector; and with the exception of a few countries, women are often over-represented in informal work, and make lower incomes than men. Work in the informal economy is, by definition, work with no social protection. Furthermore, the vulnerability of employment of informal workers means that they are disempowered, though in different ways for self-employed people, for informal wage workers, and for unpaid family members.

Informal Sector in India

Informal sector plays a central role in the Indian economy wherein more than 90 per cent of workforce and about 50 per cent of the national product are accounted for by the informal economy. A vast share of socio-economically disadvantaged section of society is absorbed in the informal economic activities. Informal employment is generally a larger source of employment for women than for men in the developing world. Other than in North Africa, where 43 per cent of women workers are in informal employment, 60 per cent or more of women workers in the developing world are in informal employment (outside agriculture). In sub-Saharan Africa 84 per cent of women non-agricultural workers; in Latin America 58 per cent for women in comparison to 48 per cent for men. In Asia, the proportion of women and men non-agricultural workers in informal employment is roughly equivalent to women and men in the informal economy.[2]

The foremost inclusive survey of 'Informal Sector' was conducted in the NSS 55th Round during July 1999 to June 2000. The NSSO during the 55th Round Survey (July 1999 – June 2000), for the first time, collected data through employment – unemployment survey, in respect of workers occupied in the non-agricultural enterprises in the informal sector. Information was collected directly from the enterprises by preparing a different interview schedule. This schedule was specially crafted for the informal sector enterprises, which enclosed all unincorporated enterprises in the non-agricultural sector. The respondents were generally owners/managers of enterprises from whom all information on workers was obtained. The emphasis was more on such details of the enterprises as their receipts, operating expenses, assets owned, etc. and very few items of information were exclusively on workers.

The ensuing survey was conducted in NSS 61st Round during July 2004 to June 2005. The Commission has prepared direct estimates of employment in the unorganised sector based on its definition (which include all of agricultural workers in the unorganised sector and defined organised employment more tightly to limit it to employees who receive provident fund and social security benefits from their employers) and the NSS 55th and 61st Round Survey results.

As per these estimates, in 2004–05, the total employment (principal plus subsidiary) in the Indian economy was 458 million, of which the unorganised sector accounted for 395 million (given in the following table). This direct estimation shows that the unorganised sector constituted 86 per cent of total workers in 2004–05, same as that in 1999–2000. Informal types of employment in organised and unorganised sectors taken together constitute 92 per cent in 2004–05 against 91 per cent in 1999–2000. Informal employment increased from 341 millions persons in 2000 to 394 millions in 2005. Formal employment, on the other hand stayed stationary at about 35 millions. Organised sector employment amplified from 54.1 million to 62.6 millions during the period, i.e. by about 9 million, which is completely on account of what is categorised as informal employment in the organised sector, workers who do not have the benefit of provident fund and social security (Chakrabarti, 2009: 3–4).

Plight of Women Workers in India's Informal Sector

In the context of India, a developing economy, the informal sector employs about 86 per cent of the country's work force and 94 per cent of its women workers. Majority of these women workers need to earn for the basic survival and sustenance of their families. However, low income women workers, especially in the informal sector form one of the most susceptible categories in the Indian economy.

The reasons for their vulnerability are:

(a) Irregular work,
(b) low economic status,
(c) little or no bargaining power,
(d) lack of control over earnings,
(e) need to balance paid work with care for children and homework,
(f) little or no access to institutional credit, training and information, and
(g) lack of assets.

The primary features of unorganised sector are that most of the women labourers are appointed as contract labourers. Neha Mittal (2012: 183–185) has expressed her concern that various studies conducted in several parts of the country indicate the awful conditions of the women workers in this sector. They persist to face unfairness and marginalisation, both slight and unconcealed, and do not share the fruits of development equally. Ignorance, traditional bound attitudes, illiteracy, lack of skills, seasonal nature of employment, heavy physical work of different types, lack of job security, lack of a comprehensive legislation to cover these workers in unorganised sector and competition in employment are resultant deprival of real wage. Wages in the unorganised sector are randomly fixed, often without regard to the minimum wage legislations, which unfavourably influence the income of the wage workers in general, and women workers in particular.

She has furthered that in the informal sector, wage workers constituted 36 per cent and the remaining 64 per cent were self-employed. The higher level of unemployment and underemployment among women means that their fraction below the poverty line is likely to be higher than men. Women who are drawn from rural areas are unskilled labourers. The life of unorganised sector worker is very tough. They are exploited in many ways. The mistreatment is not only carried on the class lines but also on the lines of male domination over females. Sexual harassment is frequent but unstated due to fear of loss of employment. Despite the advances women have made in many societies, women's concerns are still given second priority almost everywhere. Their contribution is not given due credits. Women workers in unorganised sector lag behind the males in terms of level and quality of employment. There are still cases where women workers are dispossessed of the benefits and facilities like equal payment vis-à-vis their male counterparts, maternity benefits, proper child care services and indifferent attitude of the employers towards women workers. Women often tend to work harder to save adequate money for their family and to sustain and survive through life's challenges. The ever escalating prices of private healthcare and the systematic dismantling of the public health system in these times of liberalisation are a major reason for the huge indebtedness of households in the unorganised sector. There is a pressing need to provide insurance, especially health insurance cover to the workers. Numerous factors answerable for their plight are uncaring approach of the employers towards women workers, their feeble bargaining power and in many cases the women workers themselves being ignorant of their rights.

Concept of Social Protection

The rapid growth and spreading out of the informal economy, principally in the developing countries, designates snowballing of income-related uncertainty and vulnerability of the workers. It is often competed that the concept of social protection necessities to be widened to embrace economic security and not just social security for contingencies, or what is termed here as basic security. Dreze and Sen (1991) have developed a wider concept by differentiating between two different aspects of social security called 'protection' and 'promotion'.

Social protection is a relatively new policy approach that aspires to amalgamate concerns about social security and poverty reduction into a combined framework (Kabeer, 2008). Till date, the social protection agenda has connoted different categories of poor, excluded and vulnerable social groups, distinguished on the basis of age, health status and relationship to formal labour markets. This prominence on the formal sector has sidelined women in particular. In spite of some measures designed principally for the female-headed households, gender is seldom used as a tool to comprehend the poor's exposure to risk and susceptibility. This often hinders the proper design for social protection measures. At the same time, however, social protection programmes are rarely gender neutral, and poorly designed programme can aggravate or add to inequalities (Luttrell and Moser, 2004). In contemporary times, various terms are used in different parts of the globe and by different international agencies concerned with social protection for the poor and marginalised. Terms like social security, social insurance, social assistance, safety nets, social funds and social protection are used quite frequently.

In the year 1952, with Convention No. 102 on Social Security (Minimum Standards), the International Labour Organisation (ILO) consolidated the notion of social security. A wide-ranging definition was suggested which included nine core contingencies leading to the cessation, or substantial reduction, of earnings which should be sheltered by social security. These included benefits in the case of sickness, maternity, employment injury, unemployment, invalidity, old age and death, as well as the provision of medical care and subsidies for families with children. This definition provided by the ILO covers two types of social security, i.e. social insurance and social assistance. Social assistance comprises of persons with various types of disability such as old age, illness, disability, etc. It is more likely to be non-contributory. Social insurance covers workers of different categories and refers to a system through which they contribute to their future security, e.g. injury at the workplace.

By social it could be implied that only market is incompetent of sustaining such unforeseen events. The social safety net connotes to compensatory actions for alleviating the negative impact of structural adjustment programmes in developing and transition economies in the 1980s and 1990s. Social funds, propagated by the World Bank, were a means of financing the social safety net programmes. The term 'social protection' is a novel term used to cover all these concepts as an umbrella term to depict social security. It is related to poverty reduction or alleviation, unlike social insurance and assistance (Lund and Srinivas, 2000). In developing countries, a major segment of the population is occupied in self-employment and in informal activities and it is a challenging task to refuge them under formal schemes of unemployment benefits, insurance and other benefits. The approach followed in the developed world, therefore, may not be appropriate to, or operational in, developing countries.

Countries and regions across the globe have diverse traditions of social provision and different acceptance of the links between economic and social policy. These govern the basic components that get included in and excluded from the domains of social policy, social security and social protection. There is an increasing collective awareness that the development should not only aim at attaining economic growth but also strive to achieve social justice. In other words, economic growth is worthwhile only if it hints to social justice in the form of equitable distribution, reduction in poverty, reasonable incomes, meets basic securities such as health and education and promotes political, cultural and economic freedom. Standing (1999) suggests 'a good society is a just society'. 'A just society, and by inference a good labour market, requires policies and institutions that augment self-control and basic security'. Distributive justice entails that every person in society should have basic security and self-control (Standing, 2000). Basic security and control together is empowerment or the feeling of control. In Standing's view, fundamental security for all constitutes freedom from mortality, autonomy from fear, being in control of one's development, sustainable self-respect, minimal income security – a 'floor' to downside risk, and voice representation security. Self-control embraces equal opportunity for occupational security. Elson and Cagatay (2000) indicate at the requirement to review the reliability of macroeconomic policy not by market-based criteria, but by predictable social outcomes such as distributive justice, equity, freedom from poverty and discrimination, social exclusion and development of human capabilities. In the countries predominant with huge large informal segment in the labour force, the idea of social justice would directly imply at social protection measures to cover both basic daily-based needs and economic security. Sloppy worth of employment on a large scale indicates that economic growth would not cater to the needs of many workers.

Social protection thus encompasses many different areas and traditions of policy response (Norton, and Conway Foster, 2001: 21–23). Many of these are highly technical and specialised in character (such as insurance systems, pension reform, welfare transfers, or public employment schemes). Definitions that seek to locate social protection within a broad context can go further to include famine relief, or even in some cases most activities that relate to public policy to support the well-being of citizens and reduce poverty. We are aware that the definition provided above could, pedantically, be read in this way. Arguably, for example, providing an education system is a way of mitigating deprivation. It is important therefore to read the above definition as referring to the protection of those who fall momentarily or steadily under levels of livelihood deemed acceptable or are likely to do so, rather than the promotion of a general standard of opportunity and livelihood for all citizens. While the definition remains broad, it can thus be distinguished from areas of general development policy, although issues of overlap with promotional policies will inevitably remain. It is also important to locate social protection in the context of significant relationships with other areas of policy. Firstly, social protection comprises part of the broader field of social policy. The linkage between social protection and broader social policy analysis is important to the analysis and prioritisation of public expenditures and public policy choices. Particularly in poorer countries, hard preferences are required to be made in relation to the capacity of the state and the necessity to direct financial, institutional and human resources to different fields, including health, education and water, as well as social protection. Secondly, it is significant not to see social protection as a field that deals only with left over problems of human welfare, but as a form of policy which releases human potential and encourages equality of opportunity as well as of outcome.

Women, Informal Economy and Social Protection

Highlighting social protection for informal women workers should commence from the fact that informal work is by definition work without access to work-related measures of social protection. All over the globe, girls and women are inexplicably characterised among the severe poor in many parts of the world. They not only limit women's access to the labour market, but also often confine working women to more poorly remunerated, more casual and more insecure forms of waged and self-employment, particularly in the informal economy, without access to social protection. Increasing informalisation of women's work and mounting sources of vulnerability (e.g. due to rising food prices and climate change) affect women's ability to provide for their families and cope with insecurity. Moreover, women are particularly affected by the human rights violations, pervasive poverty and physical insecurity that often characterise brittle states. These factors accentuate the need for greater understanding about the rationale and policy and programme implications of a gendered approach to social protection.

Informal women workers, whether self-employed or wage workers:

- cannot frequently have the funds to purchase private insurance against risk;
- stay in poor communities which cannot co-insure against risk;
- are excluded from contributory schemes (such as unemployment insurance, and workers compensation against accidents at work);
- may be included in social assistance schemes, such as cash transfers – but these are usually designed to go to target groups of non-working age, such as younger children, and elderly people, or who cannot work, such as people with severe disabilities;

Figure 2

Approaches to Achieving Gender Equality and to Social Protection

Gender Equality

A strategy often used to achieve the goal of gender equality in different sectors is based on a dual or twin-track approach. *Gender mainstreaming* is the integration of a gender perspective into every stage of the policy process – design, implementation, monitoring and evaluation – with a view to promoting equality between women and men. Gender mainstreaming is not concerned only with women, but with the relationship between women and men for the benefit of both. *Gender-specific* actions are required in addition to transform the inequalities between women and men that have been identified through gender analysis and mainstreaming (EC, 2008).

Social Protection

The full range of social protection interventions comprises protective, preventive, promotive and transformative measures (Devereux and Sabates-Wheeler, 2004).

- Protective measures are narrowly targeted safety nets for income and consumption smoothing in periods of crisis or stress (e.g. social assistance programmes for the chronically poor).
- Preventive measures seek to avert deprivation (e.g. social insurance such as pensions and maternity benefits).
- Promotive measures aim to enhance real incomes and capabilities, and provide springboards and opportunity ladders out of poverty.
- Transformative measures seek to address concerns of social equity and exclusion through social empowerment (e.g. collective action for workers? rights, building voice and authority in decision-making for women).

Social protection measures can have different and often overlapping objectives and impacts (e.g. simultaneously 'promoting' incomes as well as 'preventing' deprivation). Kabeer's (2008) 'generative' model emphasises that social protection measures can contribute not only to more livelihoods security for poor and vulnerable groups, but also to some of the mainstream goals of development, including economic growth, human development and good governance.

Source: 'Gender and Social Protection', Sarojini Ganju Thakur (Commonwealth Secretariat), Catherine Arnold (DFID) and Tina Johnson (DFID), PROMOTING PRO-POOR GROWTH: SOCIAL PROTECTION – © OECD 2009

- may be included in temporary public works schemes, but these do not usually have a training component that would help attain better long-lasting employment.

Social protection measures are extremely essential for informal workers, chiefly for women workers, to protect them from contingencies and scarcity. However, there are apparently meagre social protection measures in place for informal workers in India that barely address the enormous insecurities faced by them.

Social protection measures that benefit the informal sector include, crèches for children of working women implemented by the Central Social Welfare Board, monetary assistance of ₹ 300 under the National Maternity Benefit Scheme to pregnant women for first two childbirths, in the situation of death of the breadwinner of the family, a lump sum amount of ₹ 5,000 is given to BPL families under the Family Benefit Scheme, and under National Old-age Pension Scheme men and women who are 65 years and above are paid a monthly pension. There are also welfare funds administered by central and state governments provided to particular segments of the informal sector. The fund is created by charging a cess on the produce of the sector, for example, for the centrally administered Bidi Workers Welfare Fund, a cess of about ₹ 0.50 is charged on 1,000 *beedis*. Similarly there are welfare funds for mineworkers. Besides the central and state government's social protection schemes and social security funds, social assistance is also offered by many voluntary organisations as well as co-operative societies.[3]

Provision of social protection is enshrined in Articles 38 (securing a social order for the promotion of welfare of the people), 39 (certain principles of policy), 41 (right to work, education and public assistance in certain cases), 42 (just and human conditions of work and maternity relief) and 43 (living wage, etc.) of the Constitution of India as a part of the Directive Principles of State Policy. Important social security, poverty alleviation and social welfare measures are being implemented by various ministries/ departments of Government of India, state governments and civil society.

Sudha Pillai (2011: 5–6) has outlined a number of social protection measures adopted by the Government of India to ensure welfare of workers in the unorganised sector which, *inter alia*, include weavers, handloom workers, fishermen and fisherwomen, toddy (local brew) tappers, leather workers, plantation labour, *beedi* (local cigar) workers, etc. *The Unorganized Workers' Social Security Act, 2008* has been enacted which entails formulation of schemes to provide for life and disability cover, health & maternity benefits, old age protection and any other benefit as may be determined. *Rastriya Swasthya Bima Yojana* (RSBY) is a health insurance scheme providing for smart card-based cashless cover of ₹ 30,000 to a BPL family of 5 covering all pre-existing diseases, hospitalisation expenses and transport cost. The benefits are portable by splitting the card value for migrant workers. Over 25 million smart cards have been issued and the coverage of the scheme is being expanded to construction, domestic, *beedi,* non-coal mine and MGNREGA workers, railway porters and street vendors. *Aam Admi Bima Yojana* (AABY) provides for death and disability insurance cover to rural landless households amounting to ₹ 30,000 in case of natural death, ₹ 75,000 in case of accidental death and total permanent disability and ₹ 37,500 in case of partial permanent disability. Under the scheme two children of the beneficiaries studying in 9th to 12th standards are given scholarships at the rate of ₹ 300 per quarter per child. The government has set up welfare funds for providing welfare measures to the *beedi,* non-coal mine and cine workers. The funds are used for providing financial assistance for children's education, recreation, medical and health facilities, construction of houses, etc. Similar facilities exist for construction workers. Some Indian states like Kerala and Tamil Nadu have constituted welfare funds for specific categories of workers in the unorganised sector.

Handloom Weavers' Comprehensive Welfare Scheme: The scheme benefits the weaver, his wife and two children. Ancillary handloom workers like those engaged in warping, winding, dyeing, printing, finishing, sizing, jhala-making, jacquard-cutting, etc. are also eligible. The scheme covers all pre-existing as well as new diseases. The annual limit per family is ₹ 15,000 out of which OPD cover is ₹ 7,500. *Handicraft Artisans' Comprehensive Welfare Scheme:* It has two components, namely, (i) Rajiv Gandhi Shilpi Swasthya Bima Yojana, and (ii) Bima Yojana for Handicrafts Artisans. The scheme covers the artisan's family of four comprising self and any three members of family and provides for annual health package amounting to ₹ 15,000 including ₹ 7,500 for OPD. An insurance cover of ₹ 0.1

million is also available for the personal accident, death, and disability of the insure artisans. *National Scheme for Welfare of Fishermen and Training & Extension:* The scheme provides for group accident insurance for active fishermen, development of model fisherman villages, saving-cum-relief and training-cum-extension facilities, etc.

Conclusion

However, notwithstanding the dire necessity of social protection measures for the informal economy workers, particularly women, the social security coverage is actually stumpy and weakening. According to the NCEUS, only about 7 per cent of the total workforce in India has any form of social security. With increased flexibility, even among wage employees in non-agricultural establishments, social security coverage is declining. Furthermore, findings of the NCEUS on protective social coverage shows that, only 6 per cent of unorganised workers are estimated as receiving protective social security through governmental or non-governmental interventions. Major areas of vulnerability identified as: (i) illness requiring hospitalisation, (ii) untimely death of bread winner, (iii) unemployment, (iv) maternity episodes, (v) retirement from work.

Modern and superior technology, if used, could help in enhancing the social protection programmes, faster delivery, and better monitoring and evaluation of the schemes. Social protection schemes need to be decentralised to take benefit of local strengths and knowledge and furnish to local needs. Acknowledgement of women's dual responsibility in production and reproduction by providing support services such as child care centers for children of working women. Extended opportunities of employment for the informal sector, particularly for women, by skill enhancement and other vocational training employment programmes. Convergence of related schemes is critical for better delivery of programmes and to reduce the scope of corruption in implementation of the schemes. Also to generate awareness among staff and citizens about the schemes (benefits, eligibility criteria and procedures) and take advantages of complementarities (particularly in delivery of schemes where there are manifold systems and multiple windows for multiple schemes or for various components of the same scheme

Social protection, therefore, constitutes those steps which intend at preventing, reducing and eliminating economic and social vulnerabilities to poverty and deprivation. Regardless of swift development over last decades, poverty and deprivation persist to affect vast populations and an estimated 80 per cent of the population remains without access to adequate social protection cover (Srivastava, 2013). The fact that such large numbers of people, especially women, absorbed in the informal sector, continue to bear from various deprivations and have low human capabilities represents tremendous squandered human and economic potential.

Social protection helps in the realisation of human rights which are enshrined in Universal Declaration of Human Rights, international conventions, and national constitutions. Social protection measures can help to stabilise aggregate demand during economic crisis.

Notes

1. http://www.oecd.org/dac/povertyreduction/43280700.pdf.
2. Kamala Kanta Mohapatra. 'Women Workers in Informal Sector in India: Understanding the Occupational Vulnerability'. *International Journal of Humanities and Social Science, 2.21* (November 2012).
3. http://www.in.boell.org/downloads/briefing_note_5.pdf.

References

Chakrabarti, Satyabrata. *Gender Dimensions of the Informal Sector and Informal Employment in India*. Accra, Ghana: Global Forum on Gender Statistics, 2009.

Chen, M. *Self-employed Women: A Profile of SEWA Membership*. Ahmedabad: SEWA Academy, 2006.

——. 'Informality and Social Protection: Theories and Realities'. *Institute for Development Studies (IDS) Bulletin*, 39.2: 18–27, 2008.

Dreze, J. and A.K. Sen. 'Public Action for Social Security'. In E. Ahmed et al. (eds), *Social Security in Developing Countries*. Oxford: Clarendon Press, 1991.

Elson, D. and N. Cagatay. 'The Social Content of Macroeconomic Policies'. *World Development*, 28.7: 1347–1364, 2000.

Jhabvala, R. 'Social Security for Unorganised Sector'. *Economic and Political Weekly*, 33.22 (30 May – 5 June) L7–L11, 1998.

Kabeer, Naila. *Mainstreaming Gender in Social Protection for the Informal Economy*. London: Commonwealth Secretariat, 2008.

Lund, F. and S. Srinivas. 'Learning from Experience: A Gendered Approach to Social Protection for Workers in the Informal Economy'. International Labour Organisation (ILO), Strategies and Tools Against Social Exclusion and Poverty (STEP) and Women in Informal Employment Globalizing and Organizing (WIEGO), Geneva, 2000.

Mittal, Neha. 'Women Workers in Unorganized Sector: Socio-Economic Perspective'. *Asian Journal of Multidimensional Research*, 1.3: 2278–4853, 2010.

Norton, Andy, Tim Conway and Mick Foster. *Social Protection Concepts and Approaches: Implications for Policy and Practice in International Development*. London: Centre for Aid and Public Expenditure, 2001.

Pillai, Sudha. *The Social Protection Floor in India*. Planning Commission of India, 2011.

Sankaran, T.S. 'Can the Best be the Enemy of Good, If the Good is Not Good Enough?' *Economic and Political Weekly*, 41.32 (12–18 August) 3491–3495, 2006.

Srivastava, Ravi. *A Social Protection Floor for India*. A Joint United Nations Study, 2013.

Unni, Jeemol and Uma Rani. *Social Protection for Informal Workers: Insecurities, Instruments and Institutional Mechanisms*. Geneva: International Labour Office, 2002.

CHAPTER 12

Work Without Fear

Combating Workplace Sexual Harassment

SHIKHA SHARMA

Employment has always been considered as one of the variables leading/providing empowerment to the female population of the society. In 21st century, participation of women in workforce has increased where diverse range of female individuals is participating across a broad spectrum of occupations, workplaces and industries. The scholarship dominating 1950s era argued that male and female functions at workplace were necessary to be differentiated to minimise competition between the sexes, to sustain cohesion and minimise imbalance in the traditional loci of powers. Ann Oakley (1974) criticised the functional differentiation between sexes and called it convenient for men in family to exercise control and domination. The same has been applied in its patriarchal form to the public space. The occupational differences created between men and women give men the convenience to exercise and control power. The dominant values of patriarchy and women's dependency on men hindered their socio-economic growth and mobility. What about those women who have been able to attain social and economic mobility? Are such women free from exploitation and suffer no denial of personhood and human rights? It has been argued by policy makers and social scientists alike that entry of women into gainful employment help them attain social status, economic autonomy and equal participation in the decision-making process.

Work participation itself has many important issues and problems. Working women find themselves in environments largely dominated by masculine values; individualism and competitiveness rather than connectedness and emotional sensitivity. Tripathy (1996) comments that women's access to paid work may give them greater sense of self-reliance and greater purchasing power, but if it is undertaken in conditions that erode their health and exploit their labour, its cost may outweigh its benefits. With regards to organised sector or unorganised sector, occupational hazards faced by working women that are common have been discussed in this paper. The article focuses on sexual harassment that women workers face irrespective of their field of work.

Sexual harassment is major occupational hazard affecting women all over the globe. In the Indian context, the situation is even more serious as majority of working women are in the informal, unorganised sector of economy where they do not get any statutory protection. Sexual harassment at workplace affects the well being and dignity of the victim and causes frustration, low self esteem, insecurity and emotional disturbance which in turn could affect business efficiency, leading to loss of production and loss of reputation for the organisation or the employee. Bina Shah (2013) blogged that Tehelka sexual harassment case has got people alarmed, upset and aware that a huge problem exists all over the world that involves women trying to hold on jobs, earn an honest living, but being prevented from doing so because of sexual harassment.

The problem relates not so much to actual biological differences between men and women – rather it relates to the gender or social roles attributed to men and women in social and economic life, and perceptions about male and female sexuality in society that can lead to unbalanced power relationships (Haspel, Kasim, Thomas and McCann, 2001). Frank Saal (1996) in his study found out that harassment is more commonly found in female-dominated workplaces where majority of women earn low-wages and the management is predominantly male.

Besides sex and age, lack of labour and provision of social protection is also a factor where the chances of being subjected to sexual harassment increases. The high risk groups are:

- Young women in education and training institutions who are on work assignments
- Domestic workers
- Migrant workers
- Workers with little income and job security
- Women in male-dominated occupations or sectors
- Women working in sectors or professions where large number of women is supervised by small number of men.

McDonald and Charlesworth (2016) in their study said the complaints across categories were categorised by a 'wide range of intimidating, offensive physical and non-physical conduct' in a 'variety of workplaces'. Their study shows that regardless of the sex of the complainant or alleged harasser, sexual harassment causes significant psychological and workplace damage and that it is under-reported compared to its prevalence in workplaces.

It is clear that from any point – human rights, human dignity or human resources – sexual harassment is considered to be unacceptable form of conduct that should be prevented, prohibited and sanctioned.

What is Sexual Harassment?

Sexual harassment at the workplace has been one of the major problems that women participating in the workforce generally face. Sexual harassment is defined by its impact on the victim/woman rather than the intent of the perpetrator.

As defined in the Supreme Court guidelines (Vishakha v/s State of Rajasthan, August 1997), sexual harassment includes unwelcome sexually determined behaviour as:

- physical contact
- a demand or request for sexual favour
- showing pornography
- any other unwelcome physical, verbal or non-verbal conduct of a sexual nature.

The law prohibits teasing, offhand comments, or isolated incidents. Harassment is illegal when it is frequent or severe that it creates a hostile or offensive work environment or when it results in an adverse employment decision. The harasser can be the victim's supervisor, a supervisor in another area, a co-worker, or someone who is not an employee of the employer, such as a client or customer (U.S. Equal Employment Opportunity Commission [EEOC]; Title VII of the 1964 Civil Rights Act). It has many dimensions. Advancements, gestures, indicative looks, pun, taking vengeance etc. Sexual harassment at workplace has been recognised as evil almost by all progressive employers. More so it is applicable to female employees as they are worst affected.

Recognising the gravity of the offence, various national and international efforts to eliminate sexual harassment have been initiated. The United Nations General Recommendation 19 to the 'Convention on the Elimination of All Forms of Discrimination Against Women' defines sexual harassment as:

> Such unwelcome sexually determined behaviour as physical contact and advances, sexually coloured remarks, showing pornography and sexual demands, whether by words or actions. Such conduct can be humiliating and may constitute a health and safety problem; it is discriminatory when the woman has reasonable ground to believe that her objection would disadvantage her in connection with her employment, including recruitment or promotion, or when it creates a hostile work environment (CEDAW, General Recommendation 19).

The International Labour Organization (ILO) addressed sexual harassment as an illegal and prohibited form of sex discrimination under the Discrimination (Employment and Occupation) Convention (No. C111).[1] Unlike the international definitions that describe what constitutes sexual harassment at workplace, in India three levels of harassment have been distinguished: physical, verbal and non-verbal sexual harassment.

Although there is no one comprehensive universal definition of sexual harassment, certain actions and behaviours can be termed as prohibited conduct (Webb, 1994):

1. [the action] is related to sex or sex conduct;
2. [the conduct] is unwelcome, not returned, not mutual; and
3. [the conduct] affects the terms or conditions of employment, in some cases including the work environment itself.

While explaining extensively, Susan Webb (1994) draws on what constitutes a conduct that can be considered as sexual harassment.

Conduct of a sexual nature includes a range of behaviors or actions, since there is a very wide range of activities which are expressions of sexuality or have sexual connotations in our society. Therefore, behavior which may appear relatively innocent (such as joking, innuendos, flirting and asking someone on a date) to behavior which is blatantly illegal (such as forced fondling, attempted or actual rape and sexual assault) can all constitute conduct of a sexual nature. In order to qualify as sexual harassment the behavior must be deliberate and/or repeated. Some forms of sexual behavior are so offensive that the first time they occur they are considered deliberate, inappropriate, and sometimes even illegal actions. Other behaviors must be repeated over and over again before they become harassment. Whether the particular behavior is defined as sexual harassment depends largely on whether the behavior is unwelcome to the target, along with the circumstances surrounding those events.

Sexual harassment conduct is when the sex or sexuality of the person and everything culturally related to it – from her/his body, to her/his manner of dress, to her/his intimate relations – is made the object or target of the conduct, as something desired to be obtained, or appropriated, or trivialised with, whether through physical, verbal or other forms of conduct (Ursua, 2001)

The complexity of modern relationships and social media in today's workplace environment often leads to inappropriate workplace interactions. Employees who are on the receiving end of such unwanted behaviour have a legal right to press charges against such incidences.

The Issue: The Effects

There is a need to rethink the concept of sexual harassment. It is not only the physical workplace that requires attention and concerned relations are not only between supervisors and staff or between colleagues, but usually covers a broad spectrum of working relations. Sexual harassment has negative consequences for employees, employers and societies as a whole.

Sexual harassment has a serious negative impact on women's physical, emotional and mental health. These include anxiety, depression, sleep disturbance, weight loss or gain, loss of appetite and headaches. The consequences are devastating both while the harassment is occurring and when the employee decides to take action. Sexual harassment also leads to frustration, loss of self esteem, absenteeism and a decrease in productivity. Victims (in this case, women) may lose their job or job-related experiences such as training or may even resign. Women from lower income group often surrender to such incidences as they cannot afford to lose the income they need for survival and support for the family. Compliance with unwanted sexual demands is accompanied by a sense of loss of self worth and a loss of self confidence. It also takes lots of courage and planned procedures to lodge complain and take action against the crime. It is also not uncommon for the victims to face further harassment or violence and threat. Long drawn battles also take economic and mental toll. The Commission of the European Union states,

> Sexual harassment pollutes the working environment and can have a devastating effect upon the health, confidence, morale and performance of those affected by it. The anxiety and stress produced by sexual harassment commonly leads to those subjected to it taking time off from work, being less efficient at work, or leaving their job to seek work elsewhere. Sexual harassment may also have a damaging impact on employees not themselves the object of unwanted behavior but who are witness to it or have a knowledge of the unwanted behavior. (European Union Commission, 1991)

Angelica Chan (1994) points out another dimension. She explains that the law still remains unclear whether a woman 'who is not herself the object of sexual harassment might still have a hostile environment claim'. U.S. psychologist Louise Fitzgerald (1993) had studied sexual harassment in private companies in the US using the Sexual Experience Questionnaire (SEQ). The SEQ brings out the psychological anguish harassment victims experience. It also found that there is a link between sexual harassment and Post-Traumatic Stress Disorder (PTSD).

The consequences of the vicarious harms that sexual harassment at workplace can do differs with the ratio of non-targets to targets, different employment contexts, different power structures, gender ratios and interpersonal relationship norms at the organisational level. Another important aspect in definitions of sexual harassment includes the notion that it occurs along a continuum, from sexist remarks to non-verbal seductive gestures to career threats, sexual assault and rape. Along this continuum, sexual harassment can take place once or can be repeated (Jack, 1999).

The sexual harassment also affects the employers leading to workplace tensions which in turn, may hamper teamwork, collaboration and work-related performance. Increased absenteeism and lower productivity results and it may also cause losing valuable employees. It also causes loss of faith among the employees and a poor image of the organisation is created. Where the cases are solved successfully and compensation is paid to the victim, it leads to financial risks and damages to the companies.

In societies or social groups where women are seen as inferior, both women and men often consider that sexual harassment is part of life and work and it is very common that under such circumstances they push the incidence behind a wall of silence. The laws dealing with securing justice to victims of sexual harassment relate or identify with more overt and physical forms of sexual assault and violations of dignity. These laws are not well-equipped to tackle the more subtle instances of work-related sexual harassment. Another problem that the victims face is how to prove the occurrence of the incidence. To succeed in any prosecution, the law requires that the offence against the accused be proved beyond reasonable doubt. Further there is no guarantee that action will be taken against the harasser. This generally happens when in an office complain has been lodged against a higher authority who has the capacity to influence the actions and decisions taken by the complaints committee. Women victims in such cases are not in a condition to recover damages or costs. Another issue that arises is the lack of guarantee that immediate relief is going to be provided to the victim in cases of sexual harassment. The grant of interim relief to restraint the behaviour of the perpetrator is generally pending till any decision is reached in the case and until that time the victim faces the trauma which can be severe.

Sexual Harassment: The Law in India

The challenge to the soft and cultural perception of sexual harassment first came from women's movement in India. After the strong protest campaigns that challenged the laws and the eventual amendment of the rape law in 1983, it was recognised that many forms of violence have existed but were normalised in social discourses. There have been several campaigns[2] and legal interventions[3] against sexual harassment, recommending and asking for reform in the laws.

Sexual harassment is a civil/criminal issue and the "statute of limitations" for a sexual harassment case depends on the organisation that is dealing with it. Before 1997, women who faced sexual harassment at work were supposed to lodge a complaint under Section 354[4] of the Indian Penal Code that deals with the 'criminal assault of women to outrage women's modesty', and Section 509[5] that deals and punishes an individual(s) for using a 'word, gesture or act intended to insult the modesty of a woman'. However these sections of the IPC could be easily misinterpreted and left interpretation of the 'outraging woman's modesty' to the definition and discretion of the officers, employers and often the victims had to suffer further.

In 1997, the Supreme Court of India, in Vishaka and Others vs. State of Rajasthan and Others[6] acknowledged the gravity of sexual harassment of the working women at the workplace and laid down guidelines making it mandatory for employers to provide the mechanisms in order to secure the resolution, settlement or prosecution of acts of sexual harassment. The guidelines issued by the Supreme Court were treated as law declared under the Article 141[7] of the Constitution of India. It was held by the Supreme Court that the guidelines framed by the Supreme Court would be strictly observed in all workplaces for the prevention and enforcement of the right to gender equality of the working women.

The increasing workforce participation of women made it imperative for framing and enacting a legislation that focused on prevention of sexual harassment as well as providing a redressal mechanism. Vishaka guidelines apply both to the formal/organised as well as informal/unorganised sectors and to all women whether full-time, part-time, on contract or in voluntary/honorary capacity. These guidelines encompass a broad framework which put emphasis on prevention and within the framework of which all the preventive measures at workplace can be adopted. It encourages and makes it mandatory for the organisations or workplaces of all kinds to adapt to a preventive sexual harassment policy and provide effective grievance procedure. The guidelines say that it will be the duty of the employer or other responsible persons in workplaces or other institutions to prevent or deter the commission of acts of sexual harassment and to provide the procedures for the resolution, settlement or prosecution of acts, of sexual harassment by taking all steps required. The guidelines mandate all companies, whether operating in private or public sector to set up Complaints Committee within the organisation to look into such offences. The Complaints Committee should be headed by a woman and not less than half of its members should be women. To prevent the possibility of pressure or influence from senior levels, such Complaints Committee should involve a third party, either NGO or other body who is familiar with the issue of sexual harassment.

The Indecent Representation of Women (Prohibition) Act (1987) is among those laws whose provisions have the potential to be used in two ways:

- If an individual harasses another with books, photographs, paintings, films, pamphlets, packages, etc. containing 'indecent representation of women';
- A 'hostile working environment' argument can be applied under Section 7 (Offences by Companies) provides that companies where there has been 'indecent representation of women' on the premises are guilty of offenses under this act.

The Sexual Harassment of Women at Workplace (Prevention, Prohibition and Redressal) Act, 2013 was enacted for prevention of sexual harassment against women at the workplaces. The act is enacted to provide protection against sexual harassment of women at workplace and prevention and redressal of complaints of sexual harassment and for matters connected therewith or incidental thereto. The act has adopted the definition of sexual harassment from Vishaka judgment and the term "sexual harassment includes any unwelcome acts or behaviour (whether directly or by implication) such as physical contact and advances, demand or request for sexual favours, making sexually coloured remarks, showing pornography or any other unwelcome physical, verbal or non-verbal conduct of sexual nature". This act is extensive and detailed and very minutely covers all the areas of sexual harassment of workplace and seeks to prevent, prohibit and redress the issue. The key points of this act are:

1. No man can file a sexual harassment complaint.
2. As per Section 2(o), the definition of the "workplace" includes any place visited by the employee arising out of or during the course of employment including transportation provided by the employer for undertaking such journey. Therefore as per this definition even areas outside the control of the employer such as office of the clients, taxis, hotels, etc. become a workplace. Therefore, during an official tour the place of stay (i.e. hotel), travel mode (i.e. taxi) and office of customers/clients are all included as workplace and the employer is liable if any incidents happen with the women employee.
3. Section 3 defining sexual harassment also contains clauses such as 'implied or explicit threat about her present or future employment status' and 'interferes with her work or creating an intimidating or offensive or hostile work environment for her'.
4. A committee needs to be formed that needs to have 'a woman presiding officer and minimum two other employees'. Further, a member has to be from women NGO and a majority of the members of the committee must be women. The Act makes it mandatory for all offices with 10 or more employees to have an internal complaints committee to address grievances in a stipulated time or face penalty.
5. Section 10 discusses the complaint handling provisions.
6. Section 11 states that the committees shall have the same powers as vested in civil court.
7. As per Section 12, during the pendency of the complaint the aggrieved woman may request for, 'transfer to another workplace', 'a paid leave and when this leave is over then privilege leave to be granted by the organisation'.
8. Section 14 states that in the case of false complaints, action will be taken as per the service rules of the organisation. If allegations against the accused turn out to be false and after inquiry are found to be made with a malicious intent, the complainant may face similar penal provisions as listed for the accused.

Sexual harassment at workplace may lead to termination of service of the accused, withholding of promotions and increments, and payment of reasonable compensation to the complainant. The Act also encourages the documenting of the harassment. It asks explicitly to save any emails, texts, voicemail or answering machine messages, letters and gifts. Also document any adverse actions that are taken against the woman and keep copies of performance evaluations that attest to the quality of work or work performance.

Traditionally, the workplace was understood as the physical space within which paid work is performed. In this Act the workspace has been extended to cover those women also who do not work in closed offices. These include the plantations, domestic workers, export processing zones, telephone and portable computer work, transportation as well as hiring and recruiting. Thus, this Act covers major aspects of sexual harassment at workplace and ensures to secure the dignity of a working woman.

Despite all these actions taken by the government and various other national and international measures, the victims of sexual harassment that takes place at work spaces find these remedies as inadequate.

The employers' duties also need to be highlighted to ensure safety of employees. The employer does not have an absolute duty to ensure his employees safety but he is under obligation to exercise mechanisms required to take due care and provide safety. A common law duty of an employer towards employees extends to ensure that they will not be subjected to sexual harassment at work. Under recent law it was held that if an employer anticipates or has reasons to anticipate misconduct which may be dangerous to fellow employees, the employer is in duty to her employees to take reasonable steps to avoid harm arising from it. At another occasion if the employer has the knowledge that an employee has on past sexually harassed someone than employer is under obligation to take steps to ensure that it does not happen again. However it is imperative to note that that the employer is not responsible for the negligence of the employee committed outside the scope of employee's employment space.

The problem arises as to distinguish that employer's accountability is or not extended to incidences of annoyance, worry, grief and emotional disturbance. Generally an employer can be sued for the physical or psychological harm only if it is established by the victim that they have been sexually harassed and are entitled to damages. Further the victim also needs to establish that harassment amounts to breach of her contract of employment. The employer is further responsible if he is himself found indulging in seducing employee or exerting undue influence on her. Certain actions on part of employer can also make them culprit or responsible where the worker is issued an order of transfer or demotion or asked to retire after the employee has complained of sexual harassment. These constitute dismissal of employee and the employer's liability to ensure safety is under direct question.

The protection under law still does not guarantee the reporting of the incidences of sexual harassment. The employer must take prompt investigative actions and build trust with the employees so that high rate of reporting can occur. Employer needs to designate and train personnel who are to receive complaints.

Suggestions

Sexual harassment at workplace is a social challenge that warrants attention. Public advocacy and participation is needed to raise awareness about the issue. The presence of actors at different levels entails that they can play role in preventing and offering protection and support for victims. It is important to identify that these actors are present not only on organisational or company levels but can also be found at state levels, at the levels where legal machinery comes into play for securing, protecting and supporting victims of sexual harassment at workplace. These actors provide support in the form of creating support mechanisms for the recipient or by raising their voices against the crime.

The government too can ensure justice by implementing policies and programs that define and enforce clear guidelines on preventive and remedial measures. This will help in creating an environment that is zero tolerant towards sexual harassment and put employers into direct charge of social and economic responsibility and provide for safe-conducive working environment to their employees. Even after the enforcement of Vishaka guidelines and the Sexual Harassment of Women at Workplace (Prevention, Prohibition and Redressal) Act 2013, it has been noted by various researches that the companies and organisations fail to comply with these laws. Employers should consider establishing policies that prohibit sexual harassment and constitute clear mechanisms to address complaints and provide for training to staff to recognise and deal with such problems.

Organisations and associations such as counseling centres line voluntary welfare organisations, community legal clinics, industrial associations and trade unions are instrumental in providing much needed support and services to individual who experience sexual harassment. These institutions also encourage the victims who are reluctant or afraid to report incidents or who lack awareness about the procedures and formalities required to file such reports.

More efforts and work is needed to draw and recognise the scope and field of the extent of workplace sexual harassment. There is also a need for extensive research into the occurrence and impact experienced by the victims. This accounts for encouragement into development of research interests in study of specific groups or categories like migrant workers and domestic workers or students of universities or colleges. The extent of sexual harassment and severity of the crime also varies from section to section of society. Generally it has been observed that the lower paid section and lower sections of society suffer more with such incidences. The culture of silence prevails in these groups where women tend to settle down under silence after the crime happens to them just because they feel vulnerable and are often misjudged. There is need for research and interventions to increase awareness among all the different groups of working women and instill in them the confidence that their complaints and any such actions are going to be tackled and justice will be delivered.

Both academic as well as policy interventions are needed to assess the feasibility of specific legislation to deal with sexual harassment as well as possible establishment of administrative mechanisms to handle complaints. Administrative mechanisms can be helpful solutions as generally the legal process may be lengthy and expensive.

It is essential that members of a workplace remain aware of the regulations that govern the workplace behaviour and report any violation that occurs thereof. The effects of harassment can change the dynamics of a workplace. Therefore, steps needed to be taken immediately to minimise effects. The employer as well as employee needs to be trained from the beginning and a strong policy on retaliation and a sensitive approach to the emotional affects on the victim should be a part of company policy.

Notes

1. Discrimination (Employment and Occupation) Convention (ILO No. 111), 362 U.N.T.S 31, entered in force JUNE 15, 1960.
2. Delhi based group initiated campaigns against sexual harassment of women on trains in 1998. Jawaharlal Nehru University students have been fighting a long drawn campaign against specific episodes of sexual harassment. Students of LNJP college in Delhi in March 1996, came out strongly against a head of a department for sexually harassing students. In February 1999, a national level consultation took place at Hyderabad to draw anti-sexual harassment policy in all Indian universities.
3. K.P.S. Gill, former Director General of Police of Punjab, was sentenced to three months rigorous imprisonment and fine for sexually harassing Rupan Deol Bajaj, an IAS officer of Punjab. She filed a complaint after Gill molested her at a party.
4. Section 354 IPC: Whoever assaults or uses criminal force on any woman, intending to outrage her modesty or knowing it likely that he will thereby outrage her modesty, shall be punished with imprisonment for a term which may extend to two years, or with fine, or with both.
5. Section 509 (*Words, gestures or act intended to insult the modesty of a woman*) is included in chapter 22 entitled 'Of criminal Intimidation, Insult and Annoyance', and is cognizable, bail-able and tri-able by any magistrate. It holds; 'Whoever, intending to insult the modesty of a woman, utters any word, makes any sound or gesture, or exhibits any object, intending that such word or sound shall be heard, or that such gesture is seen by such woman, or intrudes upon the privacy of such woman, shall be punished with simple imprisonment for a term which may extend to one year, or with fine, or with both.
6. Vishaka Judgment August 1997, Supreme Court of India guidelines. AIR 1997 SC 3011.
7. Article 141: The Law declared by the Supreme Court shall be binding on all courts within the Territory of India.

References

Chan, Anja Angelica . *Women and Sexual Harassment: A Practical Guide to the Legal Protections of the Title VII and the Hostile Environment Claim*. New York: Harrington Park Press, 1994.

Committee on the Elimination of Discrimination against Women (CEDAW). General Recommendation 19. Violence Against Women (Eleventh Session, 1992), U.N.Doc. Retrieved from https://www1.umn.edu/humanrts/svaw/harassment/explore/whatis.htm.

EEOC Title VII of the 1964 Civil Rights Act. Retrieved from http://www.eeoc.gov/laws/types/sexual-harassment.cfm

European Union Commission (27 November 1991) Recommendation on the Protection of Dignity of Women and Men at Work. (92/131/EEC). Retrieved from http://europa.en/scadplus/leg/en/cha/c/0917b.htm.

Fitzgerald, Louise. Sexual Harassment: Violence against Women in the Workplace. *American Psychologist*. Vol. 48 (1070, 1072), 1993.

Gutek, Barbara. A and Mary P. Koss. Changed Women and Changed Organizations: Consequences of and Coping with Sexual Harassment. *Journal of Vocational Behavior*. Vol. 42. (28, 33), 1993.

Haspel, N., Z. Kasim, C. Thomas, and D. Mclann. *Action against Sexual Harassment at Work in Asia and the Pacific*. Bangkok: ILO, 2001.

Jack, Lee Tsen-Ta. 'Workplace Sexual Harassment in Singapore: The Legal Challenge'. *Singapore Academy of Law Journal*, 1999.

McDonald, P. and S. Charlesworth. 'Workplace Sexual Harassment at the Margins'. *Work, Employment and Society*. Vol. 30 Issue 1, 2016.

Oakley, Ann. *The Sociology of Housework*. Oxford: Robertson Publications, 1974.

Saal, Frank, E. 'Man's Perceptions of Women's Interpersonal Behaviors and Sexual Harassment'. In *Sexual Harassment in the Workplace: Perspectives, Frontiers and Response Strategies*, ed. M.S. Stockdale. Thousand Oaks: Sage Publications, 1996.

Shah, Bina (November 27, 2013) A Story of Sexual Harassment. Binashah.blogspot.in. Retrieved from http://binashah.blogspot.in/2013/11/2013/11/a-story-of-sexual-harassment.html?=1

Tripathy, S.N. *Unorganized Women Labor in India*. New Delhi: Discovery Publications, 1996.

Ursua, Evalyn, G. Addressing Sexual Harassment in the Workplace: The Philippines Experience. Working Paper for the ILO (unpublished). Manila, 2001.

Vishaka and Others vs State of Rajasthan and Others. Indian Supreme Court Ruling. August 1997.

Webb, Susan. *Shockwaves: The Global Impact of Sexual Harassment*. New York: Mastermedia Publishing Company, 1994.

CHAPTER 13

Domestic Violence Against Women

A Study

CHANDRA KUMARI

Domestic violence, as it is generally understood in its broader sense, is violence among members of family or members of a household. It implies any type of discrimination or violence that is inflicted by any member of the family or the household upon another member of the family. When we talk about family, it could be both natal and nuptial.

Domestic violence implies the misuse of power by one adult. It controls another by abuse of power. The abuser tortures and controls the victim by calculated threats, intimidation and physical violence. Both men and women can be the abusers as well as the abused. However, in most of the incidents the victims are women.

Consequences of Domestic Violence

The consequences of domestic violence can result in physical-mental pain suffering and can be as serious as causing even death. Domestic violence not only makes women feel insecure at home, but also endangers their independence, self development and human rights. Forward-Looking Strategies for the Advancement of Women adopted by the Second World conference on women held in Nairobi in 1985, has identified violence as an obstacle to women's right and development. The viewpoint is reiterated by the

Committee for the Elimination of Discrimination against Women (CEDAW). It emphasises violence as 'the essential and ultimate social mechanism by which women are forced into a subordinate position as compared to men'. It is not only on impediment to development but also perpetrates inequalities and gender based violence. At the same time, domestic violence results in a large economic loss to the nation.

Justification of the Study

Violence against women takes many forms. Far too frequently women are the objects of violent acts by men. More often than not, they are beaten or harassed or confined or threatened by men they know, often in their own homes. Other women are sexually assaulted and raped even by police officers or doctors in whose charge they are supposed to be safe. Some experience the violence of a stranger in each case and in all situations violence against women whether, it is rape, causing hurt in some other way, battering, harassment for dowry, forced confinement or threatening to do harm is a crime, punishable, by law. It is the everyday fact of life that a huge percentage of women all over the world are victims of domestic violence. Wife beating knows no class, race or religious distinction. Women battering are not just an aberration in the behaviour of a violent manifestation of male domination over women and the patriarchal attitude that sees women, especially wives, as the property of men.

In Indian family cases of domestic violence are generally not reported. Even if reported it is not directly reported by families. Hence, effort was made to conduct study on the topic taking help from NGOs where such cases were reported.

In the light of the above discussion the present study aims at enlisting the various types of domestic violence, exploring the abusive situations under which women live in the family, identifying causes of violence, studying the pattern of adjustment after shocking incidents, and exploring the ways and means for preventing/reducing violence against women.

Null Hypotheses: Domestic violence is independent of education level, age and income group.

Methodology

The sample was collected from NGO's working in Sharanpur (Mahila Samakhya and Disha). After collecting the names and addresses of the respondents, the researcher personally contacted the respondents (of Saharanpur) whose names were obtained from the NGOs. About 105 names were collected from the records of 1998–2004 and 50 names were collected from Disha from the records of 2001–2004. Then chit system was used to select the respondents, i.e. by random sampling. Hence, the final sample size was 100 (65 from Mahila Samakhya and 35 from Disha).

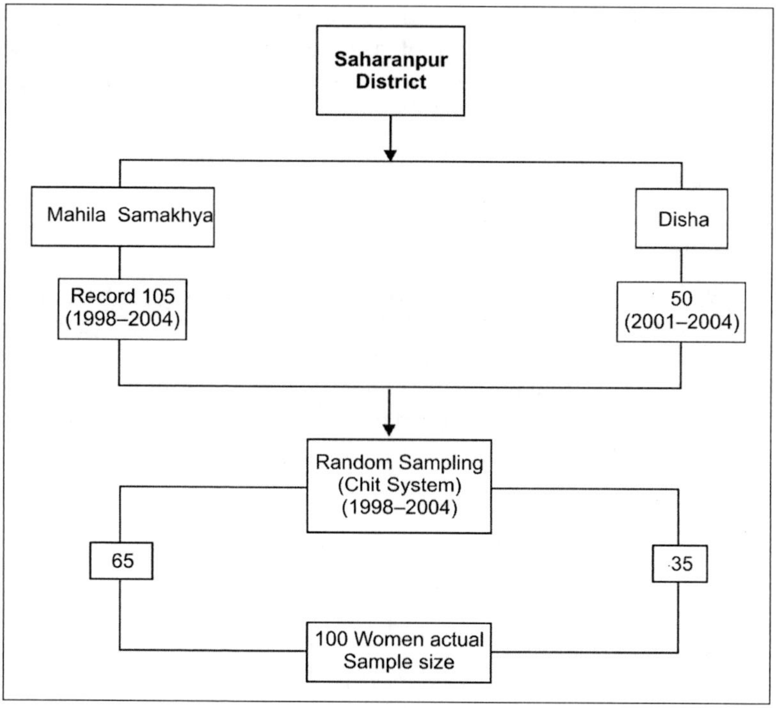

Tools used: Two tools were used for collecting the data.

1. Questionnaire on domestic violence developed by investigator
2. Domestic violence abuse checklist
   (a) *Questionnaire on domestic violence developed by investigator:* It consisted of fifteen questions, which were both closed and

open ended. The schedule had two subsections. First part dealt with general information of the respondents. The second part consisted of questions regarding violence.

(b) *Domestic violence abuse checklist*: The second tool comprised of a checklist with 23 questions which aimed to decide whether the respondent is living or had experienced abusive situation.

Results and Discussions

After the data have been collected, it is necessary, to pay attention to results and discussions, a process consisting of number of closely related operations. It is the purpose of results and discussions to search for broader meaning of available knowledge. Both these purposes govern the entire research process. All proceeding steps have been undertaken in order to make their fulfillment possible.

The data on domestic violence against women of Saharanpur have been tabulated, analysed and interpreted.

Various Types of Domestic Violence

Table 1 shows the majority of respondents were sufferers of physical violence (57%). Other types of violence as stated by respondents, are psychological violence (49%) and sexual violence (17%), least percentage of respondents faced emotional violence (14%). Thus, it can be said that a great number of respondents were sufferers of physical violence.

Table 1

Frequency and Percentage Distribution of Respondents on Domestic Violence

Violence	*F*	%
Physical Violence	57	57
Psychological Violence	49	49
Sexual Violence	17	17
Emotional Violence	14	14

Table 2 shows the indulgence of respondent's husband into addictive behaviour. Majority of respondents, husband (46%) were involved in alcoholism, while (38%) were involved in smoking, (16%) were involved gambling. This is followed by that fact that least percentage of respondent's husbands were involved in drug abuse (3%).

Table 2

Frequency and Percentage Distribution of Respondents Depicting Addictive Behaviour of Husband

Addictives	*F*	*%*
Alcoholism	46	46
Smoking	38	38
Gambling	16	16
Drug (Heroin, Cocaine)	3	3

Table 3

Frequency and Percentage Distribution of Respondents of Consumption of Drugs

Time	*F*	*%*
Daily	45	45
Sometimes	19	19
With Friends	8	8
On function	4	4

Table 3 shows that, when asked the alcoholic tendency of the husbands of respondent, majority of women (45%) had husbands who drank regularly, (19%) sometimes, (4%) on function, and (8%) when they were with friends.

Abusive Situations Under Which Women Live in Family

Table 4 depicts that majority of respondents (52%) fell in moderately abusive category. These respondents definitely live in a home where they had experienced some violence at least one in a while. Respondents (28%) can be categorised into a class of non-abusive relationship in which the respondent have not had experienced any

Table 4

Frequency and Percentage Distribution of Respondents on Abusive Relationship

Scores	*Category*	*F*	*%*
0–14	Non-abusive relationship	28	28
15–36	Moderately abusive	52	52
37–93	Seriously abusive	20	20
94 – above	Dangerously abusive	–	–

kind of violence. Respondent (20%) can be categorised under seriously abusive. These respondents have been under outside pressures, or with the strain of a family emergency. Serious injury is probability and much of the abuse can be termed as assault abuse. No respondent was found to be under dangerously abusive situation.

Table 5

Frequency and Percentage Distribution of Respondents Stating Type of Behaviour by In-laws When They Do Not Turn Up to Their Expectation

Violence	*F*	*%*
Beating	50	50
Misbehaviour	48	48
Abusive language	35	35
In-laws don't talk	20	20
Normal	8	8

Table 5 shows that when asked about the behaviour of family members towards respondents, majority of them (50%) replied that their family member had beaten them. While (48%) believed that their family members misbehaved, (35%) respondents family members used abusive language and (20%) respondent's family members preferred not to talk. Least number of the respondent's family members behaved normally.

Causes of Violence

Table 6 reveals that respondents believed that alcoholism (47%) is the major cause for their violence. Some of the causes tracked by the researcher were financial problems (26%) and extra marital affairs (13%). This is followed by the fact that least per cent of respondents stated sterility among women (3%), illiteracy among women (2%), mental retardation among men (2%) other causes like not attractive, maladjusted with in-laws (2%). Thus, it can be interpreted that a great number of respondents believed that alcoholism is the major cause for their violence.

Table 6

Frequency and Percentage Distribution of Respondents Regarding Causes of Violence

Cause	*F*	*%*
Alcoholism	47	47
Financial problem	26	26
Dowry	20	20
Extra marital affair	13	13
Sterility	3	3
Illiterate	2	2
Mental retardation	2	2
Other cause	2	2

Pattern of Adjustment after Shocking Incidents

Table 7 indicates that the respondents remain silent (41%). Other adjustment patterns as respondents were sent to parent's home (31%), law (17%). This is followed by the fact that least per cent of respondents took support from NGOs (15%). Thus, it can be interpreted that a great number of respondents prefer to remain silent while facing violence. Otherwise they would be knocked out of the house.

Table 7

Frequency and Percentage Distribution of Showing Adjustment Pattern

Adjustment	*F*	*%*
Silent	41	41
Go back to parent's home	31	31
Law	17	17
NGOs	15	15

Table 8

χ^2 Value Calculated Showing Association Between Age/Education Level, Income Group and Domestic Violence

S. No.	*Variable*	χ^2
1	Age and domestic violence	9.8386 NS
2	Education level and domestic violence	9.5291 NS
3	Income group and domestic violence	13.0809*

* Significant at 5% level
NS – Not significant
Degree of freedom – 6
Table value – 12.6

Since the calculated value of chi square for the variable age and education level is less than the table value, the hypothesis is accepted. On the contrary, the chi square calculated value for the variable income group is more than the table value. Hence the Null hypotheses, i.e. there is no significant difference between the income group of the respondents and domestic violence.

Ways and Means for Reducing/Preventing Violence

The suggestions given by respondents for preventing/reducing violence against women:

- Provide/learn self-defense techniques so as to fight against violent situations.
- Attain/provide education to girls/women regarding their rights so they become efficient in safeguarding themselves against violence.
- Keeping a more strict watch on daughters by parents.
- Introducing legal reforms which may reduce difficulties in prosecution.
- Restraining mass media from practicing an indecent exhibition of women in all types of advertisements and humiliation of women in serials and movies.

Implication

The legal/judicial system has to become more responsive and gender sensitive to women's needs, especially in cases of domestic violence and personal assault. Existing laws should be reviewed to ensure that justice is quick and the punishment meted out to the culprits is commensurate with the severity of the offence. More over psychological counseling of victims of domestic violence is recommended.

References

Carter, L., L. Weithorn and R. Behrman. 'Domestic Violence and Children: Analysis and Recommendations'. *Domestic Violence and Children*, 9.3: 4–20, 1999.

Celine, Sunny. 'Domestic Violence Against Women: Report on a Situational Analysis in Ernakulum District, Kerala'. *Social Change*, 33.1: 26–54, 2003.

Kapoor, S. 'Domestic Violence Against Women and Girls'. *Innocenti* Digest, 6, 2000.

Michael, P.J. and J.F. Kathleen. 'Research on Domestic Violence in the 1990s: Making Distinctions'. *Journal of Marriage and Family*, 62.4: 948–963, 2004.

'Violence and Exploitation Against Women and Girls'. *Annuals of the New York Academy of Science*, 1087: 279, 2006.

CHAPTER 14

Nutritional Status of Middle Aged Urban Women in Jaipur

KANIKA VARMA AND AACHU AGARWAL

Why Women are at Higher Risk: Chronic Diseases Risk from a Gender Perspective

The relationship between dietary pattern, lifestyle and disease has long been investigated (Popkin, 1994). Assessing and characterising nutritional status of populations may be helpful in controlling and preventing nutrition-related chronic disease. In India, studies have been done to assess nutritional status in mothers in the reproductive age and children because they are vulnerable groups (Gopalan and Kaur, 1989). However, knowledge on the nutritional status of middle aged Indians is limited. India is now facing transition changes in the demography, socioeconomic indicators and health which induce the changes in the morbidity and mortality pattern in different age groups. Decades ago deaths and morbidity due to communicable diseases was a major threat but now non-communicable diseases (NCDs) especially coronary heart disease (CHD), cerebrovascular disease, hypertension, diabetes mellitus (DM) are sweeping the world. Earlier, developed countries were the victims of these diseases but now economically developing countries are also increasingly affected. Importantly, these diseases begin at earlier age in developing countries than its counterparts.

These diseases are largely preventable and their risk factors are almost common such as, unhealthy nutrition over a prolonged period, physical inactivity, tobacco consumption and excessive use of alcohol (WHO, 2007).

The prevalence of risk factors in various age groups is different in women when compared with men. Age is an important risk factor for both genders, but women on an average develop cardiovascular diseases 10 years later than men. More women than men develop hypertension as they get older, particularly women over 45 years (Mosca et al., 2004). Tobacco use represents an important risk factor for both men and women. Although the prevalence of smoking is higher in men than in women but in young women who smoke, the use of oral contraceptives further increases the risk (Castelli, 1999).

In both genders elevated cholesterol levels are associated with increased risk for cardio vascular events. Total cholesterol levels in women peak between 55 and 65 years of age, about a decade later than in men (Kannel, 1987).

Prevalence of diabetes is increasing in both men and women (Mokdad et al., 2001). The risk of CHD mortality associated with diabetes appears to be higher in women than in men. However, when mortality is adjusted for the other cardiovascular risk factors the gender difference is no longer present (Kanaya et al., 2002).

Obesity is also more prevalent in men until 45 years and in women after that age (Mokdad et al., 2003). The risk of cardiovascular events is increased especially in subjects with central obesity, (Rexrode et al., 1998) because of the concomitance of other risk factors or co-morbidities, which are very often present in obese women. In fact, the metabolic syndrome, defined by the presence of three or more of risk factors, which include central obesity, is more prevalent in women than in men with CHD (Grundy et al., 2004).

Women are less likely than men to identify their risk factors (body mass index, smoking, blood pressure, cholesterol) and this may affect the implementation of more aggressive management for women at higher risk for cardiovascular events (Bartys et al., 2005).

The interheart study which compared 15152 patients and 14820 controls found that odds ratio for Myocardial infarction

(MI)/Heart disease associated with diabetes and hypertension were significantly greater in women than in men, other risk factors like smoking, abdominal obesity, fruits and vegetable intake, exercise, alcohol and Apo B/Apo A1* ratio were almost similar in both.

Focusing attention on the women's health has involved efforts mainly targeted towards issues related to reproductive health. Hence, most of the studies in the developing countries have been aimed at younger women in childbearing age group. Moreover, these have sought solutions to tackle the issues related to perinatal and antenatal health (Raymond et al., 2005). Women of postmenopausal age group suffer from multiple problems, including poor nutrition, cardiovascular diseases, obesity, osteoporosis and depression (ICMR, 2006). Ironically, in several of the studies focused on above problems in India, women, somehow, have been neglected. Additionally, gender discrimination right from the time of birth to their adulthood, poverty, unemployment, stress, restricted access to resources and illiteracy etc. in the countries like India make women vulnerable to poor health and nutritional status (Marmot and Wilkinson, 1999; Hadded, 1999).

Women in the age group of 35–60 years are most productive section of population but there is dearth of studies on nutritional status of women in their post reproductive period specially women belonging to low socio economic status. Most women are engaged in informal jobs like agricultural works, domestic helps, labourers, small scale industry jobs, etc. The field of women's health is broader than merely issues of fertility and reproductive health or the biological differences between women and men because there is growing recognition that social as well as biological factors strongly influence health outcomes in women (Goldman and Hatch, 2000). At present international attention and resources are focused on obstetric events and recently HIV/AIDS because of the significance of these problems in the least developed nations (Raymond et al., 2005). But this concept of women's health is very limited. In the earlier years through adolescence to early adulthood anaemia, chronic energy malnutrition and maternal health are important and

* A simple blood test to assess Apo B/Apo A1 ratio which predicts heart disease.

after the age of reproduction, i.e. after 35 years morbidity and mortality from the chronic diseases become important. Thus the concept of women's health, need to be revisited in the light of decreasing fertility and increasing life expectancy in many countries where it was previously applicable like India.

Hence there is an urgent need to explore nutritional status of women and prevalence of risk factors among them. Therefore, the present study has been designed with the following research questions and objectives.

The main objective was to assess the nutritional status of the middle aged urban women 35–70 years, living in Jaipur city.

Nutrition related non communicable diseases like coronary heart disease, hypertension, type 2 diabetes mellitus are increasingly affecting low-middle socio-economic groups of society. The important issue is that appropriate and timely health and nutrition education can make positive changes in the community and improve the health scenario.

The present study was a cross-sectional study among the urban community of the Jaipur. At the study site a central point was identified and the study investigators moved house-to-house and women in the age group of 35–70 years were contacted. Women who were non-pregnant/non-lactating, had no chronic diseases, belonging to low-middle socio economic group and willing to participate in the study were invited on a fixed day at the clinic to perform physical examination and interviewing to elicit required information in the pre-designed questionnaires. Ethical clearance for the study was obtained from institutional ethics committee. Written consent was obtained from each participant.

Women who fulfilled the selection criteria and willing to participate in the study were invited on a fixed day to perform physical examination and interviewing to elicit required information in the pre designed questionnaires. Ethical clearance for the study was obtained from institutional ethics committee. Written consent was obtained from each. A questionnaire was designed to collect information on age, marital status, educational level of the subject as well as spouse, family income, type of family, occupation, smoking or tobacco-intake and alcohol consumption. Socio economic status of the women was assessed using a standardised tool (Kumar et al., 2007). Physical activity of the subjects was assessed using a previously standardised questionnaire for India population (Bharathi et al., 2000) and subjects were classified into different activity levels using their physical activity levels (PAL).

Dietary information was obtained using two well established tools; 24 hour dietary recall and semi-quantitative food frequency questionnaire using interview technique (Jelliffee, 1966).

Twenty four hour recall method is the most frequently used method for assessment of dietary intake of individual; however it has a limitation that the dietary intake of individuals is highly variable. Therefore, a single day 24 hour recall is insufficient to represent the usual and long term intake of an individual. In the present study 2 days recall was taken including one holiday and average values of the two was calculated for further analysis.

Data obtained for different nutrients from two days 24 hour recall* and FFQ** was compared with the recommended dietary allowances for Indians to assess the adequacy of the diet consumed. All the data was further grouped into different age categories to see the trend in intake with ageing.

Results

In the present study 530 women were enrolled and 501 agreed to participate. The demographic detail of the subjects is given in Table 1. The mean age of the women was 45 years and around half of the women belonged to 35–44 years. Around 43.9 per cent subjects were illiterate, and 19.4 per cent subjects had education up to 5th class. Around 21 per cent subjects were educated up to 12th standard and 16 per cent were graduate and had professional

* 24 hour recall is a retrospective method of dietary assessment where an individual is interviewed about their food and beverage consumption during past 24 hours.

** Food Frequency Questionnaire (FFQ) is a retrospective method asking individuals to report their usual frequency of consumption of each food for the past few months.

qualification. To assess the SES of the subjects a modified Kuppuswamy scale was used (Kumar et al., 2007). This scale used education, occupation, and family income of the subject. According to the classification 20.6 per cent subjects had lower socio-economic status (SES), majority of subjects had lower middle SES and 31.6 per cent subjects had upper middle SES. Most were housewives and belonged to middle income group.

Table 1

Demographic Profile of the Subjects

Educational Status	*Frequency (%)*
No school	220 (43.9)
Up to primary	97 (19.4)
Grade 6–12	104 (20.8)
Graduates	24 (4.8)
Professional	56 (11.2)
Housewife	359 (71.7)
Employed for Wages	69 (13.8)
Self Employed	67 (13.4)
Retired	6 (1.20)
Socio Economic Status	*Frequency (%)*
Upper middle	156 (31.1)
Lower middle	242 (48.3)
Upper lower	103 (20.6)
Marital Status	*Frequency (%)*
Married	418 (83.4)
Widowed/Separated/Divorced/Husband Staying Away	79 (15.8)
Never Married	4 (0.8)

Table 2 describes the intake of various food groups by the subjects as per cent of their recommended dietary intakes. Wheat was the staple cereal, other cereals and millets consumed by the subjects were – rice, maize, bajra and barley mainly in the form of *khichri, rabari, daliya* and *chapatti*. Pulses in the present study, were mainly consumed in the form of bengal gram flour (*besan*) preparations like *kadhi, gatte*; and *mangodi* (made by green and black gram pulses) and sweets like *besan burfi/ladoo* and *boondi ladoo*.

The low intake of fruits in subjects may be due to the fact that mostly subjects belonged to low SES. Fruits and vegetables are expensive food items and studies have shown their intake is associated with income and income/SES (Riediger and Moghadasian, 2008). The National Family Health Survey 3 (NFHS, 2005) also reported that sixty per cent of women do not consume fruits even once a week in India, and found fruits intake to be associated with wealth index. Low intakes of green leafy vegetables were reported by most subjects. The additional water requirement for proper washing of the green leafy vegetables (GLVs) is a problem. Secondly, GLVs are available in plenty only in winter season; this may be the reason for low intake in subjects.

Consumption of milk and milk products was mainly in the form of tea, curd, *chaach* and *mava* sweets. Overall visible fats and oil intake of the subject was more than twice the recommendations. Around seventy per cent subjects reported intake of *ghee* (clarified butter), and twenty per cent used to consume *vanaspati ghee*. Use of refined oil was in cent per cent subjects, mainly in the form of groundnut, mustard and soya bean oil.

Table 2

Per Cent Intake of Food Groups in Comparison to the Recommended Dietary Intake

Food group	*Recommended Dietary Intake (grams)*	*Per cent of Recommended Dietary Intake (%)*
Cereals	270	63.93 ±21.04
Pulse	60	42.78 ± 33.55
Fruits	100	50.19 ± 56.74
Green Leafy Vegetables (GLV)	100	16.93 ± 25.59
Roots and Tubers	200	34.06 ± 23.61
Other Vegetables	200	44.52 ± 26.58
Milk and its products	300	107.54 ± 65.6
Sugar	20	139.34 ± 102.17
Fats and oil	20	230.71 ± 175.61

As seen in Table 3, none of the subjects had adequate energy intakes when compared to the Recommended Dietary Allowances (RDA). Thus energy intake of the subjects contributed 53–82 per cent of the RDA for energy in 30–60 years and 70–85 per cent in subjects > 60 years. Overall, two third of the subjects had deficient energy intake. Rastogi (2006) reported that 62 per cent urban women (30–75 years) in Jaipur had energy intake <1875 kcal, which is similar to the finding from the study. Inadequate energy consumption from carbohydrate and protein was seen in 20–25 per cent of the subjects in present study. High total fat energy per cent intake was found in 90 per cent of the subjects. Composition of fat energy per cent revealed that only 10 per cent subjects had PUFA* en per cent more than 10 per cent of total energy intake. More than 50 per cent of the subjects had <10 per cent energy from MUFA**. MUFA is associated with increase in the HDL cholesterol and lowering triglycerides levels.

Table 3

Mean Nutrient Intake of the Subjects in Comparison to Recommended Dietary Allowances for Indians (2010)

Nutrients	*Age Group*	*Recommended Dietary Allowance (RDA)*	*Nutrient Intake*	*Nutrient Intake (% RDA)*
Energy (Kcal)	30–60 Yr	1966	1615.00	82.15
	>60 Yr	1782	1519.59	85.27
Protein (Gm)		55	45.40	85.31
Calcium (mg)		600	724.10	118.63
Iron		21	10.39	56.24
Vitamin-A		600	297.44	49.57
Vitamin-C		40	60.54	151.36
Folic Acid		200	44.19	22.09
Fibre		40	18.23	45.58

* PUFA – Poly unsaturated fatty acids are vegetable oils like groundnut, soyabean, sunflower, etc. They can decrease heart disease risk if consumed in moderation.

** MUFA – Mono unsaturated fatty acids are also a healthy type of fat in olives, canola oil, nuts, etc.

Similar results were found in protein, iron, Vitamin A & B, Folic Acid and fibre intakes. Calcium intake of the subjects was 724.10 ± 280.43 mg/day. Average iron intake of the subjects was 10.39 ± 3.11 mg per day contributing to 50–57 per cent of the RDA of iron for women. Mean vitamin C intake of the subjects was around 1.5 times higher than the recommendation of 40 mg/day. Mean intake of vitamin C was 60.54 ± 43.33 mg/day. Fibre is the undigested part of the plant. Overall, fibre intake in subjects was 18.23 ± 6.07 gm per day.

The diet of these women had less quantity of fibres, iron and folic acid which may be a reflection of low fruits and vegetable consumption among the subjects.

Studies have reported that higher fat intake is a risk factor for cardiovascular diseases (Hu et al., 1997; Rastogi et al., 2004). disproportionate fatty acid intake such as higher saturated fats and trans fatty acids in diet may affect the serum LDL* and HDL** levels. Further low intake of dietary fibre may contribute in this condition. On the other hand low intakes of dietary iron and folic acid may lead to nutritional anaemia in women. Nutritional Status as an outcome may be a result of immediate factors like inadequate food intake and disease status. Social determinant of nutrition like economic, political and cultural forces affect the food supply and financial resources, they further affect the underlying causes of nutrition like access to food, maternal and child caring practices, access to water/sanitation and health services which in turn affect the immediate causes, i.e. dietary intake and disease (WHO, 2007).

Assessment of nutrition adequacy is very important in women who have completed their reproduction cycle, as this is the most economically productive phase. In India percentage of women in formal jobs may be lower compared to other developed countries but more women are engaged in the informal jobs like in agricultural works, domestic helps, labourer, small scale industry jobs, entrepreneurship, etc. Dietary inadequacy in this group may result into poor health, decreased work productivity and increased

* Low Density Lipoprotein (LDL) is the unhealthy fat in blood which promotes heart diseases.

** High Density Lipoprotein (HDL) is the healthy fat in blood which protects from heart diseases.

morbidity. However, health and nutrition programmes in India focuses on pregnant and lactating women and women after the period of child bearing and rearing is neglected. This group is especially important in present scenario as the non-communicable disease burden is increasing in India at younger age.

Imparting nutrition knowledge through health education programmes may alter the food choices and healthy eating behaviour (Wardle et al., 2000) therefore it should be given priority in these national programmes.

The burden of lifestyle related chronic non-communicable diseases are increasing heavily in developing countries like India. Awareness among the general population of the adverse health consequences of the new behaviour and lifestyle is likewise largely inadequate and as there is long delay between cause and effect, people tend to misadjust the hazards of these lifestyle. The challenge to combat this problem is to best apply our existing knowledge of NCDs in effective prevention in real life situation. To help solve this problem, carefully planned community programmes are an important component. Because merely providing risk-reduction measures for clinically high-risk people in health service settings would have only a limited impact in the whole country. On the other hand, if the population as a whole were to be targeted, even a modest risk factor and heart-healthy lifestyle change would potentially have a huge public health impact.

References

Bartys, S., D. Baker, P. Lewis and E. Middleton. 'Inequity in Recording of Risk in a Local Population-based Screening Programme for Cardiovascular Disease'. *Eur J Cardiovasc Prev Rehabil,* 12: 63–67, 2005.

Bharathi, A.V., N. Sandhya and M. Vaz. 'The Development and Characteristics of a Physical Activity Questionnaire for Epidemiological Studies in Urban Middle Class Indians'. *Ind J Med Res,* 111.3: 95–102, 2000.

Castelli, W.P. 'Cardiovascular Disease: Pathogenesis, Epidemiology, and Risk Among Users of Oral Contraceptives Who Smoke'. *Am J Obstet Gynecol,* 180: S349–S356, 1999.

Goldman, M.B. and M.C. Hatch. 'An Overview of Women and Health'. In M.B. Goldman and M.C. Hatch (eds), *Women and Health*. New York: Academic Press, 5–14, 2000.

Gopalan, C. and S. Kaur. *Women and Nutrition in India*. Special Publications Series 5. New Delhi: Nutrition Foundation of India, 153–193, 1989.

Grundy, S.M., J.I. Cleeman, C.N. Merz, H.B. Brewer, L.T. Clark, D.B. Hunninghake, R.C. Pasternak, S.C. Smith and N.J. Stone. National Heart, Lung, and Blood Institute, American College of Cardiology Foundation, American Heart Association. 'Implications of Recent Clinical Trials for the National Cholesterol Education Program Adult Treatment Panel III Guidelines'. *Circulation*, 110: 227–239, 2004.

Hadded, L. 'Women's Status: Levels, Determinants, Consequences for Malnutrition, Interventions, and Policy'. *Asian Development Review*, 17.12: 96–131, 1999.

Hawkes, C. *WHO Commission on Social Determinants of Health: Globalization, Food and Nutrition Transitions*. Globalization and Health Knowledge Network Research Papers. Ottawa: Institute of Population Health, 2007.

Hu, F.B., M.J. Stampfer, J.E. Manson, E. Rimm, G.A. Colditz, B.A. Rosner, C.H. Hennekens and W.C. Willett. 'Dietary Fat Intake and the Risk of Coronary Heart Disease in Women'. *N Engl J Med*, 337.21: 1491–1499, 1997.

ICMR. *Nutrient Requirements and Recommended Dietary Allowances for Indians*. A Report of the Expert Group of the Indian Council of Medical Research 2010, National Institute of Nutrition, Hyderabad, India, 2010.

——. *Assessment of Burden of Non-communicable Diseases: A Project Supported by* WHO. New Delhi, 2006.

Jelliffee, D.B. 'The Assessment of the Nutritional Status of the Community'. World Health Organization, Monograph No. 53. Geneva, 1966.

Kanaya, A.M., D. Grady and C.E. Barrett. 'Explaining the Sex Difference in Coronary Heart Disease Mortality Among Patients with Type 2 Diabetes Mellitus: A Meta-analysis'. *Arch Intern Med*, 162: 1737–1745, 2002.

Kannel, W.B. 'Metabolic Risk Factors for Coronary Heart Disease in Women: Perspective from the Framingham Study'. *Am Heart J*, 114: 413–419, 1987.

Kumar, N., P. Shekhar, P. Kumar and A.S. Kundu. 'Kuppuswamy's Socioeconomic Status Scale-Updating for 2007'. *Indian J of Pediat*, 74 (December): 77–78, 2007.

Marmot, M. and R.G. Wilkinson. *Social Determinants of Health*. Oxford: Oxford University Press, 1999.

Mosca, L., L.J. Appel and E.J. Benjamin. 'American Heart Association: Evidence-based Guidelines for Cardiovascular Disease Prevention in Women'. *Circulation*, 109: 672–693, 2004.

Popkin, B.M. 'The Nutrition Transition in Low-income Countries: An Emerging Crisis'. *Nutr Rev*, 52: 285–298, 1994.

Rastogi, T., K.S. Reddy, M. Vaz, D. Spiegelman, D. Prabhakaran and W.C. Willett. 'Diet and Risk of Ischemic Heart Disease in India'. *Am J Clin Nutr*, 79.4: 582–592, 2004.

Raymond, S.U., H.M. Greenberg and S.R. Leeder. 'Beyond Reproduction: Women's Health in Today's Developing World'. *Int J of Epidemiology*, 34: 1144–1148, 2005.

Rexrode, K.M. et al. 'Abdominal Adiposity and Coronary Heart Disease in Women'. *JAMA*, 280: 1843–1848, 1998.

Wardle, J., K. Parmenter and J. Waller. 'Nutrition Knowledge and Food Intake'. *Appetite*, 34.3: 269–275, 2000.

WHO. *Diet, Nutrition and the Prevention of Chronic Diseases*. Report of a Joint WHO/FAO Consultation, Technical Report Series 916, Geneva, Switzerland, 2003.

CHAPTER 15

Twilight Years

Problems and Support System Focusing Women

SHUBHA DUBE AND POOJA SHARMA

Traditionally, in India women have had a respectable place among almost all communities, but contemporary ground realities vary from this fact. In many Indian communities women are treated as second-class citizens. They have been lagging behind in almost all walks of life for centuries. They have never been financially independent. Due to less social interaction they even don't know about their rights and powers. They are always dependent on male members of the family for their basic needs, even for day-to-day requirements. Ageing women have more critical problem than older men. Ageing is the last phase of human lifecycle. It is the phase where the aged person faces multiple problems, which of course vary from person to person and from society to society. Due to social and traditional family structure ageing women are forced to live with several restrictions. Hence they find themselves marginalised and isolated all the time. As women live longer than men, most of them have to live a life of a widow in their silver years.

The elderly population especially women face a number of problems and adjust to them in varying degrees. These problems range from an absence of a secure and sufficient income to support themselves and their dependents to ill health, absence of social security, loss of social role and recognition and the non-availability of opportunities for creative use of free time. The needs and problems of the elderly women vary significantly according to their age, socio-economic status, health, living status and other such background characteristics (Kumar and Anand, 2006). Women are at special risk in this group, given their disproportionate presence in the informal sector, shorter work spans, longer life expectancies and limited access to other assets. (Bloom et al., 2010). The ageing women experience a range of changes, physical as well as psychological and this period is known as the period of serious crises. (Mathur, 2009).

Demographic Profile

Demographic is a statistic characterising human populations (or segments of human populations broken down by age or sex or income, etc.) Ageing women make up a significant proportion of the world's population and their figures are growing. The number of women aged 60 and over will increase from about 336 million in 2000 to just over 1 billion in 2050. Women outnumber men in older age groups and this imbalance increases with age. Worldwide, there are some 123 women for every 100 men aged 60 and over. The ageing population in India is the second largest in the world, next to China. This population, which was 77 million according to the 2001 Census (7.5% of the total population), is projected to increase to 137 million by 2021 (Siva Raju, 2006).

The majority of the ageing women live in developing countries, where population ageing is occurring at a rapid pace. The fastest growing group among ageing women is the oldest-old (age 80-plus). Worldwide, by age 80 and over, there are 189 women for every 100 men. By age 100 and over, the gap reaches 385 women for every 100 men. While most ageing women remain relatively healthy and independent until late in life, the very old most often require chronic care and help for day-to-day activities.

As per Census 2001, population of males and females was 3.8 crore and 3.9 crore respectively (MSJE, 2014). The share of people aged 60 years and above in the total population is highest in Kerala (8.82%), closely followed by Himachal Pradesh (8.12%) and Punjab (7.84%) (Parliament library, 2013). Invariably in all the southern states the elderly females outnumber the male elderly population. It indicates the higher expectancy of life for females. Changes in population structure will have several implications for health, economic security, family life and well being of elderly women. Currently, Indian women aged 60 are expected to live two more years than their male counterparts (Bloom et al., 2010).

India's elderly population has already crossed 100 million mark during 2011. As per analysis of census data and projections, elderly population sex ratio is in favour of females. As per the Census 2011, total Indian population sex ratio is in favour of male population in ratio 940:1000, whereas for elderly at (60+) population it is in favour of elderly women by 1022:1000 (Agewell Foundation, 2011). Widowed elderly females are greater in proportion (51%) as compared to males (15%) (Siva Raju, 2006). Changes in population structure will have several implications for health, economic security, family life and well being of elderly women.

Study conducted by Sharma (1993) revealed that the average age of the subjects was approximately 59 years. The unemployed retired women were older by five years than re-employed retired. Contradictory results are shown in other studies indicating average age of the group as 60–70 years (Muthukrishnaveni, 2011; Agewell Foundation, 2011; Singh et al., 2009; Yesudian and Singh, 2009; Rao et al., 2009). Majority of the respondents, i.e. 44.5 per cent elderly respondents were in the age group of 61–70 years while 37.2 per cent and 18.2 per cent were in the age groups of 71–80 years and 80+ years respectively (Agewell Foundation, 2014). Hariharan et al. (2010), observes in his study on the elderly women of Tamil Nadu that the majorities of the elders who were residing in joint families, belonged to scheduled castes and were illiterates. A contradictory result was given by Singh et al. (2009) indicating that majority elderly women were literate, married, living in joint family system.

According to Chauhan et al. (2009) majority of the aged women were living with spouse and had school education. While Vyas (2004) observed in his study that majority of the elderly women were graduates, teachers and living in joint family system. Astige (2009) revealed in his study on post-retirement plan of college teachers that a greater percentage of the elders had medium education profile and belonged to forward caste. Moharana et al. (2007) studied the 'Health status of geriatric population attending the preventive geriatrics clinics of tertiary health facilities'. It was reported that majority were belonged to middle income group, and were literate, married, living with spouse.

Major Concerns of Ageing Women

Social Problems

Older women, who live in cities, are prone to social alienation/marginalisation in comparison to older women of villages. Joint family system (to a certain extent) is still alive in rural areas. Older women, who live in semi urban situations/industrial townships, also find it difficult to cope with old age, particularly after their children have grown up and husbands retire. Due to lack of social protection, older women are forced to lead a life full of distress. Ignored by their own kith and kin, they don't expect any kind of social security from others (Agewell Foundation, 2011).

Lena et al. (2009) mentioned that majority of the patients thought that the attitude of people towards the elderly women was that of neglect. Tavitamma (2011) examined the care and support for the elderly women in family. It was revealed that most of them were being taken care and supported by their children's and they were happy and satisfied with that. Contradictory result was given by Agewell Foundation (2011) indicating that majority elderly women were not given respect by their family members and were felt isolated and were ill-treated.

In a study, Singh et al. (2009) investigated psychosocial profile of the elderly of Meerut city, showing that the elderly women had involvement with their family members and social contacts outside their home as well. According to Rajeshwar (2009) social discrimination, negligence from children and loneliness were the major social problems faced by the elderly women of Bhopal in their day-to-day life. Agewell Foundation (2009) examined the problem faced by the elderly in minority communities. The results showed that majority of the population in the age group of 60–69 years were more socially active and physically active.

In India, about 65 per cent of the aged population were depended on others – partially or fully – for their livelihood (Ravishankar, 2009). Lena et al. (2009) revealed that about majority

(68%) of the patients said that the attitude of people towards the elderly was that of neglect and disregard. The results of the study showed that there is a need for geriatric counseling centres that can take care of their physical and psychological needs. Bhatia et al. (2007) studied loneliness among elderly in Chandigarh. It was found that loneliness was significantly higher among the aged who were living alone as compared to those who were living with spouse, or couples who were living with the family. It is due to the fact that though the widows live with their families, they are ignored in their own homes. Agewell Foundation (2014) reported that marginalisation and neglect in old age emerged as most common problem. Almost every third elderly woman (34.3%) had no access to safe, affordable, accessible and sustainable transport facility (Agewell Foundation, 2014).

Health Problem

The idea that ageing is an age of ailments and physical infirmities is deeply rooted in the Indian psyche. People become increasingly susceptible to chronic diseases, physical disabilities and mental incapacities as they grow older. Not surprisingly, health problems and medical care become major concerns among a majority of the elderly (Siva Raju, 2006).

Declining health status is a major symptom of an individual's ageing process (Bhattacharya, 2005). Mental health of older persons is influenced not just by ageing changes in the body and brain, but by socio-economic and psychological factors. Problems related to health and economic conditions lead to suicides in older people (WHO). In India, the elderly people suffer from dual medical problems, i.e. both communicable as well as non-communicable diseases. The elderly women are also prone to abuse in their families or in institutional settings. This includes physical abuse (infliction of pain or injury), psychological or emotional abuse (mental anguish and illegal exploitation), and sexual abuse (Ingle and Nath, 2008).

It was found that the major health problems faced by women in their old age were diabetes, arthritis, poor vision, cataract, joint pain, slipped disc, hypertension, osteoporosis, musculoskeletal, respiratory and dental problem, overweight, etc. (Muthukrishnaveni, 2011; Chauhan et al., 2009; Rudra, 2004;

Agewell Foundation, 2009; Rajeshwer, 2009; Medhi et al., 2006; Moharana et al., 2007; Wason and Jain, 2010; Balan and Devi, 2010). The leading cause of death in old age in India is cardiovascular disease (Jai Prakash, 1999). Wason and Jain (2010) studied the nutritional status, dietary adequacy and health problems of institutionalised elderly; it was found that a few number of elderly rated their health condition as good and rest as not good.

Agewell Foundation (2014) found that majority of older persons were found getting proper medicines and healthcare facilities. In urban areas status of healthcare facilities was found better, where 74.5 per cent elderly respondents accepted that they have been looked after medically well while in rural areas only 71.7 per cent elderly respondents were getting regular healthcare facilities. Kumar (2014) observed in his study the health problems of rural elderly, it was reported that half of the ageing population was suffering from arthritis and this problem was reported to be more in females as compared to males. As changes in cognitive and other abilities surface, the elderly face psychological problems. Reasoning becomes slower, memory is impaired, enthusiasm decreases and cautiousness increases and sleep patterns are altered. Mental illness is also much higher among old people (Siva Raju, 2006).

Economic Problem

With increased life span of ageing women, their financial needs are also emerging as a major concern. However, today, many women have property/money but they cannot possibly use the money or take financial decisions on their own. Social traditions does not allow them to use their ancestral property/money for their own welfare. They may be rich or poor; they always have to act according to the directives of others. Since they are habitual of sacrificing their own interests for the good of other family members throughout their life, in old age they don't want to ask for their share (Agewell Foundation, 2011). Even those with pensions find their economic status lowered after retirement (Jai Prakash, 1999).

The old age dependency ratio (number of 60+ per 100 persons in the 15–59 age group) is gradually increasing in both rural and urban areas. Majority of the elderly are supported by their children, and co-residence with their children increases as they advance in age.

Unfortunately, literacy is 53 per cent among elderly males and only 20 per cent among elderly females. Elderly males are more economically active as compared to females (Siva Raju, 2006).

Mathur (2009) revealed that the level of economic status followed by education and social support are the prime factors contributing depression in aged women. Women are particularly vulnerable to economic insecurity (Bloom et al., 2010). Nearly 60–75 per cent of all aged women are economically dependent on others, usually their children (Jai Prakash, 1999). Elderly men were found in good financial command in comparison to elderly women, where 68.93 per cent elderly men claimed that they are financially independent and only half of the elderly women respondents (50.58%) were found financially self-dependent (Agewell Foundation, 2014).

Sharma (1993) investigated the management of resources and adjustment of unemployed and re-employed retired. The result showed that the average income of unemployed retired was lower, with this result they had low expenditure and saving pattern than latter and unemployed retired aged faced more problems than re-employed retired in home. Hariharan (2010) observed in his study that average income and expenditure of the elders in the age group of 60–64 years were comparatively higher to other age brackets. This population invests in government and non-government saving schemes. Children were the primary monitory source to the aged for food, medical and other daily requirements.

Agewell Foundation conducted a study in 20 states of India on the income and expenditure pattern of ageing adults. It was found that in rural areas majority were earning average income of ₹ 5000–10000. Whereas in urban it was found to be ₹ 10000–25000. Regarding the expenditure pattern, majority of the elders spent most of their income in medicine, household goods and rest of the money was invested in various financial instruments like fixed deposit, mutual funds, etc.

Welfare Schemes

The Central and State governments have already made efforts to tackle the problem of economic insecurity by launching policies such as the National Policy on Older Persons, National Old Age Pension

Programme, Annapurna Programme, etc. However, the benefits of these programs have been questioned several times in terms of the meagre budget, improper identification of beneficiaries, lengthy procedures, and irregular payment (Ingle and Nath, 2008). National old age pension schemes provide assistance to destitute women above 65 years (Jai Prakash, 1999), now it is 60 years.

Prasad and Salomi (2009) examined the implementation of old age pension scheme in Visakhapatnam. It was found that majority of the pensioners expressed happiness while very few expressed their unhappiness because of irregular distribution of pension. Suryawanshi (2010) has shown that most of the elderly women lived with their families, belonged to lower income group and viewed their pension amount to be very helpful for their last stage.

In an evaluation report given by planning department of Himachal Pradesh (2004) it was found that the pension was received in time and the socio economic status improved through pension. In another study it was suggested that the stringent rules for eligibility to social security schemes should be made more flexible to cover a larger population (Lena et al., 2009).

Conclusion

Taking an overall view, it can be concluded that there would be a manifold increase of geriatric population in coming years particularly in India. With fast growing elderly population, increased life expectancy and higher percentage of elderly women in Indian elderly population, issues concerning elderly women cannot be ignored any longer. If ignored today, this may turn into a major social development challenge. Focus should be shifted on issues concerning women. Since they have specific and individual requirements they need special attention and thought fullness.

We understand that the major health problems of elderly women were diabetes, arthritis, poor vision, hypertension, body pain, etc. Loneliness, neglect, abuse and economic dependence on others were also reported to be high in ageing women. Social isolation is also a major threat in this age. It can be said that meaningful and action oriented execution of welfare schemes could be beneficial in solving some of the glitches and improving the quality of life of greying women population leading to happier and contented twilight years.

References

Agewell Foundation *(In Special Consultative Status with the ECOSOC at United Nations since 2011)* M-8A, Lajpat Nagar-II, New Delhi. Website: www.agewellfoundation.org

Astige, B.S. 'A Sociological Study of Post-retire Plans of College Teachers'. *HelpAge India Research and Development Journal*, 15.3 (October) 12–19, 2009.

Balan, S.V. and G.V. Devi. 'Nutritional Status, Dietary Adequacy and Health Problems of Institutionalized Elderly'. *Indian Journal of Gerontology*, 24.2: 187–193, 2010.

Bhatia, S.P.S. et al. 'A Study of Health Problems and Loneliness Among the Elderly in Chandigarh'. *Indian Journal of Community Medicine*, 32.4: 255–258, 2007.

Bhattacharya, P. (2005). 'Implications of an Aging Population in India: Challenges and Opportunities'. Paper presented at the Living to 100 and Beyond Symposium, Orlando.

Bloom, et al. Economic security arrangement in the context of population ageing in India. Programme on the global demography of ageing. 2010 website: http://www.hsph.harvard.edu/program-on-the-global-demography-of-aging/WorkingPapers/2010/PGDA_WP_60.pdf

Chauhan, et al. 'Study on Knowledge and Practices of Elderly Female Self Care Givers'. *HelpAge India Research and Development Journal*, 15.3 (October): 7–11, 2009.

Evaluation Division. *Evaluation Study of Beneficiaries Under Old Age Widow and National Security Pension Scheme*. Evaluation report, Planning Department, Government of Himachal Pradesh, 2002. http//hpplanning.nic.in.

Hariharan, R. et al. 'Economic Perspectives and Life-style Characteristics of the Aged Population in Tamil Nadu'. *Language in India*, 10: 1–14, 2010.

http://www.un.org/en/development/desa/population/publications/pdf/ageing/WorldPopulationAgeing2013.pdf

http://www.unescap.org/esid/psis/meetings/ageing_madrid_2007/socialsupport_olderpersons.pdf

Ingle, K.G. and A. Nath. 'Geriatric Health in India: Concerns and Solutions'. *Indian Journal of Community Medicine,* 33.4 (October): 214–218, 2008. http://medind.nic.in.

Jai Prakash, Indira. *Ageing in India.* Geneva: World Health Organization, 1999. http://www.popbook.com

Kumar, A. and N. Anand. *Poverty Target Programs for the Elderly in India.* Manchester, UK: Chronic Poverty Research Centre, October 2006.

Kumar, P. Health Problems of Rural Aged: A Social Work Intervention. *Indian Journal of Research.* Paripex, June, 3(6): 191–194, 2014.

Lena, A. et al. 'Health and Social Problems of the Elderly: A Cross-Sectional Study in Udupi Taluk, Karnataka'. *Indian Journal of Community Medicine,* 34.2: 131–134, 2009.

Mathur, M. Depression and lifestyle in Indian ageing women. *Journal of the Indian Academy of Applied Psychology,* January, 35(1): 73-77, 2009. http://medind.nic.in/jak/t09/i1/ jakt09i1p73.pdf

Medhi, G.K. et al. 'Health Problems and Disability of Elderly Individuals in Two Population Groups from Same Geographical Location'. *Journal of the Association of Physicians of India,* 54: 539–544, 2006.

Ministry of Social Justice and Empowerment (2014) – Implementation of schemes and welfare of senior citizens (Thirty–Ninth report). Website:http://164.100.47.134/lsscommittee/Social%20Justice %20&%20Empowerment/15_Social_Justice_And_Empowerment _39.pdf(MSJE

Moharana, P.R. et al. 'Health Status of Geriatric Population Attending the Preventive Geriatric Clinic of a Tertiary Health Facility'. *Journal of Community Medicine,* 4.2 (January) 2–14, 2007.

Muthukrishnaveni, S. (2011). 'Coresidence and Well Being of Elderly in Rural Tamil Nadu'. *HelpAge India Research and Development Journal,* 17.1: 15–22, 2011.

Prasad, B.D. and N.K. Salomi. 'Implementation of the Old Age Pension Scheme in Visakhapatnam District'. *Journal of Rural Development,* 28.4: 439–449, 2009.

Rajeshwar. *Needs Assessment Study Among Elderly of Bhopal.* Project report submitted to HelpAge India, New Delhi, 2009.

Rao, S.K. et al. 'Condition of Older Persons Living in Slums in Tirupati'. *HelpAge India Research and Development Journal,* 15.3 (October): 20–27, 2009.

Ravishankar, A.K. 'Ageing and Family Support of Elderly in South India'. *Ageing and Society – The Indian Journal of Gerontology.* July to

December 2009, XIX (III & IV). website: http://www.cmig.in/Journal_Sep10.pdf

Senior Citizens: Problems and Welfare (2013). Parliament Library Reference Note. http://164.100.47.134/intranet/ SeniorCitizensProblemsandWelfare.pdf

Sharma, A. 'Management of Resources and Social Adjustment of Unemployed and Reemployed Retired: A Comparison'. Unpublished M.Sc. Dissertation, College of Home Science, RAU, Udaipur, 1993.

Singh, N. et al. 'The Psycho-social Profile of Elderly People in Urban Area of Meerut City'. *Journal of the Indian Academy of Geriatrics*, 5: 165–170, 2009.

Siva Raju, S. Ageing in India in the 21st Century: A Research Agenda. 2006. http://harmonyindia.org/hdownloads/Monograph_FINAL.pdf

Surayawanshi, B.R. 'The Nature and Impact of Old Age Pension Schemes for Improving Status of Rural Aged in Parbhani Taluka'. *International Referred Research Journal*, September 2010, II.

Tavitamma, P. 'Care and Support for the Elderly in the Family: A Study of Heerapuram Village in Andhra Pradesh'. *HelpAge India Research and Development Journal*, 17.1: 23–30, 2011.

Vyas, M.B. 'A Comparative Study on Socio Adjustment of the Aged Males and Females (60–75 years age) of Bikaner City (Rajasthan)'. Unpublished M.Sc. Dissertation, College of Home Science, RAU, Bikaner, 2004.

Wason, N. and K. Jain. 'Nutritional Status, Dietary Adequacy and Health Problems of Institutionalized Elderly'. *Indian Journal of Gerontology*, 24.2: 187–193, 2010.

Women, Ageing and Health: A Framework for Action Women, Ageing and Health: A Framework for Action Focus on Gender. www.who.int/ageing/publications/Women-ageing-health-lowres.pdf

www.agewellfoundation.org

www.esocialsciences.com/data/.../esswparticle200972717815.doc

www.helpageindia.org

Yesudian, P. and D.P. Singh. 'Profile of Elderly Women Workers in India'. *HelpAge India Research and Development Journal*, 15.2 (May) 8–12, 2009.

Index

Activisms, 48–51
Adolescent Girls: Awareness, Rights and Reproductive Health (Narang), 120
Advertisements, women in, 98
Africa, national boundaries in, 32
Ageing women
  economic problems, 251–252
  health problems, 250–251
  social problems, 249–250
  welfare schemes, 252–253
All Indian Women's Conference, 17
'Anti-Cruelty Act,' 141–142
Ashe, Geoffrey, 49
Asmal, Kader, 36
Athletes, women in, 99–100
Aung San Suu Kyi, 50
Aztec society, 39

Bennett, Jane, 46
Bharati, Dharamvir, 118
Bitter Chocolate (Virani), 107–112
The Blue Bedspread (Jha), 117, 119–120
Bull, Hedley, 30–31
Buzan, Barry, 30

Cable Television Networks (Regulation) Act, 1995, 101
Chatterjee, Bankim Chandra, 118
Child marriages, Gandhi on, 22–24
Child sexual abuse (CSA), 107–115
  effects of, 110–111
The Choices We Made (Steinem), 123
Cinema, women in, 94–95
Civil Disobedience Movement, 25
Civil society organisations, 102
Committee on the Status of Women in India (CSWI), 18–19
Critical studies, 91
Cultural violence, 34

Dark is Beautiful Campaign (Das), 121
Das, Nandita, 121
de Beauvoir, Simone, 60
Declaration on the Elimination of Violence Against Women, 45

Democratic Republic of Congo (DRC), 31
Demographics, 247–249
Desh Sevika Sangh, 25
Domestic violence, 225–233
  causes of, 230–231
  consequences of, 225–226
  preventing/reducing, 226–228
  types of, 228–230
Dominator model, 39
'Dowry Death Act,' 142

Egalitarianism, 40–41
Ellmann, Mary, 118
Emotional abuse, 133–144
  continuum to wife, 135–139
  scars on wife, 139
Employment, gender inequality in, 182–183
Engels, Fredrick, 15
Exploitation, women, 4

Femina (magazine), 117
The Feminine Mystique (Friedan), 62
Femininity, in Indian society, 15–19
Feminism, 1–2, 58–64
  in India (*see* Indian feminism)
  and socialism, 63
Feminist politics, 153–154
Films, women in, 94–95
Fry, Douglas, 40–41

Gallagher, Margaret, 77
Galtung, Johan, 28, 33
Gandhian feminism, 4–5, 13–27
Gender-based violence, 45–48
  defined, 45
  indicators of, 48
Gender discrimination, 170
Gender inequality, 170–186
Gender justice, 2–3
Gender oppression, 41–44
Gender-related Development Index (GDI), 184–185
Gimbutas, Marija, 39
Greer, Germaine, 14

Hartmann, Heidi, 61–62
Hepburn, Katherine, 59
Hobbes, Thomas, 30
Honour
  traditions and, 154–156
  and violence, 156–157
Human Rights Commission, 102
Human security, 33–37
  sources of, 36

Indecent Representation of Women (Prohibition) Act, 100–101
Indecent Representation of Women (Prohibition) Act, 1986, 78
Indian feminism, 64
  first phase of, 67–68
  second phase of, 68–69
Indigenous egalitarianism, 40–41
Informal economy, 202–206
  historical backdrop, 191–192
  perspectives of, 193–195
  theories on, 192–193
Informal employment, 190–191
Informal sector, India, 195–196
  women workers in, 197–198
Information Technology Act, 2000, 101
International Conference of Labour Statisticians (ICLS), 189–190
International security system, problems associated with, 33

Jaipur, middle aged urban women in, nutritional status of, 234–243
Jha, Raj Kamal, 117, 119–120

Karnad, Girish, 121
Kemp, Graham, 40–41
King, Martin Luther, Jr., 49
Kishwar, Madhu, 20–21
Kumar, Jainendra, 118

Liberal feminists, 64
Luther, Martin, 14

Mainstream media, 85–86
Mandela, Nelson, 49–50
Manusmriti, 151
Marriage, evil practices associated with, 22–24
Marxism and Literature (Williams), 77
Marxists feminist, 60–61, 63–64
Mass media, representation of women in, 75–76, 80–84
  Cable Television Networks (Regulation) Act, 1995, 101
  changing strategies, 84–85
  civil society organisations, 102
  Indecent Representation of Women (Prohibition) Act, 100–101
  Information Technology Act, 2000, 101
  news media, 102–103
  review of literature, 77–80
  statutory bodies, 102
  as super mom, 90
  women's indecent portrayal, 89–105
Media framing, 91
Mitra, Peary Chand, 23
Monsoon Wedding (film), 107, 108, 112–115
Music videos, women in, 97–98

Naidu, Sarojini, 26
Nair, Mira, 112–115
Narang, Darshan K., 120
Narrow state-centrism, 31
National Human Rights Commission, 102
National security, 30–33
  definition of, 32
News media, 102–103
Null hypotheses, 226–227

Oakley, Ann, 209
Othering and Oppressions centres, 39–40

Patriarchy, 62–63
Phallogocentrism, 37
Political movement, women in, 25
Post-independence period, and femininity in Indian society, 18–19
Pre-independence period, and femininity in Indian society, 16–18
Press Council of India, 102
Print media, 83
  women in, 99
Productive powers, women, 47
Protection of Women from Domestic Violence Act 2005, 142

Radical feminists, 64
Rajmohan's Wife (Chatterjee), 118
Randall, Vicky, 46
Rashtriya Sevika Sangh, 25

Reardon, Betty, 33
The Resignation (Tyagpatra), 118

Sankara, Thomas, 41
Satyagraha, 49
The Second Sex (de Beauvoir), 60
Security
  based on gender, 29
  definition of, 31–32, 37
  engendering, 37–48
  human, 33–37
  international system, problems associated with, 33
  national, 30–33
Serials, women in, 95–97
Sexual harassment, 209–220
  defined, 211–213
  effects of, 213–215
  law in India, 215–220
Sexual/Textual Politics, 118
Socialism, feminism and, 63
Social protection, 198–202
Society, women in, 15–19
South African National Defence Force (SANDF), 36
The Statesman Newspaper, 122
Steinem, Gloria, 123
Stereotypes, 91–93, 142
Structural violence, 34, 35
The Sun's Seventh Horse (Bharati), 118
Superwoman, 97

Television, as medium of entertainment, 81–83
Theorizing Patriarchy (Walby), 1
Thinking About Women (Ellmann), 118
Tirath, Krishna, 107
Traditions
  honour and, 154–156
Traumatic bonding, 139

Uncivil war against women, 38–44
United Nations International Decade for Women, 79

Video games, 100
Vindication of the Rights of Women (Wollstonecraft), 59
Violence
  cultural, 34
  gender-based, 45–48
  honour and, 156–157
  structural, 34, 35
  triangular model of, 28
  against women, 2
Virani, Pinki, 107–112
Visualisation, of Indian women, 21–22

Wages, gender inequality in, 183–184
Walby, Sylvia, 1
Walker, Lenore, 135–138
Widows, condition in society, 16
Williams, Raymond, 77
Wollstone, Mary, 15
Women in Informal Employment Globalizing and Organizing (WIEGO), 190
Women's empowerment, 170–186
Women's Empowerment: Measuring the Global Gender Gap, 172